"THE NEWEST, MOST UNIQUE WAYS PEOPLE ARE MAKING MONEY"

VOLUME II

**By Chase Revel And
The Staff Of** Entrepreneur **Magazine
The World's Only Business Opportunity
Magazine**

Contributors:
John Hiatt, Managing Editor
George Murray, Research Director
Karen de Leschery
Susan Stevens Gilliland
Jay Goldberg
Rieva Lesonsky
Mitchell Milgaten
Patricia Ryan
Mark Walsh
Clay Williams
April Van Puffelen

ISBN NO. 0-932362-03-6
Library of Congress Catalog No. 79-52286

Published in United States of America
By Baronbrook Publishing Company
631 Wilshire Blvd.
Santa Monica, California 90401

FOREWORD

Within the pages of this volume in our continuing series you will find hundreds of ideas, concepts and products that are making fortunes for their creators. Some are hilarious, some may seem improbable, but all share a number of qualities in common.

They represent the best and brightest of those we uncover in our work at the International Entrepreneurs' Association. They show ways innovators have found to *fill a need* in the marketplace and make a profit doing so. And they prove the creativity that dwells within the mind of the average person, waiting to be set free.

Investigating these ideas brings us into contact with the creators time and again. Invariably we find they are not eccentric inventors. In most cases, no flash of inspiration struck them. They are not all intellectual geniuses. In fact, the majority are average people like you and me—with an important difference. They have the ability to look at things in a new way, and the ability to take *action* to turn their ideas into reality.

Without action, the brightest moneymaking idea goes nowhere; with it, anything is possible. It is our hope that the wide variety of ideas presented here—that are making money for their creators—will stimulate you to create your own ideas and act on them. Do this, and perhaps your idea will be among those we feature next time.

John T. Hiatt
Managing Editor

ABOUT THE ORGANIZATION THAT COMPILED THIS BOOK

International Entrepreneurs Association is the most authoritative and unique small business research and reporting service in the world.

Founded six years ago by multimillionaire Chase Revel, IEA specializes in finding and reporting on new small business trends and then makes those reports available to its 65,000 members worldwide before anyone else hears about them.

Members receive numerous benefits including the services of IEA's research division which answers business questions and helps to solve problems.

In addition, members can also receive step-by-step instructional help for financing a new or existing business or idea); protecting their ideas; selling their ideas; information on the hottest new products before (or just as they come on the market; insider details on dealing with banks or other lending institutions; news of the latest laws affecting small business; plus free professional information on all franchises, dealerships and other business opportunity offerings.

Each month members receive three complete start-up manuals on some new and/or unique small business concept.

To date, IEA has compiled more than 150 complete "how to" start-up manuals on various types of small businesses. These manuals are available to all members.

IEA constantly updates this material and adds to it each month. Members receive all updates.

In essence, IEA is a virtual "supermarket of assistance" for the present—or potential businessperson.

TABLE OF CONTENTS

Dieter's Fork

Millions have been made catering to thousands of overweight Americans. Weight watchers clubs, dietetic foods and computerized exer-cycles are just a few of the concepts capitalizing on the desire to lose extra rolls and bulges.

Now a new fork has been developed that provides a unique approach to weight control. Called the Diet Fork, its tines are so twisted that even dietetic cottage cheese remains harmlessly on the plate.

Perfectly nonfunctional for eating purposes, the tines are aesthetically curled into a pattern that makes eating a futile exercise in cold sweat. And there's ample space for engraving a fat friend's name on the tasteful Rogers silverplate.

Such a fork could be duplicated cheaply as a direct mail item. It also suggests a wide range of spinoff possibilities for the overweight crowd. Dinner plates cut in half, bladeless butter knives, sealed cookie jars, calorie calculators, sugar spoons with flexible handles, and prong-less bottle openers. These are all simpler than having your jaws wired shut.

When was the last time you heard of something for the underweight people? There's room here for oversized spoons for skinny friends, ankle weights for strong winds, a double water glass and, for those who want to go all out, even "conveyor" plates. These are all simpler than having your jaws wired open. For more information on the Diet Fork, contact **Things Unlimited, Dept. IEA, P.O. Box 415, Streetsboro, Ohio 44240.**

3

The Flasher

Most drivers, at one time or another, have wanted to give a piece of their mind to someone who cuts them off or is driving as if a bowl of goldfish were on the seat.

The automobile is a frustrating isolation booth at these times and you are limited to using the horn, certain facial expressions or, in the extreme, obscene gestures. Even if you have a CB radio, the "turkey" in the next lane probably doesn't.

The Flasher changes all that, and can be as versatile with words as you are. Next time you're treated rudely on the road, just flash a sign saying "You Turkey!" or "Get Off My Back!" If some snob in a brand new Belchfire 8 cruises by, his nose in the air, lean out of your Plymouth and flash "Mine's Paid For!"

If you're parked at a stop sign and a leggy brunette bounces by, flash "Hello Beautiful", followed by "I'd Like Your Phone Number." If it doesn't get a smile, whip out the sign saying "Win A Few, Lose A Few."

Created by Visual Imagery, Inc., The Flasher is simply a folder containing 24 memorable messages printed in black on two sides of a dozen sheets of heavy, white paper. Signs run the gamut of emotions from "Yecch!" and "Sit On It!" to "I Think I Love You" or the tried and true "Your Place Or Mine." Blank cards are included to allow buyers even more expression using a felt tip marker of their own.

Other in-car communicators are on the market, but this is the first we've seen that could easily be duplicated without costly production. All it takes is paper, ink, a design and a wild imagination. You could improve this "poor man's CB" by indexing the cards and binding them with wire so that it's easier to flip to the proper sentiment for the occasion.

For further information on this product, contact Take That, Dept. IEA, Villa Creek Drive, Suite 268, Dallas, Texas 75234.

End "Telephonus Interruptus"

For years the only home appliance that you can't shut off has been the telephone. This leads to the inevitable interruptions: insurance men who call at dinner time, and midshower wrong numbers that leave you "mad as a wet hen." If you're like most people, at least once in your life a romantic interlude has been shattered by Ma Bell's tyrannical instrument. In many parts of the country, leaving the phone off the hook will activate a "howler" that increases in volume until you respond.

The Silencer, developed by two Boston engineers, will end this "telephonus interruptus" for good. It keeps any phone from ringing with the flip of a switch, and installs in less than five minutes, using just a screwdriver.

Space-age microcomponents keep the phone quiet while your caller hears the same familiar ring he always has. It is available in bulk or individually packaged from Zoom telephonics and has a suggested retail price of $9.95. A sample costs $5.00 and Zoom is looking for distributors.

With 150 million phones in the U.S., and 200 million overseas, the Silencer has excellent market potential. For more information, contact Zoom Telephonics, Dept. IEA, 65 Franklin Street, Boston, Massachusetts 02110.

Telephone For The Deaf!

Those of us who hear can't comprehend the isolation felt by those who don't. Deaf people have been able to use the telephone for some years. But this involves investment in costly teletype machinery that many can't afford.

Now a Hartford electronics company has developed a $700 briefcase-sized portable teletypewriter that weighs only 5 pounds and needs only a 100-volt outlet for power.

A user nests the handset of any phone in the device and types messages on a standard keyboard. Intricate solid-state circuitry creates tonal impulses that are received by another unit across town—or across country. Messages back and forth print out on a paper roll.

Portability and price are obvious benefits. Markets, in addition to the deaf, should be police departments, fire departments, and hospitals. Perhaps an enterprising individual in a major market could rent the machines and provide a welcome central communication service.

Magsat Corporation, Dept. IEA, 56 Arbor Street, Hartford, Connecticut 06166, seeks agents nationwide.

Own Your Own Raincloud!

Balloons can be great business, but we've discovered one balloon you won't see floating above parades. A London architect has designed an artificial rain cloud that works!

Graham Stevens has designed a plastic cloud which, like the real thing, provides both shade and rain. He has demonstrated it in the Kuwait desert, and created mini-downpours!

Black panels in the "cloud" heat the air, causing the cloud to inflate and rise. The humid air condenses on other panels and falls as rain. The cloud itself is quite large, about 30 feet by 60 feet, and can be seen for miles around.

This "rain cloud" could be manufactured and rented out to businesses as a great promotional gimmick. Even to public functions like fairs or athletic events. While you can't provide much rain for hungry crops, the promotional value can prove quite profitable.

Imagine having your own private rain cloud floating overhead, like the Goodyear blimp! Curiosity seekers would come by and probably buy something while frolicking in the cooling rain. As the cloud soars, so would your profits!

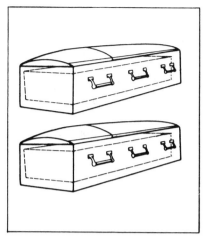

Rent-A-Casket

There are a lot of ways that your mortal remains can be disposed of when you go to "That Great Boardroom in the Sky." Nowadays, methods range from the reverent to the brutally practical.

In addition to traditional underground burial, you can be buried at sea, or have your ashes dropped from a low-flying bi-plane. Or even be frozen and kept "on ice" until a miracle cure for what did you in justifies thawing.

Most of these alternatives result from the steadily increasing cost of dying. A standard funeral now costs at least $1,000 in most areas of the country. The largest expense item is usually the casket that bereaved loved ones must select from a chilling display in the basement of the funeral parlor.

A mortuary in British Columbia is doing something about the high costs—and meeting stiff competition in the process. They offer a "Rent-a-Casket" plan that allows the dear departed to be sent off in high style for a fraction of the cost.

A "Boot Hill" style pine box is slipped inside an ornate hand-carved oak and bronze casket. Before burial, the cheaper pine box is slipped out and the shell is used over and over.

This way the funeral parlor has been able to trim costs to about $375 from the normal $1,000 or more for a regular coffin burial. And customers are seldom heard to complain!

"Check Yer Oil, Mister?"

The oil level in any automobile has to be checked regularly. Yet many people who use self-service gas stations every day don't do it. Why? Because cleaning rags are rarely available and most people don't want to risk soiling their hands and clothing with dirty, hard-to-remove oil stains!

Now, for only $1 retail, any automobile owner can have Instawipe and end the risk of oil stained hands or clothing forever! Instawipe is a simple, aluminum L-shaped device which sticks to any clean surface under the car hood.

Pull the dirty dipstick through a slotted synthetic rubber backing and presto! Clean as a whistle! The angled item is predrilled so that an automobile owner can permanently install it with a metal screw.

The nifty new product wholesales for 50 cents and should be a dynamic item for sale in service stations, auto parts houses, car washes, hardware and variety stores. The Los Arco Company manufacturer of the item, **is looking for distributors. Contact Oil Instawipe, Dept. IEA, Los Arcos Co., Arco, ID 83213.**

Pocket Breath-Alyzer!

We've reported previously on coin-op breath-alyzer vending machines and their tremendous market potential. Now there's a battery-operated pocket version on the market which we believe can be a staggering success!

The hand-held breath-alyzer not only tells you whether you're too drunk to drive, but how long you'll need to wait before it's legally safe.

By simply breathing near the device, a scale meter swings to inform you whether you're slightly intoxicated, fairly intoxicated, or really soused! Waiting periods indicated on the meter range from two to five hours for legal recovery.

This item can be marketed directly to bars, nightclubs, liquor stores, police departments, and private individuals. Considering the legal penalties as well as the danger to life and limb from drunk driving, they should move like free beer on a hot summer day.

The Japanese-made Intoximeter is available with an optional DC automobile lighter adapter, as well as an AC outlet adapter. Suggested retail price is $69.95 and the importer is looking for dealers and distributors. Contact Palmetto International Corp., **Dept. IEA, P.O. Drawer 1306, Lake City, South Carolina 29560.**

Screwball Tool

The latest twist on screwdrivers is the magnetized Screwball Ratchet Driver Kit. Featuring a round handle which greatly increases comfort and turning power, it's eleven tools in one: two sizes of slotted screwdriver bits, two Phillips bits, plus seven sockets ranging from $\frac{3}{16}$ to $\frac{1}{2}$ inch.

The Screwdriver bits are stored in slots in the 2 inch diameter Screwball handle, with sockets and adapter housed in individual compartments in the styrofoam kit.

A heavy-duty magnet in one end of the tool's metal shank magnetizes the tip so screws and nuts can't be dropped or lost. The ratchet control mechanism has forward, reverse, and lock positions.

It's a tool which we feel will be a

very hot item this year. Operators of hardware stores, tool shops, specialty stores, and gift shops would do well to stock it.

Suggested retail price is $10.99, with a 15-day money-back guarantee. Dealer inquiries are invited. **Contact S/V Tool, Inc., Dept. IEA, 301 N. Main. Newton, Kansas 67114.**

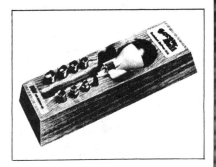

What's Old Is New

Many old time trademark names, ideas, inventions, prints, illustrations, photographs, and documents can be marketed again without obtaining permission, paying fees or royalties.

One clever company already has jumped on this idea in a big way by using the "Ipana" toothpaste trademark, abandoned by Bristol-Meyers in 1946. With a $300 investment, the young company began marketing "new" Ipana brand toothpaste, which the public nostalgically bought to the tune of $250,000 in gross profits in seven months.

The U.S. Patent Office has files bulging with expired patents. According to the government agency, 95% of all patents applied for never reach the market. These are yours for the asking.

Patents with diagrams of old fashioned hobby horses, robots for signalling car turns, high-wheel bikes, cars, rope-skipping machines, and many other odd and practical inventions could make very profitable items if marketed properly.

Browsing in used bookstores you can uncover beautiful prints and illustrations which can be inexpensively enlarged and sold for a handsome profit as art prints. These items would be perfect for sale by direct mail, to decorators, gift shops, or at flea markets and outdoor art shows.

Over 2,000 such prints and illustrations are included in The Handbook of Early American Art. This is available for $10 from Dover Publications, Dept. IEA, 920 Broadway, New York, New York.

Six million historical photographs, prints and engravings are jamming the files of Culver Pictures, Inc., 660 First Avenue New York, New York. Still pictures clipped from old motion pictures, particularly the silents, are available from Bettmann Archive, Inc., Dept. IEA, 136 E. 57th Street, New York, New York.

The U.S. Department of Agriculture has about 150,000 photos in its files, including outdoor panoramas of streams, lakes, forests, fields, and farms. There are 10 million pictures, maps, and documents in the files of the Library of Congress and the National Archives.

All these items are available free for the asking or at minimal cost. Properly framed or mounted, these "once upon a time" items can help you live happily ever after!

Zap! Hot Coffee!

If you've recently stumbled around the kitchen bleary-eyed making your morning coffee and wishing you were back in bed, you probably would like to have the Zapper.

With this remote control adapter you can turn on any electrical appliance in the home—without using cords or batteries, even while in bed!

The Zapper is a lightweight ultrasonic transmitter that activates a small receiver plugged into any standard electrical 110-volt wall outlet. The electric cord from any appliance (TV, stereo, lamp) plugs into this receiver.

The appliance switch is left on and the rest is up to the Zapper. Depress the button on the small hand transmitter and it emits an inaudible, high frequency sound. This activates the receiver unit which will then turn on or turn off the appliance.

Trying to avoid a dangerous spill at night before you reach the light switch? Just ZAP it! Investigate that noise in another room before entering the room yourself. By placing your lamps strategically you can turn them on from up to 50 feet away. It is a great convenience for ill or bedridden people.

The Zapper was developed by Data-Link Corporation of El Cajon, California. Dealer and distributor inquiries are invited. Contact Data-**Link Corp., Dept. IEA, 1282 Fayette Street, P.O. Box 1145, El Cajon, California 92022.**

No Growing Pains With Weed Seeds

You say your father was a professional gardener, but the only thing you can grow successfully is hangnails? In fact, even your plastic plants are starting to droop? Well, cheer up! Now there's a product that is guaranteed to improve your reputation with the local garden club.

Weed Seeds was developed especially for the brown thumb by Unlikely Products, Inc. Each kit contains a package of carefully selected weeds that will grow with only a minimal amount of water and neglect. The packaging container is filled with soil so it can be used as a planter box.

The product, which retails for $4.98, will do extremely well in plant shops, gift boutiques, department stores, home improvement centers, and supermarkets. Since the kits are self-contained, they can be started in the store for demonstration purposes. It is a natural for swap meets and home shows.

Weed Seeds are a good present for people who have little interest in time-consuming plants, and children will enjoy watching the weeds sprout and grow. The only possible problem is that you may have to remove an occasional unwanted flower from the planter box.

If you feel that Weed Seeds are just the item to put that green tinge back in your thumb, write to Unlikely Products, Inc., Dept. IEA, 250 Newport Center, Suite 207, Newport Beach, California 92660 for more information.

Rent a Picket

The news media are known to give disproportionate publicity to anyone who parades around with a picket sign. With enough pickets, a three-man group of malcontents can look like a whole revolution on TV!

Sy Graber, of Culver City, California, came up with the idea of renting pickets, complete with placards, to people who have a gripe. Any gripe. The cost is $8 per hour per picket, with a minimum of three hours "on the line." Rent-a-Picket pays part-time college students $3 per hour, keeping the other $5.

Rent-a-Picket's first customer was a man who was unhappy with an auto repair shop. Two of Graber's pickets carried less-than-complimentary signs back and forth in front of the shop for a whole day.

The possibilities are endless. It's a nice, clean way to air gripes about auto dealers, politicians, unpopular laws, uncooperative spouses, or even your neighbor's blaring rock music.

A picket rental service is unique, easy to set up, and requires practically no investment. You can obtain all the protest-for-pay picketers you need at local schools, and have an art student make the signs. By using replaceable messages, or a wipe-clean surface on the boards, signs become a one-time cost.

Advertising and plenty of free publicity will build the business. Just be sure that pickets keep moving, do not obstruct pedestrians, and obey lawful orders of peace officers. Your right to picket is protected by the freedom of speech guaranteed by the First Amendment to the Constitution!

Black Turns To Gold In A Licorice Store

We've been emphasizing the need for specialization for some time. Here's an example of how you can become a specialist and make good money—a licorice-only candy store!

George Mazurik's store, called the Ice Box, attracts licorice lovers from miles away, and he ships the candy all over the country. His store carries as many as 140 of 170 varieties of licorice in all colors and shapes. Some are obscure European varieties seen nowhere else in the U.S.

Part of the fun of browsing through his shop, which is nearly always packed with patrons, is selecting the right shape. Licorice windmills, coins, pipes —and even pacifiers—abound. His stock is authentic licorice.

Real licorice is made with honey or molasses, anise, wheat flour and licorice root. Some European manufacturers add ammonia salt, and many customers crave it. Many swear by its laxative value; others claim it clears sinuses and soothes sore throats. Doctors say excessive consumption can lead to high blood pressure, though.

A specialty store with an expert image like this is sure to be a hit in large metropolitan areas. Since Mazurik's place is the only store of its kind in the country, there's room for others. It's a great opportunity to capitalize on an exclusive in the marketplace with the free publicity and media exposure offered an unusual operation.

A tiny store is all you'd need for starters, provided it is located near lots of foot traffic. After all, candy is an impulse item for most buyers. You can obtain stock from wholesale suppliers located in major cities.

Mazurik can be reached at the Ice Box, 350 N. Sepulveda Blvd., Manhattan Beach, California 90266.

Be A Closet King!

If you're like most people, chances are your closets are a mess, filled with flotsam and jetsam collected over several years that don't seem to fit anywhere else in home or office.

An innovative Florida company called The Closet People has made a business out of this mess! They specialize in distinctive and functional closet interiors, custom designed for individual needs.

Storage space is often doubled using shelving, drawers, baskets, and boxes as part of the designs. They transform an unkempt, poorly utilized closet into an organized system—where everything is easy to locate!

The Closet People also market a modular system consisting of separate components that a do-it-yourselfer can use to get organized. Their patented "Closet Organizer" can be put together piece by piece or all at once, in designs that will fit even the oddest size of closet or crawl space.

Here's a business idea that has plenty of room for expansion. All you need are pre-made closet components made of wood, clear acrylics or colorful plastics, in standard sizes. They can nest together, lock together like Tinkertoys or be fastened with nuts and bolts.

Various-sized drawers, boxes or even hanging baskets can be used to organize everything from tiny closets to large office storerooms. And you can offer this service to homeowners, apartment dwellers or business offices, together with sorely needed help in getting organized.

Designed components similar to those available from The Closet People should sell well in hardware stores, do-it-yourself outlets, decorating shops and department stores. For additional details write to The Closet People, Dept. IEA, 2734 SW 28th Lane, Miami, Florida 33133.

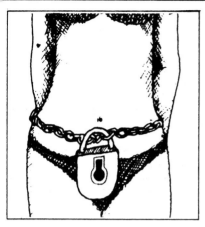

Iron-Clad Security

Chastity belts aren't new! They were designed in the 12th century to prevent wives from being unfaithful when their husbands went off to war. Chastity belts slipped out of sight for several centuries—but they are back now! Some are modern versions made out of plastic or leather.

But we've found a manufacturer in England turning out handforged iron replicas just like the real thing. Spring one of these on your best gal or guy and lock up your relationship! There is very little difference between the male and female models except the addition of ornamental flowers to add a touch of femininity.

Using the specifications of a 13th century chastity belt, David Renwick has been custom forging these delightful jailers for avid antique and curio collectors. Jealous husbands are seldom interested in paying $80 to "protect" their marriage, it seems. Anyway, each belt comes with two keys and hacksaw instructions. But can you imagine the response of guests seeing a plant imprisoned by a hanging chastity belt?

The market is, so to speak, wide open to anyone with an iron forge and eight hours to spend crafting one of these little lovelies. Chastity belts have great mail order potential. Although they weigh five pounds, they are a cinch for Christmas exposure. The key to a secure future in chastity belts is to get in while the iron is hot!

Portableachers

Much to your local high school principal's surprise, Richard Nixon has actually agreed to deliver the commencement address. The only problem is where to seat all those people.

Now you can offer a simple answer: Put the people in Portableachers. Portableachers are movable grandstands that can be attached to any standard pickup truck or vehicle and pulled along safely at traffic speeds.

There is extensive demand for temporary seating at athletic events, county fairs, parades, political rallies, church events, and other functions.

One man can set up a 40-foot Portableacher unit that seats up to 270 people in less than twenty minutes. For additional seating, more units can be placed end to end. Most operators have at least two on hand.

Providing Portableachers for rental at $200 to $300 per day per unit is a solid business opportunity. Portableachers can be delivered and installed in less time with less manpower than existing temporary bleacher facilities. They can be transported without specialized moving equipment and can be moved at the activity site.

So give the bleacher bums in your area a lift. The manufacturer is anxious for nationwide franchises.

Black Box For Cars

A tiny computer costing less than $200 promises to speed drivers directly into the Space Age. No bigger than your hand, Zemco's new CompuCruise is a push-button device that will do almost everything but steer the car!

Using the device, which mounts easily on a dashboard, drivers can monitor fuel flow, internal and external engine temperatures, battery voltage, and time and distance from departure to arrival. They can even set and maintain a desired vehicle speed using CompuCruise's cruise control feature, which directs the car to accelerate to the preselected speed.

All in all, 44 functions are monitored for numerical display. CompuCruise's fuel monitoring can help prevent drivers from running out of gas and reduce expenses for fuel and maintenance by alerting them to the need for a tune-up or warning about an impending battery failure.

The potential market for CompuCruise includes almost all of the American motoring public. Until now, motorists wanting cruise control could obtain it only on a factory installation basis, and CompuCruise's other features have been available only on recent luxury models. Now the owner of any domestic or foreign car, truck, van, or RV (with the exception of diesel or fuel-injected models) can outfit his vehicle with a CompuCruise at any time for a reasonable price.

The do-it-yourselfer can even install CompuCruise in an afternoon. Operators of truck, bus, taxi and rental fleets should be especially interested in the potential fuel and maintenance savings.

This is a great opportunity for anyone dealing in auto after-market supplies who has the necessary installation capability. Zemco is seeking qualified dealers for their hot, new "black box."

Own A Piece

Ever since the Middle Ages, when traveling monks sold "pieces of the True Cross," people have been collecting rare and interesting things. We've seen pieces of the Grand Canyon, the Golden Gate Bridge, and of course the well-known "Piece of the Rock" all successfully marketed as executive gifts or collector's items.

Latest gimmick in the "own a piece of . . . " line is a chunk of the trans-Alaska pipeline. A Washington state outfit is selling three-pound, half-inch pieces of steel pipe left over from the billion dollar project.

The chunks of steel are authenticated, numbered, and mounted on a polished teakwood base. The samples sell for $49.50 plus shipping and handling which isn't bad profit on a pile of scrap metal.

This technique could easily apply to almost anything and lends itself well to direct mail, gift shop or flea market sales. Consider old Navy ships headed for the scrap heap, infamous prisons or jailhouses, sites of battles, uprisings or riots—whatever may have intrinsic historical or emotional significance.

Nationwide marketing isn't necessary. The Golden Gate pieces, taken from cables replaced through normal wear and tear, sold out quickly in the San Francisco area.

Pieces of the trans-Alaska pipe are available from VSA, Dept. IEA, 2433 N.W. Market Street, Seattle, Washington 98107. It would be a good idea to write to them and order just one to see how they're marketed.

Bouquets By Machine

When's the last time you forgot an important anniversary or birthday? "Saying it with flowers" is pretty tough when all the florists closed for the night a half-hour before you remembered!

A Raleigh, North Carolina, florist who presumably tired of frantic calls from the love-struck, bereaved, or forgetful has put a vending machine outside his shop that will deliver a lovely floral arrangement into the hands of anyone with enough money to feed the slots.

Ken Watkins worked with an engineer for over a year to design a machine with 14 large doors opening on individual compartments holding an assortment of nifty arrangements.

Customers deposit bills in $1 and $5 denominations after making a selection and pushing a button. A timer on the machine gives them a minute to pull out their bouquet. He reports selling four or five arrangements a night from the machine, and that customers are quite pleased.

With some ingenuity, similar machines could be placed in a wide variety of locations, such as hospitals, nursing homes, restaurants, or anywhere that flowers are usually taken.

Prices for arrangements should be kept reasonable so that greater volume can be achieved because of the impulse nature of the purchase. Work with a local vending company on the design, and be sure to use a refrigerated machine so that fresh flowers keep. Use green plants and dried flowers as an alternative.

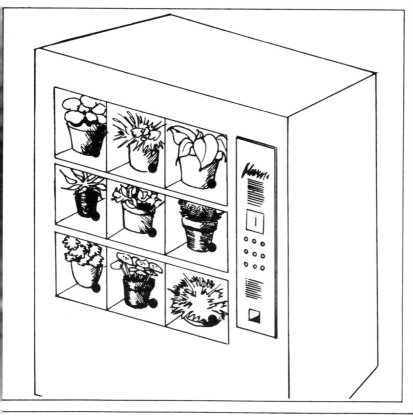

Do It In A Hammock!

Since the days of the Pharoahs in Egypt, elegant hammocks have been a sign of nobility and status. We've spotted the latest imported hammock line that rivals the most opulent creation from the days of King Tut!

A Palm Springs, California importer is introducing elegant handwoven and crocheted hammocks here in the States after much success in Europe.

Made in Central America, the hammocks come in sizes ranging from Child's to King, so everyone in the family can have his own. They're available in natural off-white, gold-yellow or cocoa brown at prices ranging from $35 to $350.

A companion line of macrame plant hangers is also available, from $7 to $45 suggested retail.

Write J.Q. Imports, Dept. IEA, P.O. Box 1116 Palm Springs, California 92262.

New Sink Trap

Ever wash a valuable piece of jewelry down the drain? Or spend money having a plumber come in to unclog a sink full of gook? We've found a product that eliminates these problems forever. The Kale Katch-All is a see-through, plastic, J-bend sink trap with a removable base that clamps in place.

If you wash that heirloom diamond down the drain by mistake, just slide two arm-like clamps out of the way and pop off the base. Inside is a tooth-like screen that traps small items like contact lenses, earrings or coins, while allowing free passage of water through the pipe itself.

Because the unit can be removed by any housewife or handy husband, drain clogs are minimized. Buildup of hair and other materials that accumulate in drains is prevented by regular removal and rinsing —without the use of caustic liquid drain openers, plungers or costly plumbers.

The Katch-All has only five parts: the bowl, barrier screen, a rubber gasket and two clamps. It is manufactured by Good Life Enterprises of Oneco, Florida, who guarantee the product for 25 years against rot, rust and electrolytic corrosion.

Distributorships are available. Good Life Enterprises, Inc., Dept. IEA P.O. Box 29, Oneco, Florida 33558.

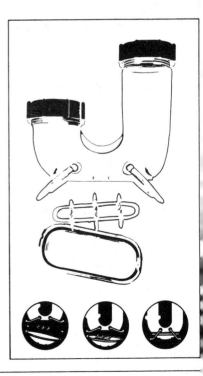

Secondhand Toyland!

Almost any family garage is bulging with old toys the children no longer want. Those unwanted but still usable toys can be recycled!

Two Oakland, California, women began Toy-Go-Round with about $1,000 and a small storefront in a business district. Their 320 square feet holds various used toys from hundreds of local children. And they have a long list of toy requests that cannot be filled.

Toys are taken on consignment, and the price of the item is split with the old owner when the item is sold. The Toy-Go-Round attracts good business from parents weary of paying high prices for fancy packaging on new toys. When sellers bring in damaged items, the cost of repair is deducted from the price before dividing the revenue with the seller.

Recycling toys can become a profitable full-time business almost any-where. If you keep your overhead low, perhaps by working together with an existing store, your profits will be much higher. The ideal spot to sell used toys could even be a garage located near a busy commercially-zoned street. Or you could take them to a flea market on weekends.

You could easily advertise in a local shopper offering to pay for certain used toys to build up a "free" inventory. You could also rummage through garage sales for used toys at bargain prices.

During holidays, donate some of the items that haven't sold well to charity, creating some free publicity. As the only operation of its kind in the area, you can bet free press coverage will help promote your grand opening.

Contact: Toy-Go-Round, Dept. IEA, 1160 Solano Ave., Albany, California.

The Bidet Is Back

The return to healthful living has revived interest in staying fit and in maintaining sound personal hygiene. It seems that every time you turn around another gadget, spray or "personal care" product enters this booming market. The latest entry in this field has its origin in Europe during the time of Napoleon.

The bidet (in French, "little horse") was originally used by Napoleon's cavalrymen to relieve the discomfort of saddle sores. In time, it became a luxury or status symbol for fashionable European aristocracy.

Rusco American Bidet Corporation has developed an updated version that is anything but antique. Its initial success in the American marketplace holds bright promise.

Rusco's bidet is designed to fit any conventional toilet, eliminating the need for a costly separate installation and extra plumbing. Costs range from $200 to $375 per unit, depending on the model chosen. It is a do-it-yourself hookup using a 110-volt outlet for power. A hose delivers water from the existing toilet tank.

Solid state electronic circuitry delivers a spray of warm water to either the perineal or vaginal area, followed by a hot air drying cycle. There's a built-in spray room deodorizer to replace aerosol air fresheners, or the proverbial book of matches.

Children seem to be intrigued by the push buttons and are easier to toilet train. Remote control models place controls within reach of the handicapped. Portability means that the unit can be taken along when the homeowner or renter moves.

Home market potential for these reasons is great, and hotels are always looking for the latest luxuries to offer guests. Hospitals and institutions can provide these units for patients at a far lower cost than previous permanent fixtures allowed. Further information is available from **Rusco American Bidet Corp., Dept. IEA, 3000 San Fernando Blvd., Burbank, California 91504.**

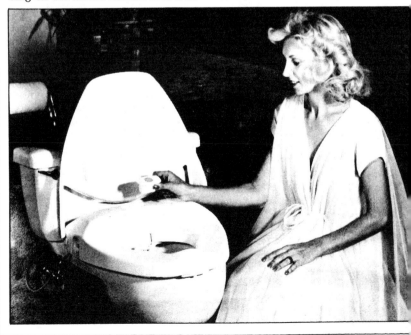

Box Office Booze

If you've ever hankered for a nice tall glass of beer while watching your favorite first-run movie, you're not alone! Most people want the same thing, and we know one Michigan theater owner who serves beer and wine. Box office business is booming!

Theaters have come into rough competition with television since so many movies are shown on TV, especially the new made-for-TV variety. Martin Shafer, the Dearborn theater owner, says people like popcorn with their beer, and it does not cut into sales of other concession items.

He adds that he has had no problem with people drinking too much. He has found that action movies and young-adult movies like "Goodbye Girl" seem to arouse the most thirst for the booze. His profit margin is high as he is able to buy the liquor at low wholesale prices.

If you don't happen to own a movie house, you might consider going into the concession business, depending on your local liquor laws. A liquor license can be very expensive, but if one is relatively easy to obtain in your area you can convince a local theater owner that he can make extra profits by providing his patrons with a little brew—wine and beer, that is. If you buy the license yourself, be sure to get an exclusive contract with the owner.

The theater would probably bear the costs of promotion, and this unique feature would bring some free publicity. As their box office business builds, so will yours!

Executive Teddy Bear

Tired of dancing to your boss's tune? Feel like you're a puppet on authority's strings? Now there's a string of your own YOU can pull that will eliminate $50 visits to an analyst and restore broken confidence.

That string is pulled out of "Teddy, the Executive Teddy Bear." When you release it, Teddy will tell you what you want to hear: "You're a born leader" or "You ARE on your way to the top."

Teddy's no slouch either. He travels in a cardboard box that resembles a briefcase and he comes nattily attired in a black and white checkered suit, grey vest, red tie and blue shirt. Small wonder he's described as ruggedly handsome.

The brainchild of Louis Stangle, Highland Park, Illinois, Teddy will be marketed throughout the world. There are plans now for translating his messages into foreign languages so anyone in the world can receive his emergency praise. Some of the other messages available are "There is nothing you can't do" and "You're a winner—Teddy knows!"

Teddy may not duly impress the psychiatric field, but he'll make those bad days at the office that much easier to bear.

For more information contact L.S. **Associates, Dept. IEA, P.O. Box 1033, 7225 Duran Drive, Tinley Park, Illinois 60477.**

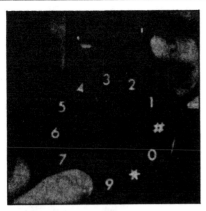

Make "Ma Bell" A Soft Touch!

Push-button telephones from Ma Bell are one of the greatest improvements in telephone technology since the mouthpiece and receiver were joined in a single unit. They save time and make dialing easier, but with installation charges and monthly service fees, they're expensive.

Now any standard dial telephone can be converted to a touchtone system in seconds with a SoftTouch push-button dialing device. This $34.95 cost-saver replaces ordinary mouthpieces and screws on without rewiring. It fits any standard wall or desk phone, single- or multi-line, in tone-capable service areas.

Soft-Touch provides accurate tone access to computers, central dictating equipment, and will even function as a portable computer. This is especially useful, as homes and businesses will be able to hook up to a computer over the phone lines, using touchtone for inputting data.

Soft-Touch is available in black, or color-matched to Bell Systems' beige, green, red, yellow, or white colors. It features a 15-day full refund and a one-year warranty.

This is a great mail-order item, and would surely move well in hardware stores, gift shops, and novelty stores as well. Dealer and distributor inquiries are invited. Contact 2001 Telephone Systems, Inc., c/o The **Hauman House, Dept. IEA. Meriden, Connecticut, 06450.**

Plants That Talk Back!

In recent years, botanists and parapsychologists have conducted scientific experiments which have proven that plants have memories, sensitivities and are even capable of emotion.

Even before then, gardeners and "parents" of indoor plants have been talking to their leafy companions in an attempt to make them feel more at home. Plant lovers claim that daily conversation with their potted friends translates into increased growth and better health.

But who ever heard of a plant that talks back?

Gabby Green, The Talking Plant, does. Hardly a miracle, the small indoor plant comes in a pastel flowered ceramic planter with a pull-string recording device that creates the illusion of a talking plant.

When the string is pulled, a cute girlish voice says eight different things such as: "Smile with me," "love me," and "be nice to me." The manufacturer is currently working on another voice: a gravelly little old hypochondriac male voice that complains about not getting enough water and if things don't change he'll leave.

The verbose plant is a natural for gift shops, florists and indoor plant shops. It makes an ideal housewarming gift, especially for people living alone. When all else fails, at least they'd have Gabby to rap with.

Gabby Green is available for $10.95 from Skalon Enterprises, Inc. Dept. IEA, 922 So. Montecito Dr., San Gabriel, California 91776. Dealer/distributor inquiries are invited.

Divorce School

Millions of couples untie the knot every year, and divorce rates are skyrocketing. An average of one in five marriages will end in divorce this year; in some parts of the country the average is closer to one in three! Sociologists predict we are headed for a time when serial monogamy will be more traditional than lifelong marriage to one partner!

Divorce is an agonizing process for most couples, and a costly one as well. Attorneys charge high fees to shepherd a case through the tangle of briefs, writs and courtroom appearances. The simplest, uncontested divorce can cost from $350 to $700 or more in some areas of the country!

What most people don't know is that the paper work involved is normally simple, forms are standard, and even court appearances are cut and dried. It doesn't take a "Philadelphia Lawyer" to get a divorce. You can do-it-yourself (or pro se in Latin legalese) in most states with a minimum of training.

A "divorce school" in Chicago, called the Pro Se Divorce Project, teaches future divorcees all of the steps involved for a tuition of only $5. Included is a manual, legal paper and training.

In a do-your-own divorce, the petitioner acts as his or her own legal counsel. He writes the allegations, files the necessary papers, and touches all the courtroom bases alone—even the final arguments before the judge.

A homemade divorce works only in cases where the action is uncontested; extended custody battles, arguments over property and the like are best left to expert legal counsel.

Depending on the laws in your state, a divorce school like this can be both a needed service and a moneymaker for the operator. Law students can act as part-time faculty for your school. You can conduct classes in conjunction with a larger free university or as a storefront entity. Access to a nearby law library would be quite helpful. In most cities, there are legal forms suppliers who can provide standard documents for student use.

For further information contact: Pro Se Divorce Project, Dept. IEA, 81 So. Walker Dr., Chicago, Illinois.

Rent-A-Shark

Tired of chasing the neighbors out of your swimming pool? Want to keep your private beach really private? Now you can buy or rent a shark of your very own just like the one featured in the hit thriller "Jaws."

A London artist has designed a menacing, razor-toothed, five-foot shark made of fiberglass and painted to look like a real denizen of the deep. Electronic circuitry inside makes the beast dive, turn and change speed (during the attack sequence) at a push of a button poolside. The operator uses a hand held radio transmitter to send signals to his ferocious friend.

Stephen Winkworth has sold several of the sharks, at $900 apiece, to customers who want to liven up their next backyard pool party or shoot realistic home movies. The price is a little high but it beats strapping a fin on the back of your dog.

This might be a great gimmick as a rental item but we wonder about the liability if you really scared the wits out of somebody.

Grow Shoe Trees!

Don't throw out those old shoes! They could be the basis of a successful new business. Two UCLA students recently took the old bronzed baby shoe craze one step further and began selling fiberglass, resin-preserved athletic shoes as planters.

They sell the acrylic-hardened shoes with plants inside for $3 apiece and have sold 2,000 in the last year. Supplies are easy to come by. Canvass athletic departments at local high schools and colleges asking for discarded basketball, tennis, football, and track shoes.

There's no reason to limit yourself to athletic shoes. Old work and cowboy boots and men's and women's shoes of all sizes and descriptions would work fine.

Salvation Army, Goodwill shops, thrift stores, and garage sales are excellent sources of old shoes. With a business license you can obtain indoor plants at wholesale prices directly from the nursery.

You'll need a garbage can for the fiberglass resin and a clothesline to hang the shoes from while they dry. Sell your shoe planters to plant stores, gift shops and novelty stores.

Profitable sidelines include preserving athlete's sneakers as gifts to parents, sweethearts, or to the jock himself. The UCLA students have preserved the slippers a man was wearing when he saved the life of a drowning child and the boots a policeman was wearing when he retired. Shoes preserved as a remembrance can be sold for up to $35.

A Doctor In The House?

For all the people lucky enough to have handymen around the house to fix things, there are many more who don't know a bevel from a hammer. Of course, you can call different specialists listed in any newspaper to do minor repairs. But finding a reliable **person with the right skills is a time-consuming chore. As are rare guarantees on workmanship.**

A Dallas firm called the House Clinic is offering guaranteed service for homeowners. They have specialists on call who'll make minor repairs, fix broken tiles, doors, screens, roofs, siding and floors. And they do windows!

A clinic like theirs can be started by anyone handy with a hammer, or friendly with someone who is. Get a list company to provide addresses of residential property in your area. A good place to start would be an old neighborhood, where houses are more likely to need repair.

Send out fliers announcing your business, and build referrals. Once you have several "handy people" working for you, knock out a pretty hefty profit by charging reasonable non-union rates. Guarantee your work and register with consumer agencies.

Contact: House Clinic, Dept. IEA, 310 Memory Lane, Dallas, Texas.

Medium-Rare Hippo?

At a loss planning what to serve your in-laws the next time they visit? Here's what you've been looking for.

Delicacies from the world over are available from Pfaelzer Brothers, a Chicago-based firm that sells exotic food through mail order.

In the privacy of your own home you can now serve and enjoy foods that princes demanded and empresses expressly requested. Choice cuts of hippo, wild boar, elk and boneless buffalo hump are just a few of the many entrees available.

Imagine your guest's delight as the aroma of medium-rare bear legs drifts up lightly from their plates. Their compliments will be outweighed only by their curiosity as to where their clever hosts acquired such tantalizing treats in the middle of Hoboken.

Bear legs, by the way, can be a little tough but rather tasty, especially with the help of a microwave oven or crockpot.

Having trouble with persnickity young eaters? They may not go for liver and onions but tell them those loins of llama are what ancient Peruvian messengers ate before they did their cross-country Andes number. What aspiring young football star or diving ace could turn down those credentials?

And for the restauranteur who wants to add a touch of exotic flavor to his otherwise ordinary bill of fare, Pfaelzer can provide other choice foods from places such as Malaysia, Central Africa, the Mediterranean and Australia.

Contact: Pfaelzer Bros., Dept. IEA, 4501 W. District Blvd., Chicago, Illinois.

Pull Their Hair Out!

Millions of people all over the world have hair on their bodies that they want to take off! The vanity business is so big that a little corner of it in your town can be incredibly profitable.

Now Space Age technology allows you to remove unwanted hair permanently and painlessly, without harm to sensitive skin tissues. A revolutionary new process uses an Ionization Computer to point harmless direct current at the hair root, reverse the pH factor and kill hair permanently.

The process takes only a few minutes to complete—depending on the amount of hair to be removed—and unsightly hair can be removed from anywhere on the body, from ugly back hair to hairy shoulders.

The process is most popular with ladies wanting to remove hair from the face, legs, midriff, or underarms.

Previously, the only way to do this was with temporary measures like messy creams or dangerous thermolysis/electrolysis, which is often harmful to the skin itself.

The House of St. James, headquartered in Los Angeles, has grown so successful removing hair with this new process that it now has national franchises available.

With an initial investment of under $5,000, their franchisees are grossing $1,500 a week with only two employees! Franchise agreements include training and assistance in setting up. The business becomes the property of the franchisee.

Charges of $40 an hour for hair removal are not unusual in this business, with $10 an hour extra for Sunday work and $5 an hour extra for difficult areas such as "bikini work."

Contact: House of St. James, Dept. IEA, 9201 Sunset Blvd., Los Angeles, California.

Create Keepsake Wall Hangings

It seems every family in America has a treasure trove of keepsakes ranging from old theatre tickets to wedding announcements and snapshots of daughter's first long dress. These items are rarely organized, let alone displayed. The extent to which most go is filling scrapbooks with memorabilia.

There is a way that anyone with an artistic bent—or a love of nostalgia—can turn a shoebox full of memories into an income opportunity. Follow the lead of Karen Watson, a Massachusetts lady who creates collages, shadow boxes, and wall hangings from these treasures as decor items for a patron's home or office.

She adds depth of feeling by using multiple images and puts a dash of humor in the works she creates for customers who pay $25 and more. Part of her service includes a questionnaire which helps her understand what the items displayed represent.

A similar service should work in almost any city in the country if promoted properly from the nostalgia angle. For openers, you could take space at craft fairs and art shows and sign up buyers based on samples you've done for friends and relatives. Keepsake creations can be put together by almost any handy craftsperson with an eye for balance and color combinations. Multiple-compartment shadow boxes, available commercially in most arts and crafts stores, are about the only materials you need. The customers will provide the "goodies" you need to fill the nooks and crannies.

For information, write Marblehead Productions, Dept. IEA, 28 Pearl Street, Marblehead, Massachusetts 01949.

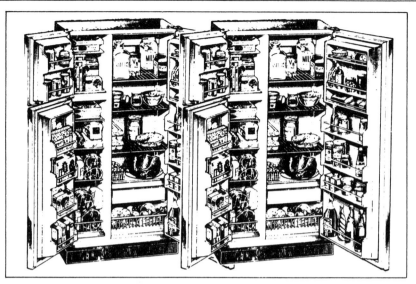

Cool Idea: Rent-A-Fridge!

With a supply of used but functioning refrigerators obtained for a song, you're ready to start a refrigerator rental service! Gerald Springer, a manufacturer and importer in Mount Vernon, New York, began renting refrigerators to college students a few years ago. Already he has 7,000 of them in college dormitory rooms from Maine to Texas.

The highly transient student market is hot for these cool items and the market can easily be expanded to apartment dwellers or servicemen if you're near a military base. Fewer and fewer apartment owners now provide refrigerators as part of the rent. And refrigerators in the barracks still aren't government issue!

When a refrigerator goes on the blink, to most people it just means it's time to buy another one. But refrigerators aren't as complicated as is generally believed.

A surprising number of discarded refrigerators are still in working order and can begin running perfectly again after minor repairs—often as simple as replacing a temperature control switch!

Running a classified ad as well as an ad in the yellow pages just offering to haul away discarded refrigerators will result in a surprising number of responses—many will offer to pay you to do it! You'll be even more surprised by how many of the "reefers" will still work!

New refrigerators are expensive, and used ones available at used furniture or appliance stores will cost $75 to $150. This is an outlay many would like to avoid in the face of move-in expenses like first and last month's rent, security, cleaning and even pet deposits!

A simple ad showing your monthly rates in college newspapers or classified sections of local papers should be highly effective. So would making contacts with local apartment rental or referral agencies.

The refrigerators that can't be repaired are candidates for the scrap dealer, and income from this end of the business alone will cover your overheads!

James Bond Jeep

In the wake of international terrorism, kidnappings, assassinations, bombings and other anarchies, a Memphis-based armored truck firm is now manufacturing an anti-terror jeep so complete that even James Bond would turn green with envy.

The $18,000 Cherokee Jeep, customized by Moore & Sons, Inc., looks like a normal station wagon. But it comes equipped with a plastic armor coating, bulletproof windows and a stabilizing system to keep the jeep going after one or more of the tires are shot out.

The "super" jeep can withstand explosive grenades, gas attacks, rammings, small arms fire up to 30-caliber size, and can elude attackers by racing off across the "boondocks" *with all four tires shot out.*

The jeep boasts roll bars, reinforced bumpers, shielded engine compartment, drive train, radiator and headlights and even retaliation equipment. Offensive weaponry includes gunports, weapons, radio communication systems, gas dispensing systems, tool kits and/or winches.

For an extra fee, the company will provide enough armor to withstand 50-caliber machine gun bullets, and add machine guns, mini-rocket launchers or oil and smoke sprays just like 007 himself uses!

For further information: Moore & Sons, Inc., Dept. IEA, 2900 Airways Blvd., P.O. Box 30091, Memphis, Tenn. 38103.

Crepes a la Cassette

Interest in gourmet cooking, international cuisine and fine wines at the dinner table is on the rise all over the country. Adventuresome home chefs can now listen as Marina Polvay, a renowned *cuisiniere*, prepares dinner on tape.

To the strains of appropriate ethnic music, a complete international menu can be prepared, from appetizer to dessert. You may not be able to pronounce Ching Chiao-Ch'ao-Niu-Jou (Green Pepper Steak), but you'll be able to serve this Chinese delicacy with confidence, and even know the correct wine to serve with it, after listening to step-by-step instructions on "Cooking by Ear" cassettes.

Ten separate meals can be whipped up, using separate tapes describing Austrian, Chinese, Creole, French, Hungarian, Italian, Mexican, Russian, Southern or Spanish menu items. Of course, the menus can be mixed for the truly daring diner.

Complete information on necessary ingredients and cooking utensils are wrapped around each tape.

This idea can be copied or adapted to a lot of different situations. The popularity of cassettes and inexpensive recorders makes market acceptance that much easier.

Why not tape step-by-step, expert instructions on auto repair, for example? Plenty of people would like to be able to do their own maintenance to save on repair bills. Yet the subject is just as confusing to a beginner as gourmet cooking.

Contact: Savannah Magazine, Dept. IEA, 402 East Bay St., Savannah, Georgia 31401.

Turn Rust Into Solid Gold!

One of the hottest new cosmetic products to hit the West Coast market in years is "Indian Earth." It's selling like wildfire at $12.50 in tiny corked crockery jars. The phenomenal success of this product shows what creative thinking and savvy marketing will do to make something ordinary into a high-margin moneymaker.

"Indian Earth" can be used by trendy buyers as a blusher, face make-up, eye shadow or lip color. It is sold as a "non-cosmetic cosmetic" that's free of artificial ingredients, harmful chemicals, and the like. It responds to body chemistry to create a unique color for each person using it—male or female.

The kicker is that "Indian Earth," for all its high-sounding claims, is nothing more than iron oxide and talc. Iron oxide, for those of you who've forgotten high-school chemistry, is commonly known as *rust*. And you can find samples of it on any used car in America!

Of course, the iron oxide used in Indian Earth is chemically pure and passes Food & Drug Administration criteria. But it's available in 50-gallon drums for next to nothing in any chemical supply house. So is talc, the second "secret" ingredient.

This proves you don't need to be Max Factor or Charles Revson to make a hit in the cosmetics business with a product like this one of your own. The ingredients are cheap and readily available. Unique bottles or jars can be produced by a pottery craftsman in sufficient quantity for a market test, and the item can be sold at arts & crafts fairs, "alternative" expos, or through the mail. When it takes off, you'll want to arrange for higher volume production with a packaging firm.

You can obtain a sample of "Indian Earth" for testing purposes from Indian Earth Company, Dept. IEA, 999 N. Doheny Drive, Beverly Hills, California 90069. Price is $12.50. You'll also receive a copy of their brochure, which you can use as a starting point for designing your own marketing plan. The company makes distributorships available, if you choose to sell their product instead of making it yourself.

Job Hunters Show

"Pounding the pavement" is a very frustrating approach to finding a job as well as being terribly inefficient.

Much of the country's unemployment problem could be relieved if it was easier for the unemployed to contact employers who are hiring.

A Miami employment agency owner is running "Career Opportunity Shows" all over Florida to do just that. More than 130 employers and 95 franchisors paid $260 apiece for booth space in the auditorium, generating $58,500 in gross rental revenue for the promoter.

Better than 20,000 job seekers paid $2.00 apiece for tickets to the convention-style show (total gate: $40,180). Eastern Airlines, one of the corporate exhibitors, got 4,500 job applications.

This would be easy to duplicate and is a needed service in many parts of the country. Tied in with the show could be inexpensive workshops on job hunting techniques, grooming, and the like.

Promoting the show should be simple using ads in the "Help Wanted" section of the local papers. Large, community-minded employers should be eager to participate.

Shows should be scheduled so they don't conflict with normal working hours; evening and weekend hours would be best.

Coin-Op Coat Check

An ingenious new coat check system takes part of the bother out of cold weather—for both customer and businessman—and presents an excellent opportunity at the same time.

There are thousands of public places like shopping malls, restaurants, night spots and auditoriums where Check-o-Matic would be a

welcome benefit. It's a coin-operated rack that gives customers a safe and secure place to hang their coats for 25 cents.

The customer inserts a coin in an empty hanger slot, wraps an attached chain through the arm of his coat, and locks it with a coded key. The key—not the coat—is carried while shopping, dining or dancing.

The Intercheck Corporation, a Canadian outfit, designed their unit to be weight sensitive, so the hanger will not support a coat unless a coin is inserted. Available in free-standing or wall-mounted versions, Check-o-Matic can be obtained without the coin-op feature for situations where security checking is to be offered free.

Prices range from $995 to $1,495 for the units, which have done quite well in Canada and are used by Holiday Inns there. Intercheck wants to expand into the U.S. market and is looking for distributors, making this a dynamic opportunity for those able to move quickly.

Each rack has 21 hangers, and that adds up to quite a piece of change.

Make Red tape Pay Off!

It should come as no surprise that people are sick of bureaucratic red tape. They hate standing in long lines to register cars, take out permits, or fill out mountains of paperwork that government thrives on. And the "you stupid jerk" attitude of the paid-out-of-your-taxes employees behind the counters infuriates people more than anything else.

Now Services Unlimited, a glutton-for-punishment organization, will go to the bureaucracy for you and take care of birth certificates, hunting licenses, passports, vehicle registration and everything you've always needed from city hall or the statehouse but were afraid to ask for!

Services Unlimited is a one-man operation in a tiny room in New York. Charges of from $1 to $5 are quite reasonable, considering that the uninitiated could waste a half day trying to fill out the proper forms at city hall.

Almost any town is large enough to offer an excellent potential for this much needed service. Investment would be absolutely minimal: an office, telephone (preferably with an answering machine for use when you're out), and some ads in the local papers. The consumer affairs reporters of local news media would be a sure bet to publicize your efforts, especially if you offered to tip them off to any particular problems with the bureaucrats.

You would have to have an excellent working knowledge of how to expedite the paperwork entrusted to you, and you should spend a lot of time observing and talking to people at city hall. Naturally, being on friendly terms with the appropriate government employees would be a big help.

One market to go after is contractors, who waste much of their valuable time waiting for permits.

Contact: Services Unltd., Dept. IEA, 112-37 Roosevelt Ave., Corona, New York.

Get Bent!

As an Illinois inventor recently discovered, getting bent out of shape might not be such a bad idea after all. In fact, it's an idea which could be worth millions and revolutionize everything from cooking to baseball!

John Bennett of East Peoria, Illinois, is the inventor of Hand-Tastic, which is simply a new angle on an old idea, namely handles.

The invention is a handle with a 19 degree angle, which Bennett maintains follows the natural line of force which passes along the arm and wrist into the instrument being held.

Mechanical tests show a 42 percent power gain over conventional handles and the inventor is now negotiating with manufacturers in an attempt to mass market bent-handled equipment.

Bennett realized that conventional handles require a user to fully rotate his wrist, wasting muscular energy to maintain the wrist in that position. While a 19 degree angle is the most effective, his patent covers handles angled from 14 to 24 degrees.

The inventor claims the Hand-Tastic principle will work on anything straight. He says, "It's a bent world."

Heralding his invention as perhaps the most revolutionary breakthrough since the invention of the wheel, Bennett plans to apply the bent principle to golf clubs, baseball bats, tennis rackets, frying pans, hammers, hockey sticks, wheelbarrows and other commonly used items with handles.

The inventor is now talking with representatives from Brunswick, Rawlings and Spalding sports equipment manufacturers. They're interested in Bennett's claim that use of his bent handles would increase home runs in baseball by 300 percent, prevent tennis elbow, and improve golf putting dramatically.

For further information, contact John at Dept. IEA, 2500 North Main Street, East Peoria, Illinois 61611.

Chairs From Flower Pots

An Atlanta entrepreneur has come up with an innovative idea you can duplicate easily—flower pot chairs that plant lovers are crazy about.

Sixteen-inch, clay flower pots form the base for chairs which are durable and comfortable. A three-by-sixteen inch, fabric-covered, foam cushion is mounted on a one-half-by-sixteen inch plywood round and placed in the opening of the flower pot.

This idea could start a new trend in environmental furniture. You can make matching tables by gluing two flower pots end to end and adding an appropriately sized plywood round. Or how about hanging lamps made from inverted flower pots!

All of the materials are easy to obtain. Pots can be purchased from nursery or garden supply centers, and it is possible to get quantity discounts. Plywood rounds can be ordered pre-cut from lumber yards; foam rubber cushions, fabric and staples for fastening are available through large fabric outlets or hobby shops.

Visit local furniture retailers with a sample chair and see if they will stock a few on consignment. If so, leave swatches of fabric so customers can select their favorite or offer to customize using their material. Consider displaying chairs, tables and other creations at swap meets, fairs and home shows to attract a wide market. And don't forget to point out the adaptability of the furniture for indoor or outdoor use.

Moveable Munchies

Here's a new idea you can really sink your teeth into: mobile gourmet lunches! We found one entrepreneur who started with three young women going into office buildings at lunch time with picnic baskets loaded with delightful goodies.

The Moveable Feast now has 50 maidens delivering high quality sandwiches and fruit to busy executives who can't make it out for lunch. While this service is now only 25 percent of their total catering business, we think you could turn this idea into your own delicious moneymaker!

You can start with less than $500, and some young female employees attired in attractive, "earthy" outfits. The key is to provide customers with good-tasting lunches—and you can almost name your price!

Prepare your sandwiches with fresh bread, and use good quality meats and poultry. You can also sell cheese, fruit, yogurt, juices, and homemade desserts.

Maidens can work out of their own cars, with picnic baskets. Simple coolers in the car will keep food fresh. Make the rounds in a downtown business district to boutiques, law firms, accounting offices and ad agencies—anywhere busy people can't make it out for lunch.

Your business should grow fast by word-of-mouth, as you become an alternative to the lunch truck or junk food machines. If you already have a restaurant or deli, this can become a unique promotional idea. As a first in your area, you should get plenty of free publicity from hungry local news media.

For further information contact: Moveable Feast, Dept. IEA, 3380 Robertson, Los Angeles, California.

Outhouse Back Indoors!

A Swedish firm has updated the old outhouse, and brought it indoors! The Mullbank Compost Toilet can save up to 2,500 gallons of water a month, eliminate plumbing problems, and even fertilize the garden!

The compost toilet is a self-contained unit which brings together the right combination of heat, oxygen and humidity so human wastes can decompose naturally under controlled and accelerated conditions.

The unit takes no more energy per month than two 60-watt bulbs.

The compost toilet can be installed in less than two hours, and is approved by health authorities. These units retail for about $736, and can be purchased in large lots for as little as $479 each!

This energy-saving Swedish product is still in its infancy, and the market is sure to grow, as more families can afford their own homes.

The best market for this product

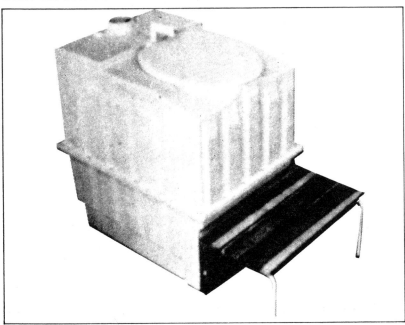

A regular toilet requires expensive plumbing hook-ups and a sewage system. The compost unit merely requires an airvent, and 120v. a.c. power. At the end of a normal year of use, all that remains of excrement and toilet paper is a powder dry residue of earth-like humus; about enough to fill a coffee can.

Other than emptying the unit twice a year, and occasional watering, the device is maintenance free! There is no odor because an electric fan removes all odors continuously.

would be "hip-affluent" homeowners. Since this product is so new and unique, it is a natural for demonstration at do-it-yourself fairs.

The right type of direct mailing lists for an entire area would be an excellent source of leads on this item, as well as close association with homebuilding companies.

It can be marketed to government agencies, which may be willing to install one to set an "energy-saving" example. This type of deal could bring lots of free publicity!

Talking Tombstones

The closest thing we've ever seen to immortality is a solar-powered headstone that will play a recording of the dearly departed's voice at the push of a graveside button.

At the same time, a video screen will flicker to life and present biographical data, genealogy and a computerized photograph.

There's more. The talking headstone has "add-ons" that can include sensors to tell when a visitor approaches, or the grass needs watering. A nozzle can spray incense and a mechanized arm can emerge to trim the grass.

Developed by John Dilks III, head of Creative Tombstone, Inc., the programmable headstone sells for $39,500 in a vandal-proof version featuring bullet-proof glass. There have been at least 50 inquiries from potential customers, who may or may not be dying to have one for their very own.

Because of stiff competition in this business, we would expect that the next "generation" in graveside hardware will include three-dimensional holograms of the loved one delivering his own epitaph in living color. After all, the technology does exist.

Horses Draw People, Too

We've found a handful of cagey entrepreneurs who have built thriving businesses by giving short hansom cab rides, carriage rides or even hayrides to romantic lovers, tourist groups, and mobs of kids—in the city, at a dollar a head.

What it takes for highest profit potential is a well-known and heavily trafficked tourist or entertainment area that draws people looking for something new and unusual to do. The more pedestrian traffic, the better. Simple visibility will bring riders.

At amusement parks, resorts, large swap meets or fairs it should be relatively simple to make arrangements with the operators to offer such a service on their property. A downtown entertainment area or romantic city park can be even better, but may pose city ordinance and permit problems, depending on the area.

Some cities have ordinances on the books preventing horses from being used on streets because of sanitation problems. Other laws date from the time when "horseless carriages" scared hayburners half to death, causing accidents.

In this situation, you would need to obtain a variance from the city fathers to go into the carriage trade. Approached properly, variances are not as difficult to obtain as you might think, especially in smaller to medium-sized towns where civic pride can be appealed to.

It would be vital to guarantee that sanitation won't be a problem—one operator we found uses a *diaper* on his horses!

Have Your Cake . . . And Eat It, Too!

Erotic desserts might seem nasty to some, but they're bringing the sweet smell of success to at least one lusty baker. The display windows at The Erotic Baker in New York City are a veritable peep show.

Inside are breast loaves, bun loaves, and rump cakes. "His" and "Her" breads, cookies and cakes in the shape of genitalia, with candy lips, hearts, derrieres, lower torsos, and other indescribables serving as decorations.

Other baked erotica includes a wedding cake showing the bride and groom nestled on top in an icing bed. The bride's breasts peep above the sugar frosting covers.

In addition to baked goods, erotic forms lend themselves equally well to candies. Imaginative lollipops, jaw breakers, and other candies can be made at home in novel molds for sale at adult bookstores and other "discriminating" shops.

One woman in the Midwest is now producing imaginatively-shaped, all-day suckers in even more imaginative flavors: macaroon, guava, tangerine, tea, lettuce, spiced apple, and other wild tastes.

She makes them in her own kitchen and has all the orders she can handle. This is an idea that should be workable in any liberal metropolitan area.

Contact: Erotic Bakery, Dept. IEA, 73 W. 83rd, Manhattan, New York.

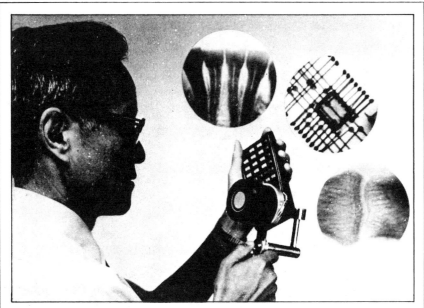

X-Ray Eyes!

Now you can have X-ray vision! Just use a new pocket-size X-ray machine that promises incredible industrial, medical and dental uses.

There are thousands of uses for the hand-held Lixiscope (Low Intensity X-ray Imaging Scope); ranging from on-site injury examination, to detection of welding defects or gas leaks in pipes.

The availability of such a device means that medical emergencies can receive instant, on-the-spot diagnosis in hospital emergency rooms—rather than losing precious moments while a portable X-ray machine and technician are brought to the emergency room. There's no wait for the X-rays to be developed either. The physician can know instantly what the problem is!

The device was developed by Dr. Lo I Yin, an X-ray researcher at NASA's Goddard Space Flight Center, Greenbelt, Maryland. The Lixiscope is based on a concept under study that will use energy sources in space by converting their X-rays to visible images.

The pull of a trigger unshields a radioactive source, sending a low dosage of X-rays into the object being examined. The X-rays passing through the object are absorbed by a phosphor screen which converts them to visible light.

Instant pictures of X-rayed objects can be made quickly with an attached camera, using a radioactive exposure a thousand times weaker than that of a conventional X-ray machine. Medical advantages include the ability to survey physical injury at the site of an accident and screening soft tissue tumors. The device is perfect for use in a dental office for simple X-ray and root canal analysis.

Although the device, powered by a single penlight battery, is not yet on the market, it's estimated that production units could cost less than $5,000. Additional industrial uses for the Lixiscope are to be covered by a NASA conference.

Contact Don E. Witten, Office of Public Information, Goddard Space Flight Center, Greenbelt, Maryland.

Newest Moped!

The hottest new answer to the fuel shortage and air pollution problem is Vesuvius—a steam-powered bicycle. David Sarlin of Berkeley, California, worked nearly three years perfecting a steam power plant which can be mounted on and detached from any 24- to 27-inch bicycle in three minutes, without major changes.

Actually, steam-powered bicycles aren't new. More than 30 have blown hot air in the course of bicycle history. In fact, the copper boiler Sarlin uses on Vesuvius is a modified, drop-tube design quite similar to that used by Lucius Copeland in an 1884 high-wheel steam velocipede.

Sarlin's single-cylinder, water-and-fuel-powered engine turns a hollow shaft held by two ball bearings. A four-inch diameter, spoked aluminum flywheel is added to this shaft.

With a few turns of an adjustment knob on the bracket holding the power plant, the engine is lowered so that the flywheel presses against the bike's front tire, providing friction drive. When the engine is raised, the bike may be ridden with the power plant disengaged.

The power unit weights 38 pounds. When added to the average 42 pound bicycle frame, you have an 80 pound machine capable of top speeds in excess of 16 miles per hour!

Vesuvius averages 55 miles per gallon of gasoline, and five miles per gallon of water. Since the power bicycle is equipped with a one-pint gas tank (gas is used to heat the boiler) and a four-pint water tank, extra containers of fuel and water will have to be carried for long trips.

Though a steam-powered bicycle may not be the ultimate answer to fuel shortages and air pollution problems, it's a great novelty gimmick which lends itself to numerous publicity and promotional uses.

Vesuvius could stoke the fires of a grand opening campaign for a bicycle shop, and add the necessary hot air to almost any publicity stunt. A single Vesuvius could be used over and over again, paying for itself by leasing as a promotional device.

A Vesuvius power plant, tested and ready to mount on your bicycle, sells for $2,300 plus shipping costs. If you'd like to build one yourself, Sarlin will send you a 25-page book for only $11 which includes complete plans and parts lists. Four pages of construction and operation notes are included with a history of steam-powered bicycles. Write David Sarlin at 1247 Glen Avenue, Dept. IEA, Berkeley, California 94708.

A Robot That Plays Table Tennis

Table tennis has been popular in America for many years as a recreational activity and competitive sport. But finding a good partner who can do more than play ping pong is another story. Now devotees can match wits with a robot opponent!

The *table tennis robot* provides all the heated excitement of match play anytime. Just plug the unit into any 120 volt outlet and use a remote control to customize ball delivery. The robot can smash them at you from its storage container as fast as 120 balls *per minute* and at speeds of 60 miles per hour.

For beginners, the robot can be programmed to release one ball per minute to any location on the table. It will put top, bottom or sidespins on shots and recycle balls through the system automatically when they're hit to a retrieval net.

The robot retails for $394 and is currently sold through the mail. Retail sales outlets should include sporting goods stores, department stores, and electronic game stores. Health and recreation centers and schools are markets as well as existing table tennis leagues in major cities. The manufacturer seeks representatives. For further information, contact Sitco T.T. Robots, Dept. IEA, Box 20456, Portland, Oregon 97220.

Grow Your Own Donuts

A group of Polish scientists were taken off the Soviet space program and put to work solving the food shortage and high prices, which are as prevalent there as in the U.S. Their latest breakthrough could run circles around the donut industry.

"Polish Donut Seeds" have recently been introduced to the U.S. market and promise to be as successful as Polish pistols (with the barrel pointed toward the shooter), Polish coffee mugs (with the handle inside), and other inventions along those lines.

The tiny seeds are actually ordinary Cheerios which come packaged in an envelope with complete planting and care instructions, including the important fact that they must be planted "with the left side up," and cultivated at 3 a.m. daily.

Chances of the seeds growing are rather slim, since germination—based on extensive testing—is .0 percent. But the seed packets can grow into a real moneymaker as a novelty gift item or a promotional gimmick for the *real* donut shops. Don't forget the home gardening market, either.

Packets are available for 25 cents wholesale, from Shamrock Reports, Inc. The suggested retail price is 50 cents. You can obtain a sample of their product for $1 by writing to Dept. IEA, at 2633 Wood Warbler Lane S.W., Roanoke, Virginia 24018.

Follow The Yellow Brick Road

Used brick is one of the most popular materials for patios, pool decks, fireplaces and walls. There's still a very strong market for *real* antique paving brick, fire brick and structural brick from old houses. In fact, the price rises depending upon the city of origin.

Of course, there's plenty of manufactured "used" brick available on the market as well as phony stick-on veneers. But these substitutes don't have the authenticity or charm of the real thing. Many people will pay extra if they can find it.

Here's where a smart entrepreneur can make a quick profit.

Any building demolition or road construction projects, especially in older cities, can yield a fortune in used brick.

Often, especially with government or municipal projects, you can have the brick for free by paying the cost of removal from the work site. In other cases you may have to pay a small amount for the brick.

An excellent approach is to prowl through smaller towns and cities scouting for buys. If you are located in one of these smaller towns, so much the better. You can obtain the brick there and cart it into a nearby metropolitan area for resale at prices ranging from 25 cents to 50 cents per brick, depending upon the going rate in your area.

A Fortune In Shredded Money

You can get millions of dollars from your local bank—for almost nothing! Millions of dollars in shredded money, that is. New pollution control laws have forced banks and the Federal Reserve to shred their old money—2.7 billion pieces in 1977. And they have to dispose of it somewhere!

Novelty companies have already started manufacturing gift items, such as paperweights and writing pens, using the shredded money in sealed containers. Others have used it for insulation and roofing supplies.

Instant Fortune, Inc., a New York novelty company, makes a complete line of resin products filled with shredded money. Their dollar sign, which contains a million shredded dollars, sells for $150. Their biggest selling item is a resin pen filled with $2,000 of shredded money. Another Connecticut firm markets money-filled plastic eggs with nests, which sell for $5.95.

The shredded money can sometimes be obtained from your local bank for nothing, or at the most $5 to $10 per ton. These novelty items are already being marketed in gift stores, department stores and through mail-order, and their sales show money is still a hot item!

The government has set guidelines for regulating the resale of shredded money. It must be permanently sealed in glass or plastic, and cannot be used in the manufacture of paper suitable for commercial printing.

Anyone wishing to buy the shredded currency must write to the U.S. Treasury Department in Washington D.C. and submit their product ideas. The proposed product must be approved by the Treasury Department and the producer must send a sample of the product to the government. About 95 percent are approved.

Despite the products currently on the market, banks still report difficulty in disposing of their old cash.

Contact: Instant Fortune, Inc., Dept IEA, 919 3rd Avenue, New York, New York.

A School For Fishing

There are approximately 28 million people in the nation who have been bitten by the fishing bug.

If you're hooked on fishing, you know what it's like to get up in the pre-dawn hours to soak a line. You also probably spend any spare moment perfecting casting skills or testing a new fly that is guaranteed to outfox the wiliest of fish.

The Orvis Company, a leading manufacturer of fishing equipment, introduced the country's first fly fishing school at its headquarters in Massachusetts. They charge $195 per person for a three-day session of lectures, coaching and casting.

This idea can be adapted to, say, three consecutive Saturdays at a riverside. Or if you can rent a private pond, you can offer a two or three day fishing school and camp-out.

There are many fishing magazines on the market in which you can advertise. The best bet is to establish a schedule of classes so potential students can easily arrange reservations. Request payment in advance with a 75 percent refund for cancellations. The balance will cover your paperwork.

If you cannot rent a pond and must use a public river or lake, keep your advertising localized. Flyers in bait and tackle shops, licensing depots and local newspaper ads will provide you a sizeable class.

For further information: Orvis Company, Dept. IEA, Manchester, Vt.

Join The Big League!

When a baseball star gets his name branded on a line of baseball bats he knows he's made it! Surely every young boy and girl playing little league baseball dreams of such big league fame.

Now even little leaguers can make the big time and have their names branded on their own baseball bat! And they don't even have to be the team's most valuable player.

R. Lindell Specialties, Dept. IEA, 728 Nina Lane, Foster City, California 94404 is now marketing Adirondack baseball bats with the Little Leaguer's name branded on where the major league player's name would normally be.

Wholesale price is $6.55 postpaid, and the suggested retail price is $7.95, though some dealers are successfully retailing them for $8.95.

Delivery time for the professionally turned, lacquer finished baseball bats is two to four weeks. Kids apparently don't mind the wait, as the company claims proud owners usually increase their batting average with the personalized bat.

The bats are suitable for children up to 12 years of age. They can be sold successfully in hardware or sporting goods stores, gift shops, or directly at the Little League field—perhaps as part of a fund-raising drive.

While kids can use the bats on the playing field, they can also be wall mounted as trophies or much appreciated gift items for fledgling Babe Ruths.

Transmitter Turns Anyone Into Dick Tracy

Want to know if the kids upstairs are *really* listening to records? Or if the guy in the next office has designs on your job? Use the *Micro Mike,* a revolutionary new product that can turn anyone into a super-sleuth.

Weighing less than an ounce and only one cubic inch, the Micro Mike can be placed in a child's room, at the front door, or any place that requires noise monitoring.

Then turn an FM radio to any open frequency between 88 and 108 megahertz and stay tuned. Conversations or other noises will be broadcast through the radio for a distance of up to 100 feet indoors or 300 feet outdoors. If you converse with another person while carrying the Micro Mike, it will even broadcast the conversation to a third party in another location.

Although other wireless microphones are on the market, none are as small, and none feature an on/off switch that saves battery power. Other advantages include the ability to use Micro Mike as a PA system or alarm.

Manufactured by MLI Industries, Micro Mike retails for $24.95 including a 1.3 volt battery and a money-back or replacement guarantee. In addition, MLI has a Micro Mike/Export model at the same price which offers a slightly wider band of 88 to 110 megahertz for foreign travel. (The Federal Communications Commission has approved it.)

At the present time, the main sales channel is direct mail, but the product has great potential for radio and television stores, electronics shops, hardware stores and even department stores. It is a perfect demonstration item at home shows, security exhibitions and trade shows and should appeal to a variety of people from business executives to homeowners.

MLI Industries is currently looking for distributors for Micro Mike.

Coal On The Rocks

Anyone know a good cure for a coal hangover? The morning-after effects of a future cocktail party may well be caused by alcohol made from that black mineral used for heating. The thanks(?) go to several scientists in Illinois who have discovered a way to convert coal into booze!

The discovery was actually an accident—so say the scientists! They were just doing research on how and why coal reacts to a catalyst, in this case tetracarbonylcobalt hydride.

For all you science buffs, the scientists used a water or synthetic gas—a product of carbon monoxide and hydrogen—commonly made from steam, air and coal. When they combined the water gas with the catalyst mentioned above they got ethyl alcohol, the active ingredient in gin.

Ethyl alcohol has other uses, such as in making plastics and fuel oil for motor cars.

Contact: **Argonne National Laboratories, Attn: Harold M. Feder, Dept. IEA, 9700 So. Cass Ave., Chicago, Illinois.**

Beautiful Remake

Good looks never go out of style, but they can (believe it or not) get boring after awhile. Especially if you are a model's agent and photographer who is sick and tired of working with perfection day in and day out.

Dan Blitman is a Philadelphian who now gets his kicks creatively by working with "flawed" women. He'll take your mate or date and do a complete "makeover" in a single day.

A couple of hours at the makeup table are usually followed by a new hair style and some instructions on posing, all designed to accentuate the positive.

Then he shoots five or six rolls of film and makes a professional model's portfolio of photographs.

The kinkier customers have asked to be made into vampires, snake-charmers or wolfwomen. Usually he just discovers the ultimate "you" and captures it on film, all for about $200 including wine and lunch.

With or without the photography session, reasonably priced make-overs can be a big hit almost anywhere in the country. At present all but the most affluent women must go to a hair stylist for one part of a new look, and then to a cosmetics expert for the rest.

For further information contact: Structure Guild of Professional Models, Dept. IEA, 1126 Walnut St., Philadelphia, Pennsylvania.

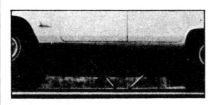

Automatic Jack

At one time or another most of us have had to jack up a car or truck to fix a flat or put on snow tires or chains. In foul weather this is a nasty task. On a slope or soft shoulder it's downright dangerous.

A San Jose, California inventor has patented a hydraulic jacking system that can be permanently installed on any vehicle. It's available for use at the push of a button and works on slopes where ordinary jacks can fail—without blocks.

Hydro Jack, developed by Stan Silva, is powered by take-offs from a standard power steering hydraulic pump or from other simple pump installations.

A set of two jacks is installed on each side of a car or truck frame. Each cylinder has a non-slip steel "foot" that holds the vehicle securely in position on almost any terrain.

After use, the jacks automatically retract back into place next to the frame. The motorist can continue on his way quickly, secure in the knowledge that his jack will always be there when needed.

Installation price of the system should range from $200 to $400 according to the inventor, who is looking for an automotive manufacturer or distributor to handle manufacturing and marketing on an exclusive license basis.

For more information, contact Stan at Dept. IEA, 3801 McKee Road, San Jose, California 95127.

Convert Pickups Into Fork Lifts

Millions of small manufacturers across the nation have a need for a forklift, but few can afford the expense of owning or leasing one for the amount of time it is in service. So they come up with jerry-rigged systems to lift and move heavy items or products from place to place.

We've found a way to turn a standard company pickup truck or van into a full-service forklift. For less than half the cost of a regular forklift, you simply hitch the Hy-Power Forklift to a truck with two latches. The whole operation takes less than a minute. Mounting and removing the unit is a snap because of the bracket fixture which is installed with no cutting or welding involved.

The Hy-Power Forklift works exclusively off the truck's battery. The control box can be attached to the steering column in the cab for operation in bad weather. Or you have the option of remote control.

The Hy-Power Forklift can handle 1500 pounds with load centers of 15½ inches. It has 10 degree forward and rear tilt and a maximum height capacity of 7½ feet. A full one-year guarantee is provided on all parts and workmanship.

Distance driving and rough terrain are no problem. The lift folds down in a three-stage, self-contained hydraulic process. This permits highway-speed driving with good over-the-hood visibility and plenty of road clearance, and leaves the truck bed available for carrying loads.

Solex Engineering, Inc. is the manufacturer of Hy-Power. They have designed the bracket so it will carry other truck accessories when the forklift is removed. Snow plows, cable winches and loader bucket scoops can be attached with extreme ease. In addition, the forklift unit can be mounted on a stock roll-around stand for inside-shop jobs.

Solex Engineering, Dept. IEA, 1811 No. 25th Dr., Phoenix, Az. 85009.

Flip-Top Game Table

The "rec" room has always been a favorite haven in American homes, whether it's a remodeled basement or part of the original floor plan. It's a great place to unwind and enjoy the company of family and friends.

Until now, table games rested on top of existing pool or ping pong tables. When not in use, space had to be made for storage. Setup was usually cumbersome and required at least two people. With all that aggravation, relaxing seemed like work!

Victory Games, Inc. of Seattle, has developed a convertible game table that is space saving, unique, easy to convert and fun to use. The table offers your family a choice of pool, ping pong, croquet or golf in just seconds.

Called the Johnny Bench Family Flip-Top, the table switches quickly to the four different games by pulling two pins at each end of the table and flipping it over on a pivot. Lock in the pins and you're ready to play! A child can easily convert it.

One side is a par 17, 9-hole golf course complete with traps and water hazards. If you bogey too many times, flip it over and you've got a beautiful (44" x 88") feno slate pool table. It's guaranteed not to crack or pit and has a glassy-smooth felt surface.

Stored on a rack beneath the Flip-Top, in two halves, is a regulation 4' x 9' ping pong table top. Easy to mount! If the croquet urge strikes, place the sturdy rack of wickets on the table's surface and you're ready!

This should be a natural line addition for sporting goods dealers and others focusing on the booming home entertainment field. For more information, write Victory Games, Inc., **Dept. IEA, P.O. Box 70367, Seattle, Washington 98107.**

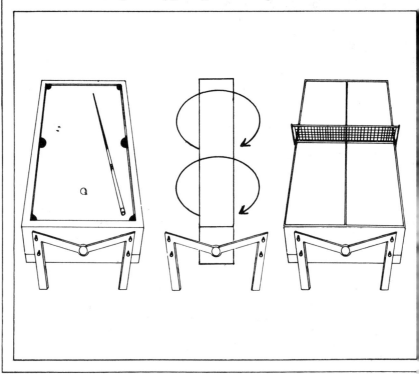

Build A Coffin Table!

The next coffee table you see may be a *coffin* in disguise. Many do-it-yourselfers across the country are building their personalized final resting place and enjoying it *now* as a functional piece of furniture.

We found an enterprising designer, Dave Zamzow, who is making a bundle selling coffin blueprints. The plans give creative ideas for converting the basic box to a bookcase, stereo cabinet or clothes closet. And well tuned to today's soaring economy, Zamzow shows how building one costs less than a tenth of the store-bought model.

The blueprint package is a perfect mail-order item. Advertising it in magazines geared to the hobbyist or do-it-yourself craftsperson will draw responses from inflation fighters.

A model bookcase on display in a hardware or lumber store is certain to guarantee inquiries from curious shoppers. And as blueprints retail for only $2.75, the questions should result in a number of sales. This concept has tremendous potential for carpenters and handymen. It can easily be developed into a lucrative custom building business by a bright operator.

The most difficult aspect of the business is convincing potential customers that a prebuilt coffin is not morbid, but extremely practical. It is necessary to have photographs showing the adaptability of the product as a tasteful piece of furniture.

Miniature models could be constructed as working examples. Mr. Zamzow, in fact, has already built a model which can serve as an urn following cremation. His wife uses it as a bench for her doll collection.

The copyrighted blueprints are now available to distributors and inquiries are invited. Write to: IPC, Dept. IEA, Post Office Box 4610, Santa Clara, California 95054.

Easier Cornering

Carpenters, cabinet makers, furniture makers or handymen, professional or not, will be interested in an amazingly simple new three-corner brace now available from Stanley Hardware.

The new reinforcement hardware device is designed to hold three surfaces securely without tedious and error-prone measuring and aligning.

The two-inch brace is made in one piece of zinc-plated steel, retails for $1.06 for a package of two, and is specifically designed for the do-it-yourself market.

The brace promises to save time and bother since it fits inside corners perfectly. All that's required is to drop it in place and screw it down. There's no need to measure or align.

Its application provides solid reinforcement for cabinets, drawers, tables, benches, chests, shelves, planter boxes, hutches, tool boxes, or anywhere three pieces of material

form a corner.

For additional information on this product, which is a natural line addition for hardware and do-it-yourself outlets, write to Stanley at P.O. Box 1800, New Britain, Connecticut 06050.

Cosmic Headgear!

The unexplainable energy forces generated inside a pyramid-shaped enclosure will sharpen razor blades, germinate seeds quicker, and keep fruit from spoiling. So say growing numbers of "pyramid power" advocates nationwide.

The four-sided geometric shape is apparently an "energy trap" that

even has healing powers. Broken bones mend and diseases are cured under a pyramid, devotees claim.

Now you can sharpen your wits as well, by wearing a pyramid crowned cowboy hat developed by Bobby Paul, who makes the cosmic headgear in his shop at Dept. IEA, 1508 Indiana Street, Houston, Texas.

Theory states that a pyramid generates the most power when one of its four sides is perfectly aligned with magnetic north. Some wearers of Paul's hat claim to receive a warm, tingling sensation most of the time.

We've also seen homemade wire pyramid headgear perched atop enthusiasts. This would seem to be an easy-to-do item for funky gift shops or even mail order.

Put the prototype you come up with on your head to help plan ways to merchandise it in volume!

For Sale: City Air

More and more people are leaving hometowns or cities for greener pastures. And when they make the break, many carry a memento to the new place of residence. Posters of the city hall, a pile of local soil encased in a paperweight and a framed roof tile from a childhood home are but a few we've seen recently.

Now we've discovered a way you can capitalize on runaway nostalgia—a sealed container of air from specific cities. There's only one company we've found doing this and the market is wide open. Their product is Nostalgair and claims to be a "breath of being there." Air from Los Angeles, New York, Chicago, Boston and other major cities is offered. But most cities are not included.

The idea of "air-to-go" has great potential and can be easily set-up to attract gift buyers in airport shops, boutiques or stationery stores.

Although it's a wonderful way to see the country, filling up each container with the actual air of each city is a costly proposition. So the secret to selling this idea is in the packaging. Nostalgair is packaged in a glass dome which serves as a backdrop for a graphically designed skyline under the name of the location. But a plexiglass bottle or cube with a cardboard wrapper describing the contents would be ideal. Plastic containers would also work and are the least expensive. Contact "Plastic Container Manufacturers" listed in the yellow pages for price estimates. A unique cardboard label can be designed.

Any city can be used; in fact, the more you have the better your profitability. A small display ad in your local newspaper will give you an idea of the air the public misses most.

For further information: Holst Bowen Associates, Dept. IEA, #316 Brack Shops/East 649 So. Olive St., Los Angeles, California 90014.

Snap-On Fenders Cover Dents, Rust

We've found a new product to revolutionize auto body repair: inexpensive *fiberglass overlay panels* that snap over dented or rusted fenders, door panels and other body parts!

The prefabricated panels, developed by a New Jersey auto body repair pro, can be installed by an unskilled person in minutes at a fraction of the cost of traditional methods. No more time-consuming removal, hammering, contouring, patching, or other steps that drive bodywork prices through the roof.

Designed by Larry Cetrano of Glassline Industries, Inc., the "second skin" panels are produced from slightly oversized molds that reproduce the exact shape and contour of

the original panel. Priced from $6.50 to $44.00, kits are currently available for Ford and Chevrolet pickup trucks and vans as well as certain passenger cars.

Initial marketing has been aimed at fleet owners; several public utilities and airlines have tested the Glassline panels on fleet units with excellent long-term results. Expansion of the panel line and further entrance into the consumer market is planned—do-it-yourselfers should welcome the idea.

Kits allow the man on the street to repair minor damage in the family garage or driveway *in half an hour or less*. They should sell quite well in auto parts and accessory stores.

For additional information on this "bang-up" new product, write Glassline Industries, Dept. IEA, P.O. Box 265, Tuckerton, New Jersey 08087.

Practical Cat Houses

Cats are the lazy man's choice when it comes to selecting a pet. Unlike their canine counterparts, they don't have to be walked, bathed, brushed or entertained.

Felines are more popular than ever. There are now an estimated 40 million domesticated cats in the United States. Though they won't eat their owner out of house and home, they did manage to gobble up 796.5 million dollars worth of cat food in 1975.

When it comes to food, what goes in must come out. This important biological law translates into a 60 million dollar litter sand market in 1975.

But litter boxes are what separate the true cat lover from the mere feline fancier. Where to store the litter box, putting up with the unpleasant odors and mess, as well as the need to sift or change the sand, have always been the major drawback to cat ownership.

There are at least a dozen different litter box sand mixtures on the market, some of which even contain chlorophyll to mask the presence of odor. Yet no matter how often the litter box is emptied, the stench as well as unsanitary effects of exposed urine and feces is constantly present.

Now it seems this malodorous problem has finally been solved. Bill Calkins, a Southern California cat fancier, has developed the In And Out House. It's a small, totally enclosed unit which can easily be attached to a human home. Feline pets enter their private outhouse through a tunnel created in the wall of the master's home.

The unit is attached to the house by two steel angle irons that bolt directly to the floor plate. The unit is supported on the back by two legs cut to the necessary height to keep it level with the main house.

The In And Out House is serviced from the outside by means of a door on the back of the unit. It's vented and totally enclosed for all-weather use. The developer currently has plans to create a modular system for the cat who has everything. Using the toilet unit as the main module, additional units can be attached to serve as a dining room and even a sun porch. Now if that isn't the cat's pajamas! To show there's no hard feelings, the developer is working on an enclosed screen sun bathing module for small dogs.

Bill is looking for a manufacturer to help him bring the patented pet products to market. For further information, write him at Dept. IEA, 7735 Pickering, No. 10, Whittier, California 90608.

Curvy Hard Ball

You may remember your kid brother trying to throw a curveball on the sandlot when he was ten—a perfect klutz! But today, even the worst pitcher can throw curves, sinkers and risers as well as Mark Fidrych, with the new Major League Breaking Ball.

Since baseball is an ever-popular sport amongst youngsters, you could score profits with this one. The breaking ball has a flat side which, depending on how you hold it, enables anyone to throw perfect curves without the usual "breaking of the wrist." It is thrown the same way as a regular fast ball.

The bat never hits the flat side, and the ball reacts like any other ball when hit. It decreases embarrassing strikeouts, and helps prevent sore arms. It comes in the official major league size, and weighs five ounces.

This ball is sure to be a hit with baseball players of all ages! It comes in a dozen-pack shelf display, and can be marketed in athletic supply stores, department and specialty stores.

The ball could be promoted by giving free samples to Little Leaguers, schools, and non-profit organizations. Publicity could be obtained by persuading a leading local baseball star to demonstrate the ball at some large event or fair.

Contact: Curvy Hard Ball, Dept IEA, Pick Point Enterprises, Inc., P.O. Mirror Lake, New Hampshire 03853.

The Player Piano Is Back In A Big Way

The multimillion dollar home entertainment field will soon have another entry.

Imagine what it would be like to hear a Debussy prelude as Debussy *himself* played it, not recorded or amplified, but his interpretation as he *actually* played it with all his dynamics and pedaling.

Pianocorder is a magnetic tape,

and a built-in version that can be in stalled prior to sale. Built-ins will re tail for $1,400 to $1,800. The roll-u version, without record capabilit should go for $1,700 to $2,000.

Built-in units can be used as teach ing aids because they will record an play back a student's piano lesso note for note.

A buyer will receive 10 pre-selec

cassette-controlled recorder and player piano. It'll perform "live" music on any upright or grand piano using special computerized "albums" that span every type of piano music from classical to ragtime.

Two types of Pianocorder will be available. A separate one that can wheel up to any upright or grand,

ed, 45-minute tapes with the unit an be able to order 90 more of his ow choosing from a catalog of ove 18,000 titles. Subsequent tapes wi cost $7.95 apiece retail.

Contact: H. C. Lembke, Pianocor der Division Superscope, Dept. IEⱭ 20525 Nordoff St., Chatsworth, Cal fornia 91311.

Profitable Party Pranks

Suppose you're sitting quietly at a party, sipping your cocktail and trying to loosen up. Suddenly the couple across the room begins to fight.

"I told you not to have another drink, you souse," the man yells at his wife.

"Shut up, you good for nothing louse," she screams as she slaps him across the face.

Then an apparent hobo, obviously drunk, staggers into the room, trips on the rug, and falls on his face. He gets up, falls again and passes out.

The hostess doesn't bat an eyelash.

"What the hell am I doing at this party?" you'd probably ask yourself.

Unless you have bizarre friends, chances are you've had a practical joke played on you by employees of a "rent-a-guest" service.

It's not an idea to be scoffed at, since such partygoers presently command anywhere from $50 to $400 (plus expenses) an evening for the pleasure of their company. With a lot of imagination and a little business savvy, an entrepreneur can put together a stable of party professionals and collect handsome fees for open or clandestine placement at parties.

There's an ongoing demand among creative and affluent party givers for psychics, astrologers, fashion shows, strolling violinists, magicians, jugglers, jesters and bards.

But an entirely new approach to placing professionals in party situations has recently been successfully introduced on the sophisticated Manhattan and Beverly Hills party circuit. And there's no reason why the same approach can't work in any affluent suburban community.

Jack Farrell, developer of this unique concept, operates The Professional Partyguest, headquartered in North Hollywood, California.

Instead of the obvious hired entertainment, like psychics and magicians, rent-a-guest businesses are finding increased demand for the "undercover" guest. These run the gamut from fighting married couples to tipsy butlers. Imagination is the only apparent limitation in this creative business.

You might find party givers interested in hiring a phony punk rock star, a duke, count or princess. How about an Arab oil sheik, or simply a drunken gate crasher who is in reality a stand-up comic? With appropriate costumes, disguises and accents, they're sure to be a hit.

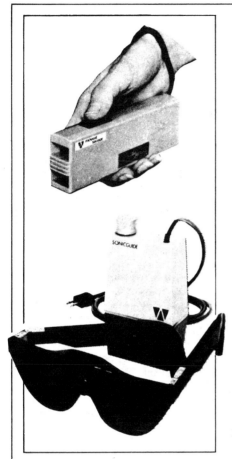

Sonar For The Blind

Until recently, white canes and dogs have been the only "eyes" available to the blind. Two new ultrasonic "seeing" devices are on the market which open a whole new world of "sound sight" for the blind.

Telesensory Systems, Inc., of Palo Alto, California is marketing the Mowat Sensor and Sonicguide; both utilize ultrasonic vibrations to help the blind detect the proximity of objects in their path.

The hand-held Mowat Sensor sells for $495. It transmits a beam of high frequency ultrasound (inaudible to the human ear) into the area the user wants to explore. The beam is reflected from objects up to 12 feet away causing the sensor to vibrate silently.

The rapidity of the vibration indicates the obstacle's distance. The more rapid the vibration rate, the nearer the object. The Mowat Sensor user's kit contains the sensor device, a rechargeable battery, battery charger, vinyl carrying case, wrist strap, and owner's manual. An earphone which provides audible sound object detection is $20 extra.

Sonicguide, which sells for $2,350, also works on the ultrasound principle. A miniature transmitter built into lightweight eyeglass frames radiates ultrasound vibrations in front of the wearer. The sound wave is reflected from obstacles back to a hearing aid where it's converted to audible sound.

Sonicguide enables the user to detect objects up to 15 feet away. The user can distinguish whether the obstacle is to one side or directly in front by the sound level in either ear or both ears simultaneously.

Sonicguide comes with three major components: the eyeglass frame, a small control unit/power pack with shoulder strap or belt loop for carrying convenience, and the battery charger. Two fluted eartubes are provided for training and a pair of metal eartube connectors allow attachment of other fitted eartubes.

Both Mowat and Sonicguide radiate an elliptical sound beam with a width of 15 degrees and height of 30 degrees. This shape best approximates the human form.

Mowat and Sonicguide are designed to complement a long cane or guide dog. Drop-offs, like street curbs, still aren't easily detectable. Both products are available in user and instructor models and come with training manuals. For further information, write Telesensory Systems, Inc., Dept IEA, 3408 Hillview Avenue, Palo Alto, California 94303.

Breakfast In Bed

Imagine waking up to a cozy breakfast in bed prepared by a gourmet chef. Complete with fine china, crystal stemware, silver and linen.

A luxury once reserved for the elite who stay in the finest hotels is now available in your home and prepared in your kitchen by a staff of cooks who come early in the morning and bring their own equipment.

An elegantly served omelette or eggs benedict is sure to beat burnt toast, cold oatmeal and a glass of what could charitably be called juice.

We've seen services like this in Los Angeles and New York but many major cities could support a small operation on low overhead. Especially at rates like $60 per couple, which is the common tab.

It's a natural extension of existing services for caterers, exclusive restaurants and others in the food business. You'd need to advertise in theatre programs and slick urban magazines to attract the affluent clientele necessary to make it go.

A Beep In Time

Time is precious for any businessman—and there's never enough of it. What's worse, mismanaged time can result in missed opportunities. But we've found a product that's virtually guaranteed to put you in the right place at the right time.

The Electronic Diary is much more than the typical humdrum desk calendar. It reminds you with a loud beep about important things such as returning phone calls or catching plane flights. All you do is write the activity on the appointment sheet and key the beeper with a special lead pencil.

At a pre-set time, the beeper sounds until you turn it off. The electronics are set to signal at 15-minute intervals, and the unit includes a clock so you can double-check your agenda.

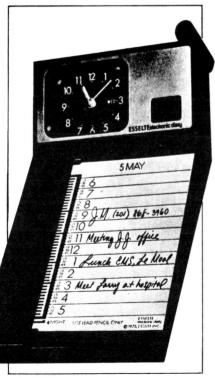

The battery-operated Electronic Diary, manufactured by Esselte Products, Inc., should sell well to executives, students, salespeople or anyone who has important appointments.

Gift shops, stationery stores, department stores, and office equipment and supply centers are perfect sales outlets for the item, which retails for approximately $80. Each unit includes 50 appointment sheets, a mechanical pencil and holder, batteries, instructions and a warranty card. Write to Esselte Products, Inc., Dept. IEA, 866 Third Avenue, New York, New York 10022 for further information.

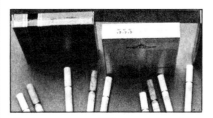

Gourmet Cigarettes

Not since chocolate and bubble gum cigarettes has smoking been so delicious! British manufacturers are now producing real flavored cigarettes for smoking in 16 flavors.

These include apple, banana, cherry, pineapple and prune. Also herbs and spices such as clove, licorice, peppermint, anise, tamarind, cinnamon, cumin, coriander and fenugreek. This might be expanded to honey, caramel, strawberry, vanilla, coffee, brandy, rum and whiskey as well.

Manufacturers are preparing for a flavor war which seems likely to be the biggest change for smokers since filters. Anti-smoking groups are concerned that flavorful smoking will make the habit too attractive to children. Purists are sure to take offense at permissable additives which include chalk, turpentine, gum arabic and shellac!

Nonetheless, flavored cigarettes are sure to sell well to a smoking public willing to try new things. Herbal cigarettes flavored with mint and cloves have been big sellers for years in India and Indonesia.

Flavored cigarettes should move well wherever cigarettes are normally sold. For information on how to obtain these British smokes, write to the Retail Tobacco Dealers of America, Inc., Dept. IEA, Statler Hilton, 7th Ave., & 33rd Street, New York, New York 10001.

Magic Pendants

Engraved jewelry is an extremely hot item these days. Now you can create your own engraved jewelry with an ordinary ball point pen! Magic? Sort of. They're soft metal pendants which are amazingly simple to inscribe.

Pen-It comes in gold or silver finishes, with chain and in a choice of round, heart, and dog-tag shapes.

The engraving is permanent. All that's required is to place Pen-It on a flat surface and press down firmly with any ball point pen. The greater the pressure, the deeper the engraving. A damp cloth removes the ink when the inscription is complete.

This inexpensive and highly original jewelry item should sell like hot cakes to the teenage market! They make gift items at parties, fairs or carnivals.

In addition to the human market,

Pen-It pendants would make great I.D. tags for dogs and cats. These could be sold in pet shops, kennels and animal hotels.

The House of This 'N That is the manufacturer. Along with the Pen-It pendants, which wholesale for $14 a dozen, the company has a complete line of other inexpensive jewelry including pendants, chains, necklaces, bracelets, anklets, earrings and rings.

Contact: House of This 'N That, Dept. IEA, 2385 Claire St., Box 244, Yorktown, New York 10598.

Afternoon Delight
At Fantasy Motel

Want to spend the night playing Tarzan and Jane? Or an afternoon suspended from the ceiling with heavy metal chains? A motel in Chicopee, Massachusetts has cashed in on the sexual revolution by becoming a "fantasy haven," transporting customers directly to the dream of their choice.

Business at the Pines Motel has never been better, according to the owners, Robert and Maya Asselin. Rental revenues have been sparked by day and hourly rates aimed at those with more desire than time.

Most customers are young couples looking to try something different or new, but the Pines has attracted many couples in their 60's. One pair received a night in the Jungle Room, under a bamboo canopy, as a gift from their children. Another couple spent their 50th wedding anniversary in Hangar No. 5, on a bed suspended from the ceiling and surrounded by exotic leather and mirrors, with red lights for accent.

Other highlights include the Mod Room, featuring eerie blacklights, and The Circus Room, where the bed is surrounded by a lion's cage. The Golden Paradise has soft gold lighting, a gold waterbed and gold-flocked wallpaper.

This easy-to-copy idea sould go over quite well in almost any liberal metropolitan area, and is a way that an off-the-beaten-path motel can become a real moneymaker. It would be important to "play it for laughs" and emphasize tongue-in-cheek humor in order to avoid developing a "sleazy" image that would limit profit potential. Check into IEA Manual No. 40, Adults-Only Motel, for further info.

Contact: Pines Hotel, Dept. IEA, 1508 Memorial Dr., Fairview, Mass.

Focus On This!

Everyone wonders now and then how they really appear to others—not just actors and models, but businessmen, salesmen, politicians, and others whose livelihood depends on sharp personal presentation.

In recent years, the use of videotape equipment has shifted from entertainment to commercial and educational applications.

Hospitals, schools, government agencies and many major corporations are now using video as a training device. Astute entrepreneurs have set up videotape real estate listings and even dating services.

With the price of video equipment now sharply reduced from when it first appeared on the scene in the Sixties, as well as the easy availability of leases, many new opportunities for the commercial exploitation of video come into focus.

Why not apply the video training techniques used by major corporations to help salesmen and manufacturer's representatives of businesses too small to afford a video training system of their own?

An experienced salesman, with the mannerisms, voice inflections and bearing of a successful salesperson, could easily establish a video sales training course.

On-camera role playing between salesmen pitching clients would allow the students to see strengths and weaknesses. After instruction, they would repeat their approach for the camera in order to see how instruction in professional techniques improved their sales effectiveness.

With as little as $1,500 you can outfit yourself with video camera, TV monitor and tape deck to visit clients in their office for private or group sessions.

Fees would depend on your expertise on the subject, but $30 to $50 for a private session on personal sales techniques would certainly be in line.

Send a flyer to businesses and organizations in your area which might benefit from your services, followed up by a personal visit and demonstration, as the most effective way to make your service known.

Contact: Weist Barron School of Television, Dept. IEA, 1216 Bay St., Toronto, Ontario, Canada.

Now Plants Can Purr!

It used to be that a plant needing water suffered in silence. The result was a premature, undignified death.

Now you can embed *Plant Doctor* in the soil, and your plant will tell you in audible sound signals when it

needs watering or fertilizing. It "purrs" when everything's okay.

Moisture meters have been available for awhile, but only Plant Doctor lets a plant catch the attention of a busy or forgetful owner. As we all know, a little nagging usually works wonders.

Plant Doctor can be used indoors or outdoors with plants, shrubs, trees, grass or vegetable gardens. It is completely maintenance-free.

The suggested retail price for Plant Doctor is $8.95. Plant stores or home and garden shops are natural outlets, but gift and novelty shops should also be interested since a device for grumbling plants will appeal to gimmick lovers.

Parking Lot War Ends

One of the most frustrating things in the world is to have your assigned or paid-for parking space taken by another driver. This happens not only out of plain rudeness but also because the other other guy didn't notice the little white labels that said "Reserved." For busy executives and the handicapped this adds up to more than an aggravation.

We've found a product that should put a stop to this inconvenience. A Reserved Parking Barrier can anchor into your parking space about a foot or more from the curb. It blocks your space and leaves no doubt that the space is reserved. The high-visibility barrier is 4 feet 6 inches tall, 6 inches wide, and anchored by six steel drive pins.

A spring coil between the barrier's base and upright allows you to drive into and over the barrier to take your space. It's made out of polyurethane and won't hurt the car's bumper or undercarriage.

For the executive who can't waste time trying to find an alternate space, the "Stop—No Parking" model is a wise investment. The handicapped will appreciate the effective "Handicapped Parking Only" model.

The market for this product is tremendous, in congested downtown areas, in company parking lots, and apartment complexes. Most small businesses have a few spaces in the lot for customers or tradesmen.

With a product like this you could start a welcome service business. Provide the barriers to customers in any area where parking is assigned or limited. Installation is easy, using only a hammer in most situations. Blank barriers allowing custom personal lettering are also available.

The barriers have been developed by RPB Industries, Dept. IEA, Tustin, California.

Anti-Smokers Spray!

There are an estimated 70 million smokers in the United States—and about 140 million non-smokers. That's two-to-one odds and war has already been declared.

The latest weapon to appear in the non-smoker's arsenal is the Anti-Smoker Spray. Paul Wright, the self-proclaimed Ralph Nader of smoking, is the inventor of the six-ounce, lemon-scented aerosol.

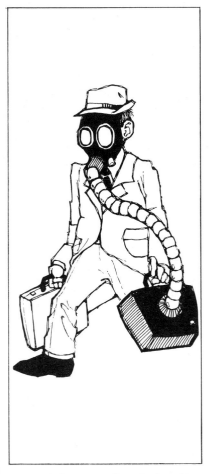

Fist fights are already breaking out on crowded New York commuter trains. Clearly, non-smokers are out to eliminate smoking in public places.

Wright's $3.95 invention seems likely to dampen the chain smoker's spirits as well as his cigarette!

The lemon-scented mist is very wet. It will put out a cigarette from 10 inches away. It will also hit the smoker in the face! Wright envisions his anti-smoking "soldiers" all armed with spray cans, roaming the streets, buses, elevators and office buildings of America, zapping anyone in the face who insists on "befouling" the air.

Over 500,000 people die each year because of cigarette smoking and a million and a half more become partially or totally disabled. Wright's army may be more merciful than mercenary!

Directions and descriptions on the can are as interesting as the product. Wright claims the product "helps prevent, control and cure air pollution by smokers in: homes, offices, cars, restaurants, bars, elevators, sports arenas, beds and parties." He says it's "fully field tested and provides non-smokers with the ultimate satisfaction!"

Directions on the can read, "When cigar, cigarette or pipe smoke is detected, aim atomizer at source and spray for one second. If smoker becomes irate, spray again. Persistent smokers may require a triple flutter-blast (three short sprays) and a few carefully selected words."

The product is "unconditionally guaranteed to stop the most offensive cases of smoking in public, at work, etc." The Anti-Smoker Spray would sell well in gift shops, department stores, novelty shops and in any public place where non-smokers are liable to become irate and in need of a weapon!

For further information, write Paul Wright, Executive Director, The National Association on Smoking and Health, Colorado Club Building, Dept. IEA, 4155 E. Jewell Ave., Suite 806, Denver, Colorado 80222.

Dolls That Look Just Like You!

If you walk into a room some day and see yourself sitting there—big as life—don't go rushing off to a psychiatrist! What you're looking at is a hot new idea that seems to have unlimited potential: a $120 "soft-sculpture" doll that has been personalized with your face, hairstyle or dress, and other characteristics that capture your looks and personality.

We found an artist-businessman combination that has created these huge fabric dolls, called "Stuffed-up People." The artists carefully craft the doll's face with the subject's features, nose, skin and eye color, and hair. Customers who want to immortalize themselves, friends or enemies are asked to submit at least two good photos of the subject.

A questionnaire accompanying the order asks for such helpful data as size of subject's breasts (large, medium, small), chest (hairy, bald, concave), moles, warts, freckles, general disposition, and male anatomy (well-endowed, average, miniscule)!

Since only one company is making "stuffed people" right now, the market is wide open and limited only by the number of parents, children, relatives, friends, and acquaintances in the world! An excellent demand should come from clubs, organizations, and businesses, which can use the oversize dolls as awards, prizes, and for the humorous effect. Banks and savings and loans are always looking for a new gimmick!

You could hire artists, on a percentage of the $120 sale price if you're not up to the detailed artwork. And you can get free publicity: just send your newsman a doll of himself—with your news release in its hand!

For further information: Dept. IEA, The Grand Gesture, Warner Plaza, 21793 Ventura Blvd., Woodland Hills, California.

Fashion Computer

Put a chic outfit on one woman and it will be just right. On another, the same clothing can make her look dumpy. That's because people are individuals, not stamped out cookie-cutter style.

Models are trained to make the most of themselves through daily exposure to fashion and beauty. But what about the regular gal who can't have a wardrobe jammed with clothes, and looks more like Olive Oyl than Farrah Fawcett-Majors? Now she can have a Paris fashion consultant of her own, by mail!

Fashionscope is a French firm that pooled the talents of several *haute couture* designers and put this information on computers. Anyone trying to achieve a new look can fill out a questionnaire with sketches of every current fashion silhouette.

Information is fed into the computer and an analysis comes back from France. If she's short, it'll tell her to wear dark, high-waisted slacks and a loose blouse to appear more "leggy." If her hips are wide, it'll tell her not to wear T-shirts and slacks and that an A-line skirt would give her a better look.

There should be an excellent market for a service patterned after this one in the States. Fashionscope has a Houston representative but there's still plenty of room for competition.

Check out the capabilities of inexpensive home computers that can be programmed to do almost anything. The nearest computer store should have experts to help with this. And there are plenty of good designers outside of Paris.

The service is a natural for fashionable boutiques and department stores. Contact the owners or buyers for these retailers to explain the exciting possibilities and advantages. Consider in-store promotions like the "trunk shows" jewelry distributors conduct regularly.

Machine Vends Hot French Fries!

What is it about the aroma of french fries that makes even people who know it's a no-no eat handful after handful? We'll leave that answer up to the psychologists, but the money-making possibilities of french-fry vending machines are sure to attract even overweight analysts.

We've found a company that has come up with a novel, patented, coin-operated machine that dispenses hot, fresh french fries. Since it's completely enclosed, the unit can be used indoors as well as outdoors. Drop in a coin, and you get a cup of hot fries in just a few seconds.

The Italian-made dispenser is easy to use, low on maintenance, and requires minimum floor space. Essential parts are made of stainless steel, sheathed in spray-varnished sheet metal. A built-in oil filter keeps the potato strips clean.

French fries are still one of the most popular snack foods in the country—just ask anyone who owns a hamburger stand. So there should be great demand for machines vending them almost anywhere there's high foot traffic and impulse buying going on. Best bet is a location where other foods are already being sold this way—sporting events, recreation areas, gas stations, cafeterias, schools and the like.

Contact Made In Europe, Dept. IEA, Reference #1-21985, Gotthardstr. 21, CH-8002, Zurich, Switzerland for more details on these machines and distributorships available. Just don't eat up all the profits!

T-Shirt Of The Month Club

We've seen record clubs and book clubs for years, but here's a new twist on the same marketing angle—a T-shirt of the Month Club. Nowadays, T-shirts qualify as fashionable attire almost anywhere in the country. There are T-shirt collectors and millions of Americans who just like wearing the latest designs.

The club, headquartered in San Rafael, California, offers members a monthly magazine chock full of T-shirt lore and previews of the hundreds of new designs that hit the market monthly. There is a T-shirt of the month selection, special edition T-shirts for members only, and even special, numbered limited editions for collectors.

The club's exposure has been limited, and there's no reason why a bright marketer couldn't use the idea in another part of the country. Even a local T-shirt shop could build business in this way on a regional basis. With all the designs available on the market, you'd never run out of new offerings. It could be a great showcase for new designers with awards and design contests.

The club costs $8 for a one-year membership, including a coupon for one free T-shirt from the first month's selection. Members are under no obligation to buy any set amount of T-shirts, but we prefer the approach taken by book clubs requiring a set number of purchases.

After accumulating several attractive designs, test market the idea with couponed ads in newspapers and youth-oriented magazines. The best way to learn more about how it works is to join the T-shirt of the Month Club. Write them at Dept. IEA, 3100 Kerner Blvd., San Rafael, California 94901.

Be A Skylighter!

Skylights can add dramatic effects to room lighting and increase indoor light without boosting electric bills. And they're so popular and simple to install that a business specializing in skylight design and installation can find bright success!

Translucent skylights made of fiberglass reinforced plastic provide a virtually shadowless light and have excellent insulating qualities. Fiberglass skylights break up the light and scatter it, providing greater brightness than a plastic or glass skylight.

Skylights are as easy to install as simple roof ventilators. All that's required is a box-type wood frame nailed into place around a hole in the roof and sealed with roofing paper. The one-piece fiberglass skylight slips into place over the wood frame and can be fastened from the side with screws, glue or even nails.

Because the skylights are one piece, there is no need for a metal frame or gaskets. Multipiece acrylic skylights with metal frames and vinyl gaskets have been known to leak, and acrylic as well as glass skylights can shatter if hit by a tree branch, falling rock or other object.

A variety of decorating effects can be created with a skylight. A liner of colored plastic or leaded glass can be installed to change colors, creating various moods.

A 15-watt fluorescent light can be mounted behind the liner for activation by a photo cell at sunset, or by a manual or time switch.

Further information on skylights can be obtained by writing Williams-Bermuda Corporation, Dept. IEA, Bermuda House, P.O. Drawer 2967, Pasadena, California 91105.

Pump Up Profits!

We've uncovered a fantastic new product for anyone who runs a full or even self-service gasoline station—and there are over 200,000 of them. It is an automatic fluid metering device that will dispense a *specific* amount of gasoline or any other fluid automatically!

Gas pumps nowadays have automatic shut-off systems, but they only work if a customer orders a full tank. With a smaller amount the attendant has to stand there to dispense, or worse, try to handle another customer while the guy who ordered $2 worth gets more than he bargained for.

The patent-pending Flo-Control gauge has a dial so the attendant can set it to shut off after a specific dollar amount is dispensed—or a given number of gallons. Using such a device, one gas station attendant can wait on many customers at the same time, and the owner needn't worry about losing sales if someone winds up driving off "in a huff."

The gauge is installed behind the existing nozzle by uncoupling the hose. It can also be installed within the pump housing and hooked up to a coin acceptor to completely *eliminate* the need for an attendant at self-service locations. All you'd need to do is regularly empty the coin boxes! The possibilities are endless. You could have unattended coin-op pumps in remote areas that would work just like Coke machines!

And the idea is not limited to gas station applications. The device will dispense nearly any low viscosity fluid simply by changing the gear ratios inside the unit.

It can be used to dispense any fluid automatically in quantities up to 2,000 gallons. Aircraft or home fuels, kerosene and turpentine are a few of the fluids that can be used.

It can be attached to a water hose or sprinkler system to water a lawn with a specific amount of water. All completely unattended! The applications of such a device on golf courses, irrigation systems, and elsewhere that water can be easily wasted are tremendous.

The Flo-Control gauge can be manufactured for a cost of about $4 and sold outright or leased for about $5, according to the designer, Robert Clarke. He is looking for a manufacturer, so write to him at Dept. IEA, 1410 Saratoga Drive, Bel Air, Maryland for more information. With eight million gas pumps in the United States alone, the market for such a product is incredible!

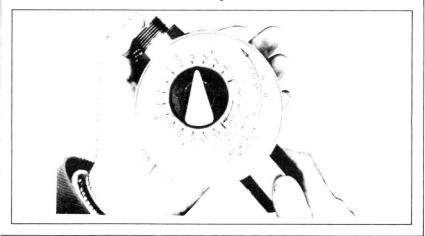

Space Age Sewage!

Sewage sludge no longer has to foul rivers, lakes or streams. It can be converted into a nutrient-rich soil additive at a processing cost of only a nickel a *ton!*

Research scientists at the Massachusetts Institute of Technology have found that bacteria, viruses, and poisonous chemicals in sludge can be completely destroyed by bombarding the gook with beams generated in an electron accelerator.

After processing, the recycled sludge is placed in the soil in landfill areas and allowed to compost for a period of time. Then crops can be raised on the land, or the dirt can be hauled away for use as lawn and garden fertilizer!

Some cities like Milwaukee are now spending fortunes to recycle their sludge by heating it. This new process is far less expensive.

Similar efforts are underway to convert animal solid waste into building materials and even livestock feed!

Contact: John G. Trump, M.I.T. High Voltage Research Lab, Dept. IEA, Cambridge, Massachusetts.

Windshield Washers Clean Up

When was the last time you thought about windshield washer fluid? Well, over 3½ billion gallons are sold every year. It is estimated that each vehicle on the road uses about two gallons every year. Even more is used in northern and eastern areas of the country, where harsh climate is a factor.

From the driver's viewpoint, washer fluid can be a pain. You always seem to run out at an inconvenient time, and refills are a hassle. But no more, especially if Royalty Research & Development, Inc. has its way. They are launching a distributorship program featuring dispensers mounted on the islands at service stations.

Each dispenser holds five gallons of fluid carrying their CW brand; an attached hose allows an attendant to easily fill a patron's washer bottle under the hood. Station owners report higher volume of fluid sales, increased customer satisfaction, and a jump in other sales that comes from popping the hood of a customer's car.

Buying into the RRD program requires purchase or lease of 400 dispensers at $47.50 apiece plus 385 refill cartridges at $4.45 apiece. After placing the units, distributors sell refills to the station owner at $8.45 apiece. The station operator can give away fluid as a loss leader or charge for it.

This winning concept is best in major metropolitan areas. But it isn't necessary to spend the $18,000 plus for a distributorship. A bright entrepreneur should be able to go it alone without this heavy investment. The patented dispenser is a simple metal box that straps high on the service island pole. It should be easy to fabricate your own version in smaller quantities.

The first market for a local operator is full-service station owners. A second is volume users like rental car agencies, fleet owners, trucking firms, cab companies, and bus lines. We see no reason why self-service stations or car washes can't become users with the addition of a coin-operated mechanism dispensing measured amounts.

To investigate this further, write to Royalty Research & Development for information about their system. They are located at Dept. IEA, 1111 E. 54th Street, Indianapolis, Indiana 46220.

Get A Grip On This One!

An ice cold can of beer or soda really hits the spot when you're thirsty. But it can be a nuisance when your hands get cold and covered with drops of water evaporating from the can. We've found a product that turns any 12-ounce can into a mug—the *Stein-Way Can Handle.*

This lightweight, aluminum handle was developed by Bob DeMars, an innovative young man who got tired of having wet hands along with every cold drink. And he's got a good market. Americans purchased over 50 million canned beverages last year, and with each can they had to figure out how to avoid drips and frostbite.

The Stein-Way has tremendous marketing potential in liquor stores, supermarkets and anywhere than canned drinks are sold. It has interesting possibilities as a vending item at stadiums, racetracks and other recreational parks. It is also a great promotional gimmick for home demonstrations and premium coupon gifts.

The wholesale price ranges from 55 cents apiece for 101 display units to 75 cents each for one to three units. Each display unit contains 48 handles which will easily retail for $1.25 each. And for a small charge, you can have any company's name or trademark embossed on the handles in a variety of colors such as brown, blue, red and green.

To get a handle on this product, write to Sunshine Manufacturing Co., Dept. IEA, 437 W. Main Street, Alhambra, California 91801 for further information about distribution.

Don't Leave Home Without It!

Once you've gotten into the habit of throwing down a plastic card instead of cold, hard cash, anything seems within your means—until the mail arrives overflowing with payments due. If you can't skip town your alternative is to eventually pay on that pile of last notices. Unless you've had the foresight to arrange for a Nothing Card.

The Nothing Card is just a small cog in the Nothing Movement that is sweeping the country. With the Nothing Card your life won't pass before you when the mail comes every thirty days. The bearer is entitled to all the comforts crisp cash can buy.

Dining out? Do it in style with the trusty Nothing Card tucked in your pocket. Decide how much you want to spend on dinner—in cash. Do not order food and drink that add up to more than the cash you have.

Going on a vacation? Go now. Pay now. Simple as that with the Nothing Card. Maybe that lamp made from salvaged scrap metal caught your eye as a souvenir perfect for the corner desk. No problem. Relax, smile and pay *cash!*

The Nothing Card is available for $1.50 from (who else?) The Nothing Company, Dept. IEA, P.O. Box 4155, Malibu, California 90265.

Cohabit Forming

Living together is becoming more and more popular nationwide. No accurate figures are available, but it's estimated that millions are forsaking traditional marriage vows for the alternative lifestyle of cohabitation.

Reasons given for living together in unwedded bliss (or "sin," depending on point of view) are many. Some young couples see marriage licenses and rings as outmoded symbols. Others want to know themselves, and each other, better before making a permanent commitment. Shell-shocked divorcees may not want to risk getting burned again.

In many cases there are sound economic reasons for not tying the knot. Two unmarried adults, filing separate income tax returns can often save significant dollars over a similarly situated married couple. A few savvy couples get divorced and remarried *every year* just to get these tax breaks!

Growing numbers of senior citizens seeking companionship will live together rather than give up Social Security benefits which are higher for two single adults than for two married ones.

And now there's a magazine for those who choose to live together, called *Cohabitation*, published quarterly for $16 a year and headquartered at Dept IEA, 3824 E. Indian School Road, Phoenix, Az 85018.

The magazine carries articles on subjects such as "Why Sex Stays Fantastic When You Live Together," how to eliminate money problems, and how to get the approval of skeptical—or opposed—parents, friends and employers.

Distributed with a subscription are instruction booklets titled "How To Do It," and "Living Together and Loving It."

We believe that cohabitation is a shift in societal values that's here to stay. Refer to IEA Manual No. 130, Roommate Finding Service, for more information.

Weather Capsule

It probably wasn't too long ago that you finally closed the door on a day full of tension headaches. If you've been wondering how you could escape to one of your favorite resorts and still make it back in time for the next day's migraine, hang on. Those soothing climates can now come to you.

Kohler Company's Environment enclosure provides its owner with enough environmental diversity, personally monitored, to make even the most chronic teeth grinder breathe a deep sigh of relief.

Start off in the warmth of the Baja sun with a soft chime halfway through to suggest shifting your position for an overall tan. Ease into warm tropic rain and, if not just right, adjust the temperature within a 60 to 100 degree range. A few minutes later be surrounded by a jungle steam that moisturizes and cleanses every pore of your (by now) grateful body, with spring showers arriving to wash, cool and refresh.

To top it all off, along come the warm Chinook Winds to gently dry and buffet your hair and skin. Warm ambiance, both before and after your Environment retreat, prevents the shock effect of outside temperature. Nothing to upset your new, relaxed state of mind and body.

The Environment enclosure at $9,000 to $12,000 comes complete with hand-crafted teak and cypress interior and hand-held shower, two porthole windows suitable for a terrarium, aquarium or closet, and six 24-carat gold electroplate spray heads. Optional features include comfort pillows, attractively colored facia panels and a stereo AM/FM, 8-track tape player to lull you through what could amount to 2½ hours of idyllic weather.

The energy required for all this is unusually low, consuming less wattage than an electric dryer and fewer gallons of water per minute than a standard shower. Whether planned for a single-family residence, condominium, hotel or health spa, the Environment offers a new relief from daily pressures not even the traditional noon-hour sauna or evening cocktail can compete with.

For additional information on this product, write Kohler Company, Dept. IEA, Kohler, Wisconsin 53044.

Attache Case With Attached Umbrella

You can guarantee there'll be rain anytime you leave your umbrella at home. Lug the darn thing around, though, and you'll probably forget it at a restaurant.

Now, thanks to an ingenious new product, you really can fool Mother Nature. The Domex *Attache/Umbrella Case* is an attache case with a built-in compartment for a handy, automatic folding umbrella.

It allows you to have an umbrella with you at all times without tying up your free hand. Losing the Domex umbrella is unlikely, but it's no problem if it happens: Any folding umbrella will fit the Domex attache case.

The Attache/Umbrella Case would make a fine gift or novelty item. It should find a ready market among executives, salesmen and college students. Luggage and leather goods stores, stationery shops and department stores are likely outlets.

The attache case is currently available in vinyl and a leather version is planned. Suggested retail price for the vinyl unit is $69.95. Leather versions are expected to retail in the $200 range.

Someone To "Be There"

Why is it that deliverymen, repairmen and installers don't think anyone else works for a living? Did you ever try to get the phone installed, the gas turned on, or the carpet cleaned at a time convenient to you? No way. The consumer has to wait for a serviceman to arrive "sometime this afternoon."

What if you work or have better things to do? Do you take the afternoon off? Do you find a neighbor who isn't working to be there when you can't? Whoever invents a better method should make a fortune.

While we wait for department stores, utility companies, and service people wake up to the fact that we're tired of dancing to their tune, something can be done by a bright entrepreneur. Why not organize a team of part-time house sitters to let in the repair people, installers, and accept deliveries.

Plenty of customers would be willing to pay a nominal fee for a service that saves time and headaches. Especially those who would have to wait weeks for a convenient delivery time—or lose a day's pay. And what about all the people moving from one place to another? Several days are involved in getting gas, electric and phone service. Few people want to ask for time off from a new employer to get this work done. Do it for them!

An even better approach is to sell utility companies, department stores and even smaller service businesses on the idea of sponsoring your operation or at least recommending your service to customers who need it.

Your fee could be paid by the deliverer and passed on to the consumer as an extra charge—or absorbed by larger outfits for better public service. This third party endorsement would virtually guarantee high volume for you and do a lot to improve the consumer relations image of many services.

Clean Parking Lots

Dirty parking lots reflect poorly on the business or organization using them! As a result many parking lot maintenance services are grossing over $50,000 a year. Numerous part-timers are hauling $15,000 and more away to the bank annually!

Look at the parking lots in your area. Grocery stores, airports, bus depots, shopping center lots and school yards are often filthy! Most parking lots are filled with cans, papers, cigarette butts and unsightly litter of all kinds.

Methods of cleaning these environmental eyesores range from simple hand operated carpet sweeper and vacuum devices to high power vacuum systems mounted on pickup trucks. It takes only minutes to suck a parking lot clean!

In addition to parking lot maintenance, such a service can be utilized for cleaning areas like outdoor tennis court complexes, convention centers, sports stadiums and other large areas which require speedy and efficient cleanup.

Much of the equipment you'll need, such as hand operated devices, is available from large janitorial supply companies.

Schwarze Industries, Inc. utilizes pick-up truck mounted vacuum system to clean parking lots. The company offers a training program and equipment, with financing available. See IEA Manual No. 31, Parking Lot Striping Service, for more information, or write to: Schwarze Industries, Inc. Dept. IEA, Route 3, Box 12, Jordan Lane North, Huntsville, Alabama 35806.

Sell Ethnic Cookware!

Americans are going crazy over ethnic foods—witness the boom in ethnic restaurants where diners sample the fare of far-off lands. And there are plenty of gourmets who would love to cook these items at home—if they only had the right cookware.

So why not open a shop specializing in ethnic cookware? Cookbooks and classes teaching the art of foreign cooking should also rustle up delicious profits!

Couscousiere, toupin, sushi press, *daubiere, pashka* mold and *wok* are names of but a few ethnic cooking utensils available from China, France, Hispanic countries, India, Italy, Japan, the Middle East, Africa, Middle and Eastern Europe, Northwestern Europe and Southeast Asia.

The International Cooks' Catalogue ($19.95, Random House) describes numerous ethnic cooking utensils and provides price information, retail and wholesale sources!

A *couscousiere*, for example, is a steamer shaped somewhat like an hourglass, used in North Africa to prepare a traditional grain dish called *couscous*.

A *doubiere*, or *toupin*, is an earthenware pot from France used to cook soup and stews. It dates back to early French provincial history.

The Japanese *sushi* press is a well-designed little box used to press a mixture of rice and vinegar dressing into cakes. *Sushi* is often garnished with seaweed, raw or cooked fish, or omelet strips.

A *pashka* mold is used to prepare a Russian cheese dessert. *Woks*, large metal bowls, are the basic cooking utensil throughout Asia. They're used to fry Chinese "stews" which include meat, fish and vegetables.

This type of specialty shop would be most successful in nearly any major "melting pot" city with a young, adventurous populace. You could whip up interest by having celebrated local ethnic chefs do demonstrations in the store!

Topless Shoeshine?

The well-dressed man is never without a good shoeshine. It rivals a good hairstyling job as an important aspect of the first impression. Combining this fact with the male penchant for pretty faces, a California man has opened over 30 shoeshine stands *managed by attractive, young lasses in fetching uniforms.*

The Great American Shoeshine Company is a featured attraction at 30 Southern California hotels. The hotels either donate the space or charge a small fee for old-fashioned, ornate brass and filigree shoeshine stands. The stands were produced in Mexico, based on a $2,500 antique prototype.

The most intriguing part is that the out-of-work models who do the shoeshines *pay him* $100 per day, per location. He provides polish and uniforms. Whatever the models take in the till and in tips is theirs. This is like the system used by cab companies to compensate drivers. And it's a good way to simplify record keeping.

Depending upon the local market, you may have to deviate from these high prices—or arrange a different type of compensation system. Either way, the idea should work quite well in nearly any major metropolitan area. It's a great tie-in to the nostalgia binge and a magnet for male patrons.

Your best bet is to find convention hotel locations, airport spots and other areas with high foot traffic around the business/financial district. You should have no trouble "cleaning up" even in a single-stand operation, depending upon the marketplace. It's an excellent opportunity for good, free publicity from the media. Contact newspaper and television stations for promotion.

Disposable Problem Bags!

For $35 and up per hour, you can go to a psychiatrist who'll let you air all your problems. But a New Jersey artist has found a much cheaper way that may be as effective. Her answer is The Guilt Bag!

Instructions on the ordinary brown paper bag say to "place bag securely over your mouth. Take a deep breath and blow guilt out. Dispose of bag immediately."

Deborah Sullivan, developer of the Guilt Bag, has already sold 2,500 kits of ten bags at $2.50 each! And she doesn't feel guilty about that at all! The bags are selling well in department stores, gift shops and novelty stores.

The Guilt Bag is a product which can be easily duplicated and even expanded upon for increased profits. All you need is a supply of paper bags, available wholesale from bag manufacturers, which can be printed at an instant print shop.

A set of bags can be marketed for all sorts of problems, printed in various colors. Red for anxiety, green for envy, black for depression and blue·for insecurity.

Why not offer something positive and constructive as well? Like a set of air-inflated plastic bags with instructions to release tab and breathe in for instant solutions to all manner of psychosomatic ills.

A set of color-coded problem solver inflated bags might be labeled: Breathe in for instant sex appeal, ego inflation, security, happiness, success and even nirvana! A disclaimer for legal protection is advised. For further information on the Guilt Bag, write to J. Burns, Inc., Dept. IEA, 225 E. 57th Street, New York, New York 10022.

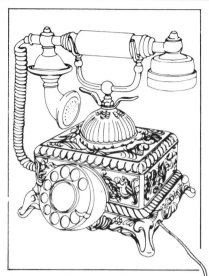

French By Phone

Interest in foreign language study remains strong. Now a method of teaching French, Italian and other languages *by telephone* has been perfected by a New York school.

Office workers can combine a stay-in lunch with a 25-minute Spanish lesson. Housewives can practice French without leaving the house.

Students set up a convenient five-day-a-week lesson plan and telephone schedule in advance with instructors at Phonelab, a New York City language school offering instruction in French, Italian, German, Spanish and Japanese.

Teachers phone students at the appointed time for 25 to 30 minute lessons. Because of the verbal practice, and rapid-fire telephone technique the new method is superior to language records or other home study methods.

Vocabulary and grammar are absorbed with the aid of printed lesson sheets and conversation practice. Twice weekly, students work 20 minutes on vocabulary and grammar using prerecorded tapes.

Courses run for at least four weeks, although most students study longer. Those who already know language basics can take intermediate or advanced courses.

This is a simple thing to duplicate in other markets with rock bottom start-up costs and ongoing overhead. Qualified language instructors should be easy to find because of the teacher surplus. Pay them a percentage of the tuition per student.

Convenience, quick results and low cost are selling points to use in advertising, which would need to be heavy initially. Testimonials are the most effective kind of ads to use.

One important point: Don't overlook classes in English as a second language. There's been a *tremendous* need for this type of instruction for many years.

Most cities are sorely lacking in education facilities that provide such classes for visiting foreign nationals.

Contact Phonelab, Dept. IEA, 200 Park Ave., New York, N.Y.

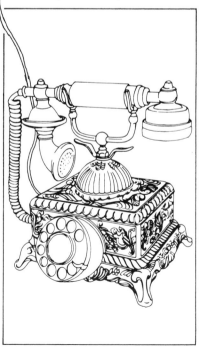

Star Wars Desk

Zoom into the Space Age behind a desk that doubles as a veritable command center for the top executive!

At the push of a button you can get the latest "Big Board" stock quotations or use a closed-circuit TV to communicate with key staff members. You can even use a biorhythm calculator to find out whether or not today's your day!

All this and more is possible with Electronic I, a fantastic new executive desk created by Paul Zell Designs with the needs of the busiest executive in mind.

Gadgets and systems built into the striking pedestal desk make running a business seem like piloting a 747!

A recessed console 74 inches long contains a touchmatic telephone with memory bank, a stock ticker and CCTV set with camera. Other features include tape recorder, dictating machine, digital temperature readout and AM-FM radio.

A control panel will lock the office doors. A standard calculator can be used to balance your checkbook. And a paper shredder can dispose of sensitive documents.

Base price is $9,100 which suggests that one item for the shredder might be the invoice!

Be A Railroad Tycoon!

In spite of the well-publicized problems of the Penn Central, and financial troubles plaguing other railroads, there's still plenty of money to be made in the railroad business!

Well, the *railroad car* business. With the nostalgia craze in high gear nationwide, railroad "theme" restaurants, motels, fast food operations, singles bars and even doctor's offices are opening up all over.

Passenger and freight cars are available for fractions of their cost when new. Belt-tightening U.S. railroads are eager to dispose of outdated stock that's hard to maintain.

In addition to the dramatic, attention-getting value of a railroad car on the property, there are excellent financial advantages.

Buying and refurbishing an antique car for stationary use can be less expensive than new construction or additions to existing property. An added plus is that railroad cars are treated like *mobile homes* to avoid property taxes!

Antique railroad cars, when restored to original condition, are increasing in value to wealthy collectors the way Model T or Deusenberg automobiles have. This will bring fantastic investment returns to those who act now while the most desirable cars are still available.

But the biggest return on investment in the next five years is going to be in *resale to foreign countries,* who will be retiring their rickety 50-year-old equipment during this period.

These countries can't afford new rolling stock—a passenger coach runs $500,000 to $700,000 when new. So lightweight cars from 20 to 25 years old will be in great demand in poorer countries in South America and elsewhere, so long as the track gauge is the same as U.S. Standard. They will pay from $60,000 to $100,000 and absorb shipping costs.

On the wholesale market, railroad cars have consistently appreciated 25% to 30% per year, but profits of 500% to 800% have been realized on sales to foreign countries of serviceable equipment.

For "active duty" resale, cars must be maintained in good enough condition to move. You'd need to have storage facilities (leased from a railroad) that allow for limited maintenance and moving the cars a few hundred feet at least twice a year.

We know of only one company now set up to buy and sell antique railroad cars for these purposes: The American Free Enterprise Train Corp. in Bethpage, New York.

Operating on tracks leased cheaply from the Long Island RR, owner Alfred M. Coleman provides storage, refurbishing and brokerage services to clients seeking railroad cars for stationary use or investments.

Contact American Free Enterprise Train Corp., Dept. IEA, Beth Page, N.Y.

Singing Telegrams

Remember when Western Union messengers would burst into song on your doorstep during the holidays or on your birthday?

Ever since Western Union discontinued the service years back, nothing compares with the melodic messages guaranteed to surprise, excite, fluster and bring a smile to the face of the grouchiest recipient.

Until now. We've found a super update on their idea called Live Wires. Costumed messengers for Live Wires will sing standard or specially composed ditties that congratulate, say hello or goodby, or happy anything.

Normally closed doors of stuffy bank presidents, harassed producers, stone-faced judges, advertising executives and purchasing agents have opened for "the singing telegram people" from Live Wires.

For these occasions, custom lyrics will plug a product, a script or even a resume. An actual wire with printed message is also given to the surprised and usually delighted recipient, along with a sample of whatever you want him to see.

Prices start at $25 for an "in-person" telegram, depending on what you want to do and where. Messengers have gotten on planes and flown to remote places to do doorstep theatre. For $10, a telegram will be delivered by phone anywhere in the world. Custom lyrics composed for special situations cost extra.

This is a great gimmick that can work in nearly any major city in the country. Live Wires is in Southern California, and there are similar services in San Francisco. But plenty of other cities could support a service similar to this one.

Operating would be simple using college students, out of work theatre folk, or adventuresome secretaries looking for an out-of-the-ordinary job. Messengers for one service get $7.50 for each message—and have delivered ten or more a day in their own cars or on bicycles.

Publicity for a service like this should be easy to obtain; it's unknown in most major cities.

Contact: Live Wires, Dept. IEA, 1680 Vine St. Hollywood, California.

Handyman's Dream

The days of fumbling in your toolbox for just the right size wrench are over! An all-purpose, self-adjusting wrench that combines ratcheting, boxend and crescent features has been introduced to the marketplace by a California toolmaker.

The Thormaster wrench will handle nuts from 3/8 inch to 7/8 inch *as well as metric equivalents* without adjustment!

Its unique design will permit use on square, hex, winged, aircraft, fiber lock or other nuts. Even damaged nuts can be easily removed.

The chrome-vanadium wrench is 9 inches long, weighs 4 ounces and will handle 200 foot lbs. of torque.

The wrench retails for $12.75 plus shipping from **Thor International, Dept. IEA, P.O. Box 91254, Los Angeles, California 90009.**

At Last—The Perfect Fit!

Using laser beams and computer programming, a new age for men's tailoring has dawned, shedding light not only on the drawbacks of conventional methods, but also on the peculiar dips and bulges of each individual that, until now, made "the perfect fit" so elusive.

English-American Tailoring Company of Baltimore, Maryland, has developed a system that automatically adjusts measurements to the actual contour of the person being fitted. The result is a handsomely crafted, custom-fitted suit of high quality that will hang perfectly on the person's unique frame. The fitting takes less than five minutes with a permanent record for future reference. Here's how PhotoMetriC works.

A series of tapes are adjusted on the purchaser to provide the exact information required by the designer. The person being fitted stands on a designated spot surrounded by four specially placed mirrors that reflect his image to the PhotoMetriC camera. In 1/10,000 of a second, the PhotoMetriC camera records a precise, scaled "blueprint" for the designer's drafting table. The four-way, optically perfect reflection is placed on one negative, correlating every detail of posture and attitude. From this negative a plate is developed and projected to perfect scale on a translucent, calibrated screen.

These calibrated grade measurements are then fed into a computer, along with pre-programmed body proportions. The computer builds the alterations, corrections and deviations into the pattern and guides the laser beam along a sheet of pattern paper. The 40 individual pieces that make up a man's suit are cut at a rate of 300 inches per minute! Eyeball guesswork and misinterpretation are eliminated!

English-American offers a wide choice of fabrics, patterns, colors, styles and models as compared to the limited choice in the nearest size offered by most ready-to-wear stores.

The price, starting around $245, is competitive with that of fine clothes from any other source, and delivery of the perfect fit is usually well within 15 working days. Licensees are wanted. Contact English-American Tailoring Co., Dept. IEA, P.O. Box 448, Baltimore, Maryland 21203.

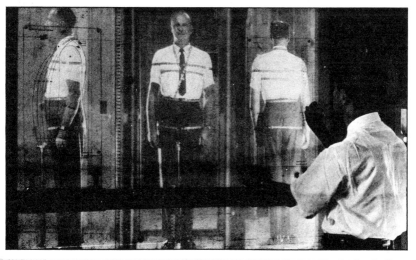

Buying Service For Printing

Costs for commercial printing vary quite a bit from one part of the country to another—and even across town. Finding a printer at the right price is tough without much experience, and it's easy to pay too much.

The concept of a "members only" buying service has now been applied to this complex field. For a small annual fee of $25 to $56, Alpine Industries of Cupertino, California, puts buyers and sellers all over the country in touch with each other in order to cut printing, stationery forms and office supply costs.

Through the mail, members get catalogs, supplementary directory sheets, bulletins and other information. A hot line for consultation is available as well.

Orders from members can be combined to achieve quantity discounts. Members who want to buy or sell surplus supplies or hardware are put in touch with each other.

Using the service, bargain prices like $9.95 for 200 printed letterheads and matching envelopes, or 500 business cards for $5.00 have been obtained by members.

This is an excellent idea, involving modest overhead, that can be applied to other areas besides printing. Catalogs are, after all, free from most suppliers, and many thousands of small businesses haven't the wherewithal to afford a skilled purchasing agent of their own.

Solar-Heated Doghouse

What next? Latest entrant in the race for profits from pet pampering is *Solar Rover*, the first solar-heated doghouse on the market. Being in the doghouse was never so good!

Developed by Solar One Limited, the doghouse is heated by "passive" solar, which means no electricity is used in the process. The sun's heat is captured by a plastic panel on the roof and transferred to a rock bed

storage area under the floor through copper tubing.

When the pet turns in for the night, heat is slowly released into the interior. Even on a cloudy day enough heat can be stored to keep Bowser warm all night. During the summer, panels can be covered with a shade to keep Rover from roasting.

A solar doghouse covers two strong market trends and has a serious side. Harsh winters are rough on animals exposed to the elements, and more deaths occur during this season because of the weather and reduced resistance to disease.

The custom-built dog domicile retails for $795, FOB Virginia. It wholesales for $495 completely assembled. Because the technology is fairly simple, do-it-yourself kits could be developed for sale to dog lovers and breeders.

Write to the ESP Division of Solar One, Dept. IEA, 2644 Barrett Street, Virginia Beach, Virginia 23452 for further information.

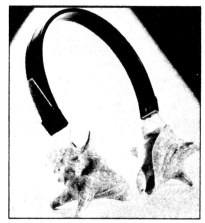

New Shell Game

Has the roaring of trains, blaring of horns, and pressure of the rat race got you down? Now you can escape to the seashore and enjoy the calming influence of the surf—without spending a fortune on beachfront property!

Concha-Consciousness is two genuine conch shells, eternally filled with sounds of the ocean! They're held comfortably on any head with an adjustable headband. With it, the sound of waves washing on a distant shore can be yours whenever and wherever you choose—behind a desk or a wheel.

The $10 headset comes packaged in a burlap sack that smells faintly of wharves and boat docks and is available from the Consciousness Group, Inc., Dept. IEA, 10 Banta Place, Hackensack, New Jersey 07601.

Concha-Consciousness is a product that can easily be duplicated and marketed profitably in a number of ways. If packaged and sold properly, it could be as big as the Pet Rock!

Sea shells of all sizes and descriptions are available wholesale. Find suppliers in the yellow pages under "Shells—Marine." Headset bands or radios tuned to easy listening can be inexpensively manufactured in plastic with adjustable fittings to accommodate different-sized shells.

Seashore headsets could be packaged cheaply in fishnet or put in "presentation" boxes. Sell through direct mail or by placement in gift and novelty stores. Outdoor arts and crafts shows and the adult games departments of major department stores are other markets. With just a little bit of work and money, the blissful sound of pounding surf can be profitable as it is serene.

Zip Out Dog Leash

When Rover has to go out, he has to *go out!* There's no time to waste hunting all over the house for the dog leash! And more and more cities have "leash laws" that require all dogs to be leashed when out of doors.

Retract-A-Leash promises to solve these problems, and provide owners with a way to safely leave the leash on their dogs all the time. It's a retractable leash that may be permanently fixed to the dog's collar or removed for easy carrying in pocket.

Another problem solved is the very real risk that the dog will break away, dragging its leash behind, and get tangled up in someone's fence, tree or thorny hedge. Every year animals are injured—even strangled to death—this way.

The new product weighs only 1½ ounces. The leash line is braided dacron with a tensile strength of 130 pounds. The overall length is 3½ feet, including the strap handle, leash and retracting unit.

Retract-a-Leash is available in either blue or yellow for $9.95, from Wildwood Products.

Retractable Dog Leash, Dept. IEA, Wildwood Products, 18107 Hwy 18, Apple Valley, Ga. 92307.

Bulletproof Clip Boards!

Not since the days of King Arthur's knights have shields been standard issue for fighting men. But nine "Blue Knights" patrolling New York City streets are now carrying them!

Disguised as ordinary clipboards, the lightweight bulletproof shields will stop a .38 slug at close range, and even a .45 bullet from farther away. The clipboards are touted as the latest weapon in the arsenal of defense against street crime.

Most violent confrontations between police and suspects occur at close quarters, within five feet—many life or death situations are at arms length!

With a strap handle on the back, the clipboard can be used as a defensive cover when attacked, and an offensive weapon as well when the officer has only seconds to react. It can be used to jab, slash or smash—and can be deadly when aimed at critical points on an attacker's body.

The shields are made of 1/8 inch fiberglass, and cost only $14. This is much cheaper than bulletproof vests, which cost $125 and more. Further, many policemen will refuse to wear the bulky vests day-to-day because they are hot and heavy.

The 10-by-14 inch clipboards are available from William J. Donovan Corporation, Dept. IEA, 5 Melrose Court, Hamden, Connecticut 06518. They should find a ready market among law enforcement agencies across the country; clipboards are usually standard issue anyway.

Better watch it, though . . . When clipboards are outlawed, only outlaws will have clipboards!

King Arthur Coming Back!

If you think the nostalgia craze has run its course, guess again. We found an armorer in England who is a year behind on orders for *full suits of chain mail* just like King Arthur wore when courting Guinevere! This could tie in with the phenomenal interest in genealogy that's sweeping the country.

Anthony Ptolomey crafts armor to fit like a custom suit, matching in detail the one worn by the knight of your choice in the Age of Chivalry. He's located in tiny Ramsden, a village outside Oxford, but sends his suits all over the world for prices ranging from $1,000 to $2,000—and can't keep up with the demand.

Each suit takes about a month and a half to produce after an exacting set of measurements is taken from would-be Lancelots. These measurements include the length of the fingers and the circumference of the biceps. Then he hammers out a suit from cold steel, forming it over an oak log in the traditional way of medieval armorers.

Of course, a skilled craftsman in the states could do the same thing and market full suits or miniatures in a variety of ways—as art objects, costumes, or historical duplications of the clothing worn by a famed ancestor. Spin-off ideas include costumes which are exact replicas of those worn by ancestors from any time period. The idea is an unlimited opportunity to capitalize on the "roots" craze.

A bright entrepreneur should be able to duplicate armor or other costumes in quantity using volume production techniques and shortcuts. And why not emblazon each suit with the family crest or colors worn in battle? Then the suits would become treasured heirlooms to buyers. Contact Ptolomey at his armory. The address is Dept. IEA, Royal Oak, Ramsden, Nr. Charlbury, Oxfordshire, England.

Cobalt Jewelry

It was only a few years ago that millions of copper bracelets were sold as the "wonder cure" for arthritic joints. Well, the bracelet craze has spawned a $20 *cobalt* necklace guaranteed to ease aching neck and shoulder muscles. It's the current rage in Japan where $20 million worth of the trinkets have been sold.

The Japanese Minister of Health & Welfare even approved it, claiming the Bio-Magnetic necklace "enhances blood circulation and softens stiff shoulders."

The necklace is made of copper and Rare Earth Cobalt, a substance developed by NASA for the space program. The jewelry contains five cylindrical magnets which perform the magic.

To "work" it must be worn in direct contact with the skin and kept dry. People with pacemakers are warned not to wear it. Considering the fantastic sales of this item in Japan, the Bio-Magnetic necklace is an item well worth duplicating.

It shouldn't be difficult to make one, even if you don't have an "in" at NASA! The necklace is being carried at Carson, Pirie, Scott & Co., at 1 So. Date in Chicago, as well as other national retailers. It would be helpful to get a sample to facilitate duplication. Copper is available from metal suppliers and the Rare Earth Cobalt can be obtained from suppliers of scientific equipment (listed in the yellow pages under "Scientific Apparatus & Instruments").

After you've come up with your own magic necklace, you can market them by direct mail, or sell to jewelry stores, department stores, gift shops.

Contact Carson, Pirie, Scott, Dept. IEA, 1 S. Date St., Chicago, Ill.

Pick-Proof Padlock

A magnetic padlock has been developed that provides much better security than conventional key or combination locks. No one can open it without a secretly coded magnetic key.

Ridges and grooves on the key are eliminated, so it can't be duplicated. No keyhole in the door means picking or clogging is impossible. There's no combination to fumble or forget.

Available from Universal Industries in Taiwan, these magnetic locks come in a variety of sizes and models. There's a 30mm and 40mm standard padlock. A long-shank bicycle lock and a 22 inch automobile steering wheel lock are also offered.

To open the locks simply place one of the two slabsided keys provided into a similarly shaped groove on the side of the lock and slide out the shackle. Keys are coded with over 10,000 combinations and your code is stored in the manufacturer's vault.

No other magnet will work on your lock, and it is made of case-hardened steel to make it virtually cut-proof.

Things Unlimited, Dept. IEA, P.O. Box 415, Streetsboro, Ohio 44240.

Plants That Never Die!

Indoor plants are easy pets compared to dogs, cats and even goldfish. Normally, all you have to do is water them. Still, millions of people manage to kill their leafy friends by overwatering or underwatering.

Unless you're a botanist, it's pretty hard to know exactly how thirsty plants are. But with Anything Groes, even people without green thumbs can guarantee their house plants a long and healthy life. These plants water themselves!

Anything Groes is a new concept in raising plants which can be used for all plants commonly grown in the home. The process calls for planting in special pots which contain a rare, imported peat soil in a mesh liner. The soil is specially processed to hold an unusual amount of air, the secret to root health.

Watering is simple! You just fill the pot's water saucer. The plant will take only as much water as it re-quires, regardless of how much water you put in the saucer. This is perfect for traveling plant owners, because you can give the plant a week's supply of water.

It works because of the "humidity chamber" between the mesh liner and the container. Plant roots grow into this humidity chamber rather than clotting together in a circle inside the pot. Since this area is filled with air, the roots thrive and the plant will grow quite large before the roots are cramped for space.

Anything Groes systems are available in potting sizes from 2 inches through 16 inches. A six-inch system, for example, wholesales for $1.75. The system can be used in any ceramic, clay, or plastic pot. The manufacturer is looking for distributors.

The product line is marketed from Anything Groes garden parties and is a natural for plant stores.

Anything Groes, Dept. IEA, 340 Nesler Center, Dubuque, IA. 52001.

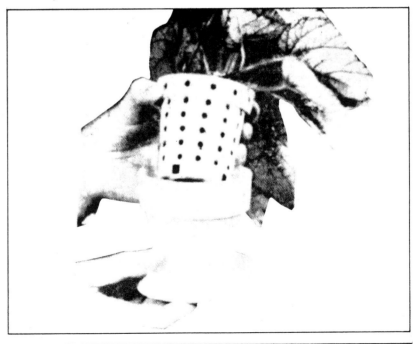

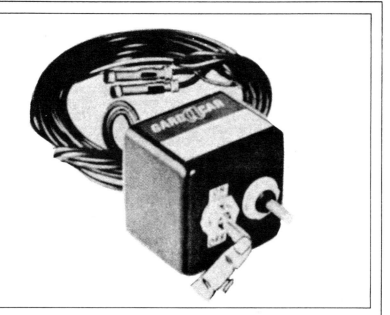

Drive Away Car Thieves!

Car thieves have to work quickly and almost anything that will delay them or make stealing a car difficult is enough to send them down the road looking for easier prey.

We've found a great device that promises to foil almost any car thief who isn't an electrical engineer. It's the Gard-A-Car Immobilizer—not much more than a black box, toggle switch and timed circuit breaker.

When the black metal box is turned on, the timed circuit breaker automatically cuts off the electric current flowing to the distributor. If a thief breaks into the car, jumps the ignition and gets the car started, the system stalls the engine in less than eight seconds! The car cannot be restarted until the device is reset.

The Gard-A-Car control box is easily hidden under the dash. It is operated by flipping a switch on when leaving the car and off when returning. If an attempt is made to start the car, the element must be reset by pressing a red button controlling the in unit breaker.

The product can be installed in a few minutes in any auto, truck or other motorized vehicle. There are no holes to drill. Two wires are connected to the 12-volt hot wire that runs from the coil to the distributor. The only tools needed are a knife to cut the one wire and pliers to crimp splice connectors.

The box has a self-adhering surface for easy hiding under the dashboard, seat or in the glove compartment. The unit is designed for any ignition system, conventional or electronic. There is no interference with normal car operation. The system can also be used in conjunction with other anti-theft devices.

Gard-A-Car comes complete with connectors and instructions and carries a one year warranty. It's a nifty product which should sell well at auto supply stores, service stations, hardware stores, department stores and by direct mail. The manufacturer is looking for distributors. Auto Alarm Gard-A-Car Inc., Dept. IEA, 8930 Macomlost., Grosse Isle, Michigan 48138.

Drive-A-Drunk Service

There's plenty of money to be made off drunk drivers by keeping them away from the wheel, as one Los Angeles business has discovered. Drive-A-Drunk, Inc., operates a round-the-clock chauffeur service for drivers who find themselves too inebriated to risk driving home.

Drunk driving is dangerous, not only to life and limb but to the pocketbook as well. There are stiff legal penalties, auto insurance problems, and even third party liability for helping the driver get drunk in the first place! Everyone stands to lose

Using a telephone answering service, the business answers as many as 75 calls a day. Saturday nights are the busiest. Drivers follow the chauffeurs in the client's car.

Customers pay in advance and sign a simple contract assuring the company that the car is insured, and releasing the service from any liability. Drivers and chauffeurs are part-timers who contract independently with Drive-A-Drunk for a percentage of the fee and remain on call for four-hour periods.

Because chauffeurs drive the customer's cars, taxi licenses aren't re-

when an inebriated driver gets behind the wheel.

A Los Angeles actor who lost an arm and leg when hit by a drunken driver was awarded $1.9 million *from the bar that served the drunk booze!*

For a fee of $15 to $100, depending on distance, Drive-A-Drunk will send a driver and chauffeur to a party, restaurant, bar or nightclub to transport the driver and his car home. It's a service aimed at drinkers with cars, not at walking drinkers who can simply call a cab.

quired. Chauffeurs have a right to refuse to drive anyone they think would cause problems. Female drivers are on staff as many women are apprehensive about having a strange man drive them home.

Setting up a Drive-A-Drunk service, putting up posters in bars and nightclubs and seeking free public service publicity with local newspapers, radio, and television stations is sure to bring staggering results.

Contact **Drive-A-Drunk Service** Dept. IEA, 7060 Hollywood Bl., Los Angeles, California.

Funeral Bards

People just keep on dying! Despite attempts to streamline funeral services and lower prices required to deliver loved ones to the "other world," eulogies are still standard operating procedure.

Jules Maitland, a Los Angeles writer, discovered there's plenty of money to made in the eulogy business. For $50 he puts together a few kind words about the deceased and for another $25 his partner, Stanley Johnson, delivers them at the service.

Their company is called Personal Words. They average about five funerals a week, deriving most of their business from recommendations by local funeral directors.

The mortuary gives Maitland the hour and date of the service. The family of the deceased provides the personal information.

Maitland explains that eulogies should be kept light. For example, after writing a tribute for a man who had enjoyed having his granddaughter dance for him, Maitland arranged to have her dance at the funeral—while the eulogy was spoken.

For a man whose greatest love in life was dogs, Maitland had the departed's two Great Danes sit beside the coffin during the services.

Writing funeral eulogies can be a profitable business for any budding poet. If you also possess stage presence and a deep rich voice, you can deliver the tribute yourself.

The best way to get started is to write a eulogy for a recently departed famous person. You can get details on his or her life at the local library. Keep it short (six to eight minutes) but meaningful.

Take the sample eulogy around to funeral directors in the area, showing them what you can do. In reading the eulogy, follow Stanley Johnson's advice: "I try to deliver them with feeling. I don't want it to sound like items from a birdseed catalogue."

For further information: Personal Words, Dept. IEA, 8489 W. 3rd., Los Angeles, California.

Sell Rolling Billboards!

When Lady Bird Johnson "beautified" the nation's highways she turned outdoor advertisers ugly! Environmentalists celebrated a victory and motorists were saddened by the passing of "Burma Shave" signs into folklore.

Now General Advertising Company, of Columbus, Ohio, has found a way around restrictive highway advertising regulations—and the super high cost of erecting permanent billboards as well.

They've signed up trucking companies to ten-year contracts and are converting 50,000 big semi-trailer rigs into moving billboards! The trailer units will be equipped with electric lighting to illuminate 40 foot paid advertising messages on the sides.

Because of low cost in comparison to other media, national advertisers are jumping at the chance to get the high exposure that these rigs offer. The approach is particularly attractive to liquor and cigarette advertisers who can't use television.

With millions of trucks on the highways, there's plenty of room for more competition in this unique new ad game. And expensive installation on the trucks isn't necessary. Lighting is only required after dark, when freeway traffic drops outside major cities. And over-the-road haulers won't deliver as many viewers as local trucking operations anyway.

A local or regional operator should be able to arrange for contracts with smaller trucking fleet owners eager for additional revenue. Payment for the use of the space for advertising should be minimal.

The next step would be to agressively contract all the advertisers in the area to sell the space. Bargain rates and high exposure are the best selling points.

Contact: General Advertising, Dept. IEA, 6497 Proprietor, Columbus, Ohio.

Plug Farming

The on-going energy shortage has sent the home insulation business booming. In insulating older homes, contractors frequently drill holes in the siding, insert a tube and blow the area between the studs full of insulation material.

While this method of insulating older homes is considered quite successful, it has a major drawback. Homeowners aren't too happy about the holes left after the insulation is blown in. And contractors aren't exactly thrilled about having to patch all the holes. About 250 holes are required to insulate an average home!

A Nebraska cabinet maker recently stumbled on a unique way to circumvent this problem. He makes plugs. And he calls his business The Plug Farm. There are no holes in this man's solution and it's a business idea which can be implemented by nearly anyone with a knack for woodworking.

The plugs must be tapered, somewhat like a bottle cork, so they can be tapped into a hole quickly, neatly and firmly and made to match the angle of the siding perfectly.

Insulators apparently are thrilled by these plugs. The Plug Farm reports that the average order is now 15,000 to 20,000 plugs! Most insulators prefer pine plugs, while many request them in redwood.

The Plug Farm needs 24 employees working in three shifts to handle back orders. Cutters turn out the plugs by the wheelbarrow load. Others are kept busy smoothing up the plugs, counting them and packaging them in plastic bags. Business just keeps plugging along.

Handicapped Store

For years we've seen clothing stores tailored to the needs of tall, skinny people or short, fat people— or any "hard to fit" size in between. Now an enlightened Japanese designer has opened a shop in Osaka that specializes in merchandise for the handicapped!

Namiko Mori has filled a real need in the marketplace and received tremendous response and public support for his store, called "Helper's." There's no reason why a shop like his can't work just as well in a major metropolitan area in the States.

Mori's shop features fashionable clothing and accessories, such as like a poncho that fits over a wheelchair and its occupant at the same time. There are ramps throughout the shop, as well as handgrip railings in fitting rooms and elsewhere. Custom tailoring is often required.

Handicapped individuals have to "shop around" to find apparel, shoes, and other items in ordinary clothing stores or orthopedic supply houses. Necessary alterations can be costly and often clothing will wear out quicker because standard garments are not designed to withstand heavy stress. This is particularly true in footwear. For example, one shoe will wear while the other doesn't, and where can you go to buy one shoe?

A comfortable store (with convenient parking, another hassle for the handicapped) could do an excellent job of promoting itself through hospitals, extended care facilities, Goodwill and other organizations. The public relations value inherent in performing a much-needed service like this should be worth a fortune in free publicity.

A down-the-road idea, once the store is established, is to develop a mailing list and catalog sales program to reach the substantial national market, as well as those who can't come to the store themselves.

Mobile Massage Parlor

Hard-charging executives with no time to relax during the day—and others who are looking for a unique way to see the sights in a strange town—can pick up a phone and call for a "massage-taxi service."

A quick back-rub by a lovely young lady on the way to the airport or a "teeth grinding" meeting with a client sure beats discussing the weather with a surly cabbie, judging by the response Dennis Sonneschein and his brother have gotten to the nation's first mobile massage-taxi service, opened recently in St. Louis.

A phone call brings a $22,000 Winnebago motor home rolling up to the door of a customer's office, home or other prearranged spot. While the driver wheels the rig down the road or around the block—an attractive lass massages the customer. Refreshments are part of the package.

Any liberal metropolitan area could support a similar service for affluent and discriminating clientele. And a fancy motor home isn't absolutely necessary. Many smaller recreational vehicles can be adapted for use in this fashion. Curtains for privacy would be a welcome touch.

Advertising in the sports section of daily papers should bring in plenty of business during a grand opening campaign. After that, word-of-mouth and reasonable rates should generate lots of repeat business.

Fees should vary with distance travelled and the type of massage requested. Rates in the $30 to $50 range are common starting points.

Install Padded Cells

Psychotic inmates aren't the only ones living in padded cells these days. An increasing number of "normal" people are padding the walls of their homes and apartments.

And it's not because they anticipate impending derangement! Padded walls not only cover cracks, but also insulate for warmth, reduce noise pollution and look pretty plush.

Medieval castle dwellers used wall upholstery to cozy up their cold, dark rooms. But the technique really took off in the 1700s when brocaded walls were the big fad.

Renewed consumer interest in wall upholstery means big profits for those who install it. It's a business which carpet layers, furniture upholsterers and even auto upholsterers (for that tucked and rolled look) can move into in a big way. Wall upholsterers are making $1.50 and up per square foot for installation.

The technique is to pad walls with half-inch-thick polyester Kodel or similar material, and then cover with corduroy, fabric prints or whatever the customer wants.

Another approach is to simply carpet the walls and even ceilings. This achieves a totally "soft" environment with pleasing acoustical results.

After you develop your product and technique, interior designers are probably the best source for work. Executive offices and waiting rooms are likely prospects, as well as private residences.

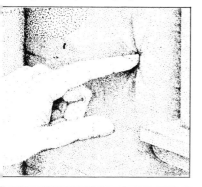

Ballbarrow

The wheelbarrow has been a workhorse in construction and gardening for centuries without change in basic components. Until now.

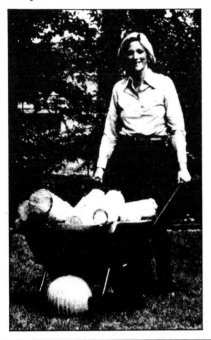

Two British designers changed the wheel to an inflatable ball and created the revolutionary Ballbarrow. A ball beats the wheel because it can't get mired in mud and doesn't leave tire marks on damp lawns.

The wider tread surface and position under the bin mean greater stability and easier emptying. A side tipping action isn't necessary. The user just tips the bin straight forward to spill contents on the ground.

The body is molded from polyethylene plastic so it can't rust, crack or dent. The smooth, non-stick interior surface means that even hardened cement just drops out!

The bin has a capacity of 4 cubic feet. The ball is 10 inches in diameter and it weights only 22 pounds, so even small children can use it easily

The barrow, to be priced at about $50 retail, will be distributed through garden centers, stores, and by mail order. It comes knocked down in a box for easy assembly.

For further information on this product, write Ballbarrow, Dept IEA, 1320 Ardmore Ave., Itasca, Illinois 60143.

Foam Pool Floor

A pool party can turn into a tragedy if an accident takes place, and every year we read about more and more of them. One reason that pool covers sell so well is the desire to prevent unattended children from falling in and drowning.

Shoved aside amid all the hoopla is the problem of diving accidents. On the increase are serious head injuries, paralysis and even fatalities.

We have a cheap and effective solution that could be as large as the multimillion dollar pool cover business. A Styrofoam pool floor!

Styrofoam is cheap, easy to work with and available in large sheets that can be cut to fit the most intriguing pool shape. A thickness of two inches should be sufficient, and is obtainable commercially from plastics concerns.

The real cushioning is done by the water itself! The underside of the Styrofoam sheeting is weighted enough so that it rides just above the existing pool bottom, so the water under the foam layer acts as a hydraulic shock absorber!

Every homeowner, school or YMCA with a pool is a prospect for such a device and the market is untouched. This is a natural add-on for existing pool sales firms or maintenance outfits. You could make it a profitable service with high margins and low operating costs in an area where backyard pools are big.

Skin Is In

Few cities of major size are without a handful of adult bookstores, or porno movie houses. Opinions vary on this subject, from welcome acceptance as a healthy shift away from "up tight" sexual taboos of the past to vehement opposition as a sign of moral decay.

Moral values aside, sex is *big business* and phenomenal profits can be made in even the tiniest adult bookshop (Report #14). And profits have been so good at Plato's Retreat, a New York City swinger's club, that its owners are hoping to *franchise* the operation across the country.

Plato's, located in a renovated bathhouse, charges admission of $50 a couple and $20 for unescorted women. Unescorted males are not allowed.

The entry fee includes all you can eat or drink, use of swimming and disco facilities, and just about any sort of sexual activity you can imagine in private cubicles or out in the open in luxurious surroundings.

On most nights there are from 80 to 150 couples there—most of them naked and engaged in sex acts of one

kind or another. Trading off partners is common, but not required. Because all are consenting adults, nothing is forced, and the booze is free. It's all perfectly legal and licensed in the liberated Big Apple. Attorneys watch this carefully.

Customers range from mid-twenties to mid-fifties, and come in a wide variety of shapes and sizes. Most are intelligent, well-educated professional types. Couples are usually either living together or married. Plato's projects gross revenues of over $1 million from fees and memberships. Overheads are in the 40% range.

With estimates of six to eight million swingers nationwide, and growing numbers of young people shedding Victorian-age values, potential for such a facility is great in permissive major metropolitan areas. Of course, the acceptance of a swinger's club depends greatly on local county and state laws.

And in smaller cities, where everyone knows everyone else, anonymous sex in public places isn't all that anonymous.

For further information: Ansonia Hotel, Dept. IEA, Broadway & 73rd, New York, N.Y.

Weave A Table

Find a product that combines beauty, handcrafted quality and low cost and you've got a winner on your hands! Macrame is one of the hottest "in" crafts and it seems to be everywhere. Beautiful wall hangings that take only a few hours to make sell for hundreds of dollars in gift shops.

Now you can get macrame *furniture* in kits. Spend an afternoon weaving an occasional table, magazine rack or plant stand. You'll have a lightweight, attractive and inexpensive piece of handmade furniture for a fraction of the cost of an all-wood item—even unfinished!

Easy-to-build furniture kits from Macramania in Bellmore, New York, sell from $6.95 to $16.95. The kits include an instruction sheet, lengths of jute, and pre-cut wood dowels. All the do-it-yourselfer adds is white glue, sandpaper and stain or paint.

For tables, a sheet of glass, wood, masonite or tile will top things off with just the right effect. A catalog of macrame furniture and hanging kits is available for 25 cents from Macramania, Dept. IEA, P.O. Box 923, Bellmore, New York 11710.

This would be a natural for art, craft and hobby stores to carry. Nothing prevents you from imitating what they've done and selling these kits by direct mail, perhaps as part of a "Craft of the Month" format.

Your Own Black Bag

About all the typical home has available in the medicine chest is a fever thermometer and Band-Aids. But most families could handle common childhood illnesses on their own, saving the doctor's time and the patient's money, if the right equipment was available along with detailed self-help instructions. Now it is.

Marshall Electronics, Inc. has developed a family Black Bag containing basic medical equipment needed for diagnosis and instruction booklets that tell what to do *before* the doctor needs to be called in.

The bag is equipped with an aneroid blood pressure sphygmomanometer, a dental reflector/tongue depressor device, and a high intensity exam light just like the doctor uses to shine in your eyes or look down your throat.

A stethoscope, oral and rectal thermometers and health history packets help you keep tabs on the family's health. Manuals prepared by licensed physicians teach you how to use each implement in the kit as part of a health maintenance program.

Marshall plans to market this product in drug stores, pharmacies and other health-related retail outlets. For further information, write to Marshall Electronics, Inc., Dept. IEA, 7440 N. Long Avenue, Skokie, Illinois 60076.

Shower Power

Most people look forward to a good, hot shower to wash away a buildup of grime and soothe nerves. The shower is a turn-on for those who use pulsing shower heads and other watersports gadgetry.

Now there's a simple apparatus that installs beneath the existing shower head and promises to make getting clean an even more luxurious (and sensual) experience.

Invented by Doil Coley of Corsicana, Texas, the device mixes liquid soap, shampoo, oils, conditioners or "signature" scents with the shower spray. The heavy duty plastic reservoir has two separate chambers so you can even mix different liquids.

It can be mounted without any special tools and requires no auxilia-ry power. A Venturi tube joined to the reservoir is threaded on between the shower head and its connecting pipe. Water flowing down the tube creates the necessary suction to draw liquid from the reservoir.

Now you can give your skin and hair a treat without a vast assortment of bottles and containers. A simple valve adjustment controls additive selection and flow from the two chambers.

For women using a signature scent it's the perfect, effortless way to get that extra fresh feeling. Shampooing becomes less harsh when mixing shampoo and conditioner with a turn of the controls.

Doil is looking for a manufacturer who can take this idea into the waiting market place.

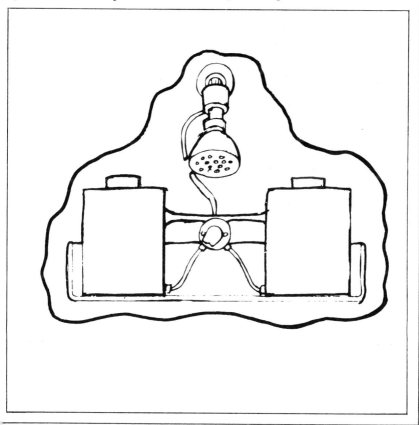

MoPed Rival!

As mounting sales of mopeds clearly indicate, America is seeking convenient, inexpensive transportation. This follows in the wake of fuel shortages and skyrocketing automobile and motorcycle prices.

Many people have purchased bicycles in an attempt to circumvent rising transportation costs and get some exercise at the same time.

While bicycles are great for short runs, pedal-powered cross-town journeys are time consuming and exhausting. Now almost any bicycle can easily be converted to a moped with the Globalman Spitz Engine!

The 11 pound, 22cc engine sells for $140, or $125 if six or more are ordered. The suggested retail price is $169.95. Spitz equipped bikes are capable of speeds up to 20 mph and boast an impressive 215 mpg!

The Japanese made engine has an automatic pedal start action and carries a full year warranty.

The Globalman Spitz Engine features a chokeless rotary carburetor designed for motorcycles—a fuel pump is utilized which allows for unused gasoline in the carburetor to flow back into the fuel tank for greater fuel economy and less air pollution.

Because any five or ten-speed bicycle can be equipped with the bolt-on engine, this product should be a great competitor with mo-peds, in any bicycle shop. In addition to low prices, competitive advantages include light weight and easy pedalling. Mopeds weigh over 100 pounds, and usually have no gear ratios, so that pedalling is a chore!

Globalman Products, importers of the Spitz Engine, is looking for dealers. Bicycle Moped Globalman-Spitz Globalman Products, Inc., Dept. IEA, P.O. Box 246, El Toro, California, 92630.

Car Wash For Dogs

While the result is pleasant, giving a bath to your favorite canine is often a headache. It's enough to make you wonder who came up with the label "man's best friend." The bathroom often ends up in a shambles and after the mess is cleaned up, you've got to take a shower yourself.

For the frustrated dog owner who has tired of these inconveniences, a Brooklyn couple has the answer—an automatic dog washer! No more yelps, no more sopping struggles, no more desperate snapping, no more "wet shakes" all over you.

Originally designed by Clem and Antoinette Blafford for their doberman pinscher, the automatic dog washer offers an effective and safe means of giving Bowser a good scrubbing without drenching you in the process. And it's *easy*.

The design provides two enclosures separated by a gate. In the first cage the dog stands under spray nozzles that discharge soapy wash water, then clean rinse water. Your dog's head is outside so no soap or water can get into his eyes, ears or nose. When the wash cycle is completed, he steps into the second compartment, head, body and tail. There an automatic blower sends a stream of heated air through the compartment to comfortably dry your companion. Presto! Instant sheen!

Now all he needs is a quick brushing, a few biscuits for good behavior and he's ready for some more dirty mischief with his pals!

With pet owners nationwide spending millions on their furry family members, this type of easy-to-copy idea should be a natural service for pet salon and kennels to offer. And a great gimmick for car washes!

Squeakless Hinge

Next time you tiptoe into the house in the wee hours of the morning, you won't have to worry about hinges squeaking if you've had the foresight to install Kra-z-ee Hinge, a flexible plastic material designed to replace metal hinges for a lot less money.

The centerscored material comes in 12-foot or 100-foot rolls that can be cut to appropriate length using shears or a mat knife. It can be used to hinge tool boxes, hang awnings or connect flexible, free-standing dividers. These and other applications have previously required use of costly, continuous metal hinges.

It can also be used as a temporary hinge when checking the fit of cabinet doors or cabinet parts. For light duty jobs, use annular nails. Where weight is a factor, roundhead screws or nuts and bolts may be used. The hinge gives a slightly greater than 90 degree swing.

It should be a welcome addition to hardware and do-it-yourself retail outlets in the 12-foot roll which sells for $11.95 retail. The 100-foot roll costs $55.00, and should find a ready market among cabinetmakers, carpenters and others in the construction trades.

A sample roll 3 feet long is available for $2.95 postpaid from the manufacturer. Write Provost Displays, Dept. IEA, 618 W. 28th Street, New York, New York 10001. Dealer/distributor inquiries are invited.

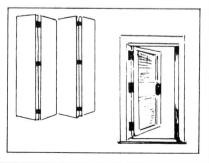

Chimney Sweep

Shake hands with a chimney sweep and good luck will rub off along with the soot. So the story goes.

In any case, good luck has followed a Harvard Business School student who has built a thriving business in New England out of Old English garb and a long-handled, wire bristle broom.

Dressed in traditional black top hats and tails, Rick Osborne and his three apprentices clean fireplace chimneys in the wealthy suburbs west of Boston. The flues fill with flammable soot from wood fires burned to warm winter evenings. So it has been since the days of Dickens.

Heavy cloths are laid on the floor in front of a customer's fireplace. The sweeper dons a face mask (courtesy of OSHA!) and goes to work pushing a broom to the top of the chimney. As clouds of soot and creosote billow down, a vacuum cleaner sucks up the dirt. Occasionally, a sweeper has to scramble up the roof and work from the top down to finish the job.

Osborne warns customers of the real danger in letting creosote accumulate. It can ignite and send flames shooting up ten feet above the chimney top. For a fee of $40 per chimney, his firm, called Master Chimney Sweepers, will prevent the hazard.

Summer is the best time to do chimney sweeping. It's a time-honored profession involving minimum start-up expense, but you have to be a combination electrician, steeplejack, gymnast and actor to do it right.

For more information, refer to IEA Manual No. 155, Chimney Sweep Service, or write to August West Systems, Dept. IEA, Box 1725, Norwalk, Connecticut 06850.

Tour Europe By Postcard!

Most travelers owe the folks back home postcards. You can shoulder this responsibility and make plenty of money doing it as Charley Stone, founder of Foreign Cards, Ltd., New Haven, Connecticut, has discovered.

He sells 100,000 postcards a year to travelers so they can address and even inscribe them before they leave. A minimum order of 25 cards sells for $4.95, 50 cards for $9 and 100 cards for $17. A good selection of postcards from major cities in Europe, Africa, the Mideast, and Asia are all you need to launch this business.

Stone buys from several printers in Europe and directly from the State in communist countries. He purchases in quantities of 3,000 cards from tourist cities like London, Paris, and Zurich, and has an inventory of over 300,000 cards.

There's no danger in stockpiling so many cards since the Eiffel Tower or Sphinx won't change. Even if they should be destroyed by war or an act of God, his cards would be valuable collector's items.

A natural extension of this idea is

to sell the cards to schools, collectors, armchair travelers, dreamers, and practical jokers who for one reason or another are seeking a jet-set image without actually going anywhere.

After customers inscribe the cards, arrange for cards to be sent overseas and mailed back, for a fee, from various ports-of-call by airline employees or foreign travel agents.

Advertising in the travel section of newspapers, in slick city magazines, airline flight magazines, and distributing sales brochures or flyers at travel agencies should bring plenty of business your way.

24-Hour Football!

Are you frustrated after watching Monday Night Football because it's too dark outside to throw the old pigskin around? Are beach parties boring after the sun sets because it's too dark to play ball?

Flamer, the illuminated football, is the bright solution to this nocturnal problem. The regulation size, battery-operated football is safe, unbreakable and water resistant. It's an ideal toy for after-hours backyard family fun, beach parties, that friendly game of pass and catch, or that neighborhood session of flag football.

Seeing the ball's flight in the dark is an artistic delight, according to the manufacturer. The spin of the ball and the resultant blur of light coming through the ball's light holes make fascinating patterns.

Flamer uses two AA batteries and retails for $5.99. The manufacturer is looking for dealers. Wholesale price is $42 a dozen (two doz. lots), $36 a dozen (six doz. lots) and $30 a dozen (ten doz. lots). Samples are available for $4 each.

The bright new product was used in half-time shows at the Chicago Bears, Los Angeles Rams and Minnesota Vikings night games.

Flamer, Pick Point Enterprises Inc., Dept. IEA, P.O. Mirror Lake, New Hampshire 03853.

Bovine Body Builder

The next mouth-watering porterhouse you bite into may come from cattle raised on a diet of cement dust! Government researchers have found that the calcium-rich dust fattens cattle at up to twice the normal rate when used as a stretcher to extend supplies of traditional feeds.

Dust filtered out of the air in Portland cement kilns has been approved for use as a feed ingredient by the Food and Drug Administration as a result of testing conducted at Maryland feed lots.

The FDA cautions that farmers may face legal action if further testing now underway reveals that any residue of dust remains in the meat. Testing to date has uncovered no such abnormalities, however.

Agriculture Department officials credit three Georgia farmers with the accidental discovery. They had limed grazing land with the dust, and noticed a phenomenal increase in the growth rate of cattle who fed there.

Controlled testing by the department has shown that cattle gain weight an average of 30% faster on a diet of 13.3 pounds of hay, 10.9 pounds of corn, and 0.8 pounds of dust. This compared to normal rations of 13.2 pounds of hay, 8.5 pounds of corn and 3.2 pounds of costly supplements.

Even more promising is the fact that dust-fed cattle produced "top choice" grade meat, while their counterparts scored only "top good" marks in quality.

Cattle ranchers across the country looking for ways to produce more and more, cheaper and cheaper, should welcome this development. While the long-term effect on consumers is yet to be determined, one thing they won't be able to worry about is hardening of the arteries. The dust doesn't contain ingredients necessary for cement to set!

Floating Snack Bar

If you live in a well-heeled yacht harbor or resort area, you could be missing the boat if you haven't considered serving the lucrative boat owners' market. A group of enterprising college students recently launched a "row-in" floating lunch counter at a resort lake.

They service several areas of the lake, and also transport food and beverages to residents and visitors along the shores and docks.

Another row-in service near Catalina Island offers to pick up items at the local store for boat owners who weekend on their boats. A cardboard sign is given to all boaters staying overnight on their crafts. If a boater needs anything, he simply marks the items on a checklist. The brightly colored sign is then put on the stern of the boat. Twice a day the sign is checked and the items are promptly delivered by the service.

The row-in service charges a service fee plus the cost of the items. They do a good business during the summer months, because boat owners are always forgetting their suntan lotion and/or Sunday papers. And if you can afford a yacht, you can certainly afford to pay for personalized service!

Be King Of The Mountain!

Has your career peaked? You can assure yourself of permanent "king of the mountain" status by buying mountain tops! A tall story? Hardly, considering that Loren McQueen has become a millionaire doing just that!

He started his climb to success in 1952 when he paid $2,500 for 270 acres atop Mt. Umunhum outside of San Jose, California. He now owns 73 peaks from Seattle to San Diego, with hundreds of tenants paying $100 to $700 a month for sky-high space.

Who wants to rent space on top of a mountain? Radio stations, highway patrol organizations, the National Weather Service, the U.S. Forestry Service and the U.S. Air Force.

With the ever-increasing numbers of citizen band radio operators and ham radio buffs throughout the nation, there's a growing need for relay stations and high altitude antenna sites. Since these are hobbies which appeal to the wealthy, mountainous rents can be levied.

Mountaintops are one of the favorite sites for spiritual as well as creative development. Space could be leased to a yoga or meditation school. Struggling writers might dedicate a novel to you, besides paying rent for an opportunity to leave the world behind and compose the "Great American Novel" atop your peak. Running ads in literary magazines should attract them like flies!

In addition to the occasional recluse willing to pay rent to get away from it all, owning your own mountaintop can come in handy next time it rains for 40 days and 40 nights!

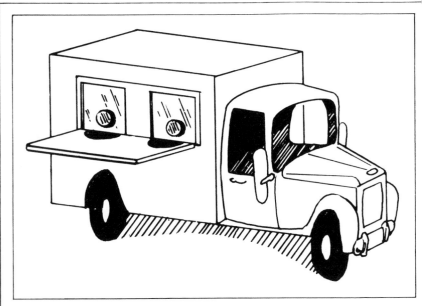

Money On Wheels

There are literally *millions* of people in the United States who don't have personal checking accounts at banks but still need to get checks they receive cashed.

Cashing checks for these people has turned into a multimillion dollar business for Money Mart, a Denver operation that specializes in cashing checks from small drive-up booths and *mobile vans!*

The Denver operation makes its profit by adding a service charge for each check cashed. Rates range from 50 cents for a check under $49.99 to $1.50 for checks up to $199.50. An additional 50 cents is charged for each $100 increment.

Business has been so good that Money Mart plans to buy two more armored vans by the end of the year.

Others using the service are workers in areas where a bank isn't readily accessible. People are obviously willing to pay for the convenience of this kind of service.

There haven't been any security

problems since the business began and the real risk is that the business issuing the checks won't have sufficient funds to cover the payroll.

Money Mart obtains permission before sending the van out on location and checks with the firm's bank to make certain the checks issued won't be rubber.

All that's needed to start a similar business is a leased armored van, an armed guard, and permission from local factories and industrial plants.

Securing a bank loan to cover the expected payroll should be no problem after you explain what you're doing to your banker. Indeed, local banks might be interested in contracting with you to function as a mobile banking branch, depending on state regulations.

The personnel or public relations departments of companies you plan to service should be delighted by your novel idea. These services can be presented by the factory or plant as a company sponsored convenience for employees.

Contact: Money Mart, Dept. IEA, 2200 W. Alameda, Denver, Colorado.

Crash Course

Teaching a spouse, friend, son or daughter to drive is enough to strike terror into the stoutest of hearts, especially if it's done in your car!

Despite the availability of numerous driving schools, many people still prefer to be taught by someone they know. Professional driving instructors attribute this to a fear of "freaking out" in front of strangers.

Even the best intentioned spouse, friend or parent is naturally going to be equally as nervous about having the student driver destroy their car.

In an attempt to cover this angle of the driving instruction business, two Toronto driving instructors recently started a student rent-a-car agency, which should do well in any locale.

They purchased five new cars, had dual brakes, steering wheels and mirrors installed and are now renting them, complete with student driver warning signs, for $24.95 a day.

The cars are insured for an additional $5 a day per student and there's no mileage limit, though the operators insist the cars be used within a 20-mile radius of the firm. Customers pay for gas and a $75 "precautionary" deposit is required.

Because of insurance considerations, the person renting the car must be 25 years of age or older, but the student can be of any age beyond the legal minimum.

This is a great gimmick, since professional instructors aren't required and the rental agency can substantially undercut local driving school prices.

There's no reason why you couldn't start with several used cars. Outfitting them with dual controls by a mechanic specializing in auto devices for the handicapped would cost only a few hundred dollars per car.

Because of the novelty of this approach to driving instruction, not to mention the humor, plenty of free publicity would be available from local papers, TV, and radio.

Rub A Dub Dub

Even though newborn babies aren't China dolls, new mothers are justifiably frightened of dropping their slippery, suds-covered infant to the floor during bath time.

Numerous serious injuries and even deaths are attributed each year to such freak accidents and any product or device designed to eliminate such dangerous mishaps is a welcome addition to the multimillion dollar baby products business.

A Washington state manufacturer has developed baby bath mitts designed to help mothers maintain their grip on slippery infants.

The mitts are made of soft terrycloth, backed with durable nylon and delicately trimmed in ribbon and lace. They come in assorted colors.

These mitts could easily be duplicated by enterprising entrepreneurs and should make an excellent direct mail item.

The mitts are perfect for baby shower gifts because they're inexpensive and highly practical. The manufacturer plans to market the safety mitts for $3 a pair and is looking for distributors.

For further information, write to **Dillard Enterprises, Dept. IEA, Box 5107, Redondo, Washington 98054.**

Be A Movie Mogul!

Now you don't have to be in Hollywood to become a movie star! You can stay right where you are and become a hot shot producer selling classic movies for home viewing!

Old movies like *High Noon, Bridge on the River Kwai,* or *The Jolson Story* are available for the first time from Universal and Columbia Pictures on an outright sale basis.

One Los Angeles company called The Nostalgia Merchant has begun marketing the oldies at retail prices of $160 and up to buyers tired of ho-hum TV fare—or Uncle Harry's slides (yawn!) of his (yawn!) vacation in (yawn!) Nebraska.

A 12-chapter series of the Adventures of Captain Marvel sells for $600. Films are available in either Super 8 or 16mm sizes.

Shorter, 20-minute versions are also available for those who don't have the patience or time to sit through a complete movie. However, required editing results in huge gaps in the plots. In *Kwai*, the bridge goes up and is destroyed before you can even gobble down a bag of popcorn!

What a fantastic opportunity this is for anyone in the booming nostalgia business! There are a variety of directions to take. Movie nuts are sure to be a ready market, along with "old time" restaurants or pizza joints looking for new ways to entertain the public.

It would be a simple matter to develop a nifty catalog of available films, using old movie stills or posters. Sell these prints through the mail or develop a rental service at rock bottom rates while you continue to own the prints.

For more information contact Universal or Columbia Pictures 8mm Marketing Divisions in Los Angeles. Also write to The Nostalgia Merchant for their $1.00 catalog, at Dept. IEA, 6255 Sunset Blvd., Hollywood, California 90028.

Do-It-Yourself Skeletons

Researchers who dug up the remains of King Tut have made a fortune from its incredible historical value, but the current skeleton shortage means you too can dig up a treasure chest of profits in old bones!

If you don't mind the smell of embalming fluid, you can capitalize on this human skeleton shortage, as they now sell for more than $750 apiece! That's more than $3 per bone.

The escalating cost of assembly, as well as the growing popularity of cremation have created a low supply of skeletons, which are in demand by medical facilities around the world. The shortage was partly caused several years ago when India's then Prime Minister Indira Ghandi banned the export of human skeletons. While people die in large numbers there, the Hindu religion mandates burning of the dead.

The ban was felt all over the world, and the black market flourished. The bones were smuggled out of Hong Kong, Mexico and Peru, and grave robbers dug into exorbitant profit potentials as the going price skyrocketed. The ban was lifted 21 months ago, but the shortage still exists.

Consequently, one dealer reports turning down one offer of $11,000 for one set of bones! A human skull with a full set of teeth brings at least $250 from a medical school.

So, if you're planning a trip to Hong Kong this year, and want a nice little write-off, you might consider this bare bones business. Since assembly is costly, and bones are known to be quite brittle, you could create a "Do-It-Yourself Skeleton Kit" and ship the bones in a padded pine box! The kit would come complete with instructions any 12-year-old could follow.

Contact: Wm. Kuerbs, Dept. IEA, MacMillan Science Co., 3200 So. Hoyne, Chicago, Illinois.

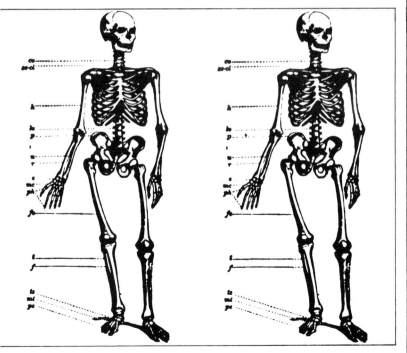

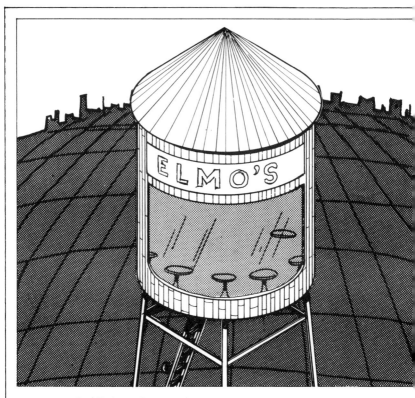

Get Tanked At Elmo's

A classic Halloween prank has always been to sneak to the top of the local water tower and hang a dummy over the edge. A trusty can of spray paint is often used to scrawl some final epitaph on the tank walls, like "I can't take it anymore!"

Two men are attracting attention to the water tower in Baxter Springs, Kansas in an entirely different, and more constructive, way. They are turning an abandoned, 125-foot eyesore into a high-rise restaurant!

Patrons will ascend to the top of the tower in an elevator built into the central shaft, and dine on a glass-enclosed balcony surrounding the tank. They expect to provide seating for 200 people, and serve them from a bar and kitchen complex built within the 100,000 gallon tank itself.

City fathers were glad to sell the structure to contractor Elmo Bur rows and architect Migdonio Seidle for only $2,000 rather than pay t have it torn down. A new, large tower was built two years ago t serve the community and the aban doned one couldn't be given away!

Imagination and creativity like thi has led to restaurants made fron railroad cars, old train depots, pos offices and other classic structure that are usually available for next t nothing when abandoned and read to be torn down.

Renovation costs are frequentl far lower than the cost of building new building in today's marke where construction costs are goin through the roof. And if you find tower like this one in your area chances are you won't have an trouble getting water to the site!

Don't Be Left Out!

Everyone has a theory about left-handed people. According to some, it's an indication of superior intelligence. Others brand southpaws as witches!

Folktales aside, lefties certainly get left out in the rain when it comes to equality. While 20 percent of Americans are southpaws, they're hard put to find products manufactured for their particular needs.

"Southpaws need love too" is the motto of Left Hand Plus, Inc., a mail order company specializing in all manner of products for this minority. The company's catalogue sells for $1 and contains a $1 gift certificate applicable to a future order.

Inside the catalogue are descriptions and photo reproductions of useful items for lefties. Included are instruction manuals for *legible* left handed writing, golf, tennis, guitar and embroidery.

Practical items include lefty address books, ruler sets, coffee cups, kitchen utensils, scissors of all sizes and even baseball gloves! Also wrist watches, playing cards, pocket knives and belt buckles. Books are available through the catalogue on all aspects of life in the left lane—from education problems for junior to adult adjustment anecdotes.

There aren't enough items in the catalogue to completely stock a shop tailored to southpaw needs. But on the other hand, a gift shop, novelty store or cookware shop could stock a complete department from the catalogue—on the left side of the store, of course! Send $1 for the catalogue to **Left Hand Plus, Inc., Dept. IEA, P.O. Box 161, Morton Grove, Illinois 60053.**

103

Make Pots Of Film

Ever wonder what happens to all that film that winds up on the cutting room floor at movie studios? Censored or cut because an actor flubbed his lines, it is useless to moviemakers.

An enterprising young craftsman in Los Angeles picks up this discarded film free from studios, film processing labs and professional photographers. He uses it to make unique flower pots, vases and other containers selling for $6.00 and more.

The rim of each pot features a strip of film from familiar full-length movies, commercials or cartoons. As it is the only part of the pot where an entire strip of film shows, the remainder can be made from different colors of leader or 35mm scrap.

The pot base is a yellow plastic 35mm film spool. These discards are available for next to nothing.

This would be an easy-to-copy idea that should sell well in gift stores nearly anywhere in the country, and you don't need access to major studio to do it.

Nearly any large city has film processing labs and professional photographers that use thousands of feet of film a year. Make arrangements with them to take scrap film and spools off their hands.

Making these pots is simple. Starting at the base, just wrap layer after layer of spliced film tightly around cone-shaped form until you complete the basic shape. Then wrap several layers on top of each other to make the rim. The final wrap should be an exposed film clip.

It is best to do this on a wood lathe ($200-$300) turning at slow speeds because a tight wrap is critical or the pot will be flimsy. Mount the spool and form on the lathe and feed the film onto the form as the lathe turns. You could modify a potter's wheel to suit your needs as well.

Chocolate Sculpture

The heavy aroma of rich mouth-watering chocolate attracts sweet-toothed buyers like a magnet through the doors of any candy shop. But when's the last time you saw anything really unusual inside?

There's always a wide assortment of small, filled chocolates, nuts, jelly beans and other goodies. But about as creative as it gets is hollow Santas and Easter bunnies during the holidays.

Gunther Heiland, an Atlanta pastry chef, has turned chocolate and pastillage (sugar work) into an art form as well as what could easily be a moneymaking idea for a sharp marketer.

His chocolate sculptured baby shoes, covered wagons and biplanes have won awards at international competitions held in Europe.

His chocolate Stutz Bearcat has individually spoked wheels, a gear shift, gas and break pedals—even a horn. A pastillage spinning wheel made of confectioners sugar is half the size of the antique original and copied from several photographs.

Pastillage is made with confectioners sugar, water and gelatin. The water and gelatin must be boiled or at least very hot. The hot liquid is mixed with the sugar until it is the consistency of almond paste. The paste is rolled out and parts cut with a knife using a template. Depending on humidity, drying takes two or three days.

For chocolate, use the semi-sweet variety. It is melted and glucose added before cooking for a stiff consistency. Next, pour it onto a paper-lined tray to cool. Then it can be kneaded into the consistency of modelling clay, rolled, cut and shaped into any desired design. In a few hours dried pieces can be glued together using liquid chocolate.

Heiland's one-of-a-kind masterpieces have taken up to 80 hours to produce. But simplified designs and assembly-line techniques can reduce this labor cost. It should also be possible to make molds for production in quantity.

What a nifty gift a pair of edible old shoes or a biplane would make! Any chocolate shop owner should be delighted to carry unique sculpture like this and would doubtlessly feature it in the window to attract plenty of attention. At a good flea market, a simple booth should attract buyers in droves, especially if you are doing the sculpture on the spot.

Contact: Gunther Heiland, Omni International Hotel, Dept. IEA, 1 Omni International, Atlanta, Georgia.

Smoke Eating Ashtray

The war between smokers and non-smokers continues. Research has shown that 68% of the smoke from a cigarette is not inhaled. It spirals up out of smelly ashtrays to fill the air with twice as much tar, nicotine and other irritants as smoke filtered through a cigarette.

This raw smoke is what's offensive to non-smokers—irritating eyes and nose and making it difficult for some to breathe.

A Chicago inventor has developed a smoke-eating ashtray that can help change that. Bob Kirk's invention draws the smoke from a cigarette resting in it through a replaceable charcoal and polymer deodorizing filter, removing all but a trace of the harmful smoke.

Particles as small as 100 microns or .000393 of an inch in diameter are filtered out by activated carbon from coconut shells.

The Smoke Eliminator uses a tiny battery-powered fan to suck smoke into the unit so it doesn't drift into the air. The item is expected to retail for $7 to $11 and distributor/dealer inquiries are invited.

For further information, contact **Norbert A. Kirk, Dept. IEA, 43 E. Ohio Street, Room 930, Chicago, Illinois 60611.**

Stick Around For Profit!

Ordinary walking sticks are turning into the most revolutionary exercise aid to hit the market in years. With sales of huff-and-puff equipment soaring in this country, why miss out on the profits? We've even found a store that specializes in selling walking sticks and canes of all shapes and sizes!

A walking stick/cane shop should work in nearly any major metropolitan area from the fashion angle though most sales will come from the geriatric trade. There's only one shop in the country doing this now and sales of antique canes, sword canes for protection and ornate hollow canes from Prohibition days for holding liquor are selling like wildfire.

Exercise buffs are always looking for new and better ways to keep in shape. And the walking stick, a fashion accessory for gentry since the days of Sir Walter Raleigh, is finding new uses as a leverage device in isometric exercises where muscles work against each other.

Only one company capitalizes on the walking stick as an exercise device and the market from this angle is wide open. The E.J. Marshall Corporation in Connecticut sells a very heavy model with solid brass fittings wholesaling for $15 apiece. So you should be able to go into the manufacturing business with this idea as well, attracting a broad market. Other applications include security for night walking, added support for the elderly—and as a stylish fashion accessory.

Sticks should be sturdy and an oak or white ash shaft is best. A rubber tip and metal headpiece are important features walkers appreciate. Wood-turning companies listed in the yellow pages will give you cost estimates based on your specifications.

Walking sticks can be marketed in gift shops, sporting goods stores and men's clothing stores. Tall baskets, kegs or customized umbrella stands are excellent point-of-purchase display ideas. You can get price breaks from wholesalers on these items. One way to get widespread market distribution is to set up a secondary marketing system using local distributors who buy stock from you for resale.

Growing Greeting Card

Ever stand for hours in a card or gift shop trying to find a card that doesn't sound and look just like all the rest? Then repeat the same exercise at the flower shop down the street?

Now you can do both with Greetings That Grow, a greeting card that comes wrapped around a can of potting soil and seeds ready for planting by the recipient.

Full-color photography and a variety of sentiments are featured on the plastic-lidded can that becomes a flower pot as soon as seeds are planted inside.

With tender loving care, the seeds sprout and grow into a variety of flowering plants that serve as a lasting reminder of thoughtfulness long after the typical card is tucked in a desk drawer or discarded.

The growing greeting cards were developed by Design Communications and should be an exciting line addition for card and gift shops nationwide. Distributorship inquiries are invited. For further information contact International Nature Products, Dept. IEA, 16055 Ventura Blvd., Encino, California 91436.

Flat-Proof Tires

Air-inflated tires were invented to take the bounce out of traveling on solid rubber. But a punctured tire can spell disaster at high speeds. Now a flat-proof tire is about to go into production, which could take the danger and hassle out of tire punctures forever!

The new tire is a venture of Goodyear Tire & Rubber Company, and was recently demonstrated at the annual New York Auto Show. When punctured, the tire is supported on a sidewall rubber compound that will maintain its shape for about 40 miles at speeds up to 40 mph—even with a severe rupture.

According to Goodyear, the new tire will make the fifth wheel, spare tire and the jack in the trunk unnecessary. A flat in the new tire makes so little difference in riding quality that the company claims it will be necessary to include a tiny radio signaling device with each tire.

The new Goodyear tire should be an instant success when it hits the market; and it's bound to be a big seller wherever tires are sold.

Contact Goodyear Tire & Rubber Co., Dept. IEA, 1144 E. Market St., Akron, Ohio 44316.

Grow A Plate of Gold

It takes about 50,000 *tons* of snails to satisfy the taste of American escargot fans. And this delicacy, which combines garlic butter, parsley and plump snails, is rapidly gaining in popularity. Whether or not the dish is among your favorites, there is a way you can capitalize on the escargot craze. Start a snail farm!

There is a shortage of good snails and restaurateurs currently import them from Taiwan or Europe. But with the increase of escargot eaters,these foreign breeders simply can't supply enough. A crop of about 50,000 snails is sure to guarantee profits.

Snails used for escargot are not the average garden variety found on lawns and flower beds. These often consume—and enjoy—large quantities of pesticides. The best snails are raised in a controlled situation on grape leaves, cabbage, bread crumbs or bulk bran.

Your farm can be set up in a one-car garage or tent in the backyard. Soil-filled boxes will give the snails a good home. The most popular breed of escargot is the Roman snail or *Helix pomatia* and the Department of Agriculture in Washington, D.C. will assist you in finding a source of breeder stock. They recently published a booklet for would-be snail farmers or heliciculturists aptly en-titled "Snails as Food," which is available by request.

The financial returns on this business are slow—in keeping with the nature of your product. It takes a snail three years to qualify as a plump contender for gourmet dining tables. But at maturity, each snail will bring in a healthy 25 to 40 cents from restaurant owners or independent gourmets.

The biggest problem is keeping the snails awake to eat. They usually spend half of the year in a state of hibernation called dispause. Some successful farmers in Europe have found that spraying snails with mist and tickling them keeps them awake and munching. It is also important to keep them out of a cold draft or they will withdraw into their shells.

So if you have an unused area in your yard, this may be just the perfect sideline business. And since snails have a relatively uninteresting personality, there will be little danger of your getting attached to them—until you brew up a plateful!

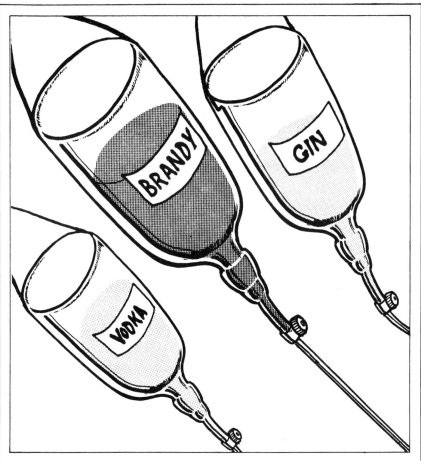

For Medicinal Purposes Only

Sometimes a hangover can make you feel like checking into the nearest intensive care unit. Well, now there's a way you can recuperate from the night before without leaving home.

Hospital Booze is the hottest new bar accessory on the market. The "hair of the dog" is dispensed into your glass from an authentic intravenous bottle complete with plastic tubing and a flow regulator. You'll *feel* better just looking at it.

The sales potential of the item is unlimited. It is the perfect gift item for the home mixologist. Cocktail lounges and bars will find it practical. And in any situation, it is a great conversation piece. We can also see it in bathrooms as a mouthwash dispenser and in kitchens for detergent.

Each bottle holds 32 fluid ounces and is easy to refill. The unit stands (or hangs) 12 inches high and comes with 11 pre-printed liquor labels. Bottles can be ordered with a serving stand for an additional $2.50 over the standard $5 wholesale price.

Dealer inquiries are invited. Write: Neoart, Dept. IEA, 6832 Val-Jean, Van Nuys, California 91406.

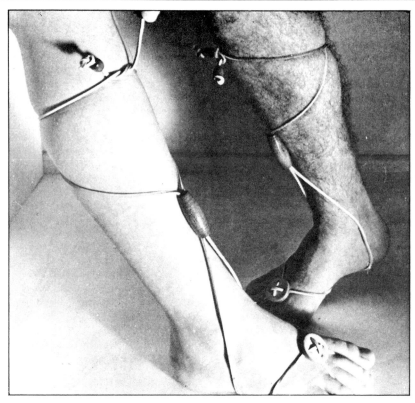

No Bare Feet!

Few restaurants allow customers to enter with bare feet. And during the summer, that can put a crimp on satisfying your hunger pangs. But there is a solution other than carrying an emergency shoe bag.

We've found a fashionable little item that will get you past any maitre d'—*Barefoot Sandals!* They are leather thongs that wrap around your feet and legs. Decorated elegantly with beads, they look like expensive Grecian style sandals without soles.

Clothing shops and shoe stores will attract a large potential market. The items will also do well in drug stores and discount marts. At gift shops, it is ideal for the person who has it all.

When not being worn as shoe decoys, the thongs can be used as a belt, necklace or even a headband. The manufacturer recommends its use as a string for small kits, but this, we feel, is a bit far-fetched.

Beach-goers and golfers who enjoy baring their feet, but want style, are good candidates for Barefoot Sandals. Teenagers will likely make up a large portion of customers and the sandals can be worn by men. Backyard barbequers will find them a fashionable addition to Sunday dinner.

Barefoot Sandals currently retail for $6.95 and should put an end to bare feet discrimination. Write to **KTNT Productions, Dept. IEA, 4409 Stern Avenue, Sherman Oaks, CA 91423** for further details.

Home-Clone Business

Cloning is not something you do at a party to get laughs, but has become serious business. It used to be that the idea of asexual reproduction of a group of objects from a single source was fantasy or science fiction. But no longer. Now there's a way you can watch dollars reproduce by selling "clones" from plants!

Once considered a passing fancy greenery has become one of the biggest businesses in America today—and cloning is the latest off-shoot, so to speak. It combines the popular trend for natural environments with a sneak preview of futurism.

The clones are just ordinary two-inch starter cuttings of healthy, sturdy plants with a humorous packaging. We found one operator who is selling "clone-grown" plants faster than he can get the little devils packaged—and seeing a very real 70 percent gross profit margin on every one sold.

The emphasis here is on packaging. It is necessary to have an outer box or wrapper explaining that the plant is cloned, although it isn't necessary to go into the technical explanation. In fact, this is where a person could really capitalize on hidden creative talent. "Home-cloned plants are orphans and need love—Allergic to household cloning fluid, feed only with hydroponic nutrients—responds to songs by Rosemary Cloney." We're sure you get the idea!

Creating a cloned plant does not require a degree in science. It works on the principle of hydroponics, that is, growth by placing the roots in liquid nutrients rather than soil. This is accomplished by using a two-inch plastic pot and vermiculite nuggets which expand when moistened.

This nifty idea is a natural business for anyone with a green thumb—or simply an interest in greenbacks. It can be started at home. All that's needed is space to work and store the finished product. And as a gift item, they easily sell for $4.50 retail figuring on operating costs of 50 cents to 75 cents per clone.

Plant shops, home and decorating centers, gift boutiques and department stores will love the response they get from shoppers. Swap meets and state fairs are also great for exhibiting and reaching the impulse market. It makes an unusual promotional item for banks, real estate companies and other service businesses wanting to attract lots of new customers.

Talking Diet Aid

There are more than 80 million overweight Americans, many of whom will go to any length to stay on a diet. Hypnosis, shock treatments and extensive support networks with other dieters are a few methods being used. Many of these attempts, however, often fall short of expected results.

We've found a novel item that will have dieters laughing their fat away. *Diet Conscience* is a battery-operated message device that is mounted inside a refrigerator or cupboard. It scolds sneaky eaters anytime the door is opened. A pressure arm activates the voice which advises the culprit to "do yourself a favor—shut the door." This follows several other comments designed to give dieters second thoughts about eating again.

The unit, which wholesales for $4.95, will do well in health food and drug stores and gift shops. It is an attention-getter as a demonstration item at home shows, county fairs and bazaars. The marketing potential is widespread because of its versatility as a thoughtful gift to a dieter, a novelty item or a serious purchase by people trying to slim down.

Diet Conscience is manufactured by a company that produces recorded messages for major toy companies for dolls and other talking toys. The unit comes packaged with instructions for easy installtion. Write to **Performance Sales Associates, Dept. IEA, P.O. Box 531, 440 W. Colfax Street, Palatine, IL 60067.**

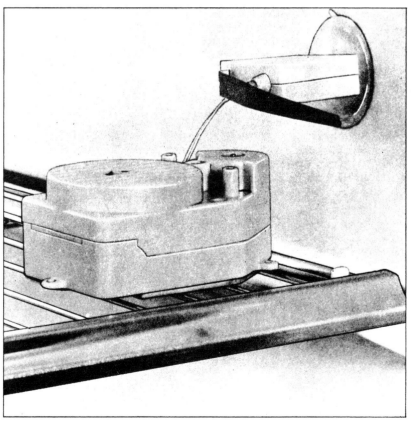

can also be used by hobbyists to hang needlework canvasses, film or work clothes.

Hardware stores, home decorating centers, bathroom boutiques and department stores are just a few locations that will attract potential customers. The versatility of this item also makes it a sure bet in boat and camper supply stores where space-savers are a prime seller.

Slax Rack is available in walnut brown, white, yellow, blue and orange. Each unit weighs two pounds and is packaged with installation hardware and instructions. The wholesale price is $12.95 each, based on a case lot of 10 units.

Contact Well-Built Inc., Dept. IEA, Box 22176, Memphis, Tenn. 38122.

A Rack For All Reasons

Making space in a clothes closet is like bailing out a sinking ship: the water—or the clothes—always win in the end. But we've found a product that will give you extra space *and* help stop closet clutter.

Slax Rack is an ingenious item that is installed on a closet door and holds eight pairs of pants or skirts and 10 or more ties and belts. It folds down for selection and back up for storage, adding 12 to 16 inches of space on clothing rods.

The Slax Rack can be used for other purposes, like hanging towels in the bathroom or kitchen. It is made of high impact plastic which won't rust so it is perfect for wet garments in the laundry room or by the pool. It

Go For Game Point

Every tennis player knows how difficult it is to keep track of the score, especially after a great rally. Several tennis scoring devices are on the market, but most require a degree in engineering to operate.

A unit has been invented by Robert Pagel, a tennis player who is familiar with the problem. The Tennis Scoring Device is worn on a band around the player's wrist. The score is entered after each point with a press of a button. And even ace and deuce scores can be entered.

The item is patented, but is not yet in production. Once it is manufac-

tured, it should do extremely well i sports shops, tennis pro depots an gift shops. The projected retail pric of $2, including a band, will make it popular accessory for every player

The Tennis Scoring Device prote type is made of simple injection-mol ed parts. A variety of standar watch bands can be substituted suit the taste of anyone.

The unit is available for produc tion and marketing. Interested pa ties are invited to write to Inventor Licensing and Marketing Agency Dept. IEA, P.O. Box 251, Tarzana, C. 91356 for more information. (The represent inventor Pagel.)

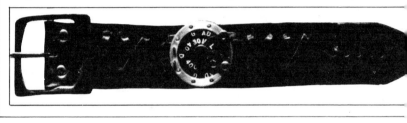

Greet Guests With A Song

The next time the Avon Lady rings your doorbell, give her a chorus of Beethoven's "Fate Knocking." Or, if it's close to Christmas, "Come All Ye Faithful" will get your guests into the spirit at the front door.

These and 22 more songs have been preprogrammed into the Philharmonic Doorbell, an innovative and musical way to say "Welcome." All you do is select the melody of your choice and the song will play everytime the doorbell is pressed. When you get tired of one, simply select another!

Homeowners and apartment dwellers will sing the praises of this unique device. It is simple to install and selections are made at the turn of a dial. In addition, individual controls permit adjustments of volume and tempo to suit your preferences.

Although mail order is currentl the primary form of distribution, thi item should ring up sales in har ware and home decorating store The "Star Spangled Banner," "Go Save the Queen" and "The Mai sailles" give the Philharmoni Doorbell international appeal as a unusual gift item for specialty store

Two nine-volt batteries operat the solid-state microprocessor, s there are no extra charges on you electric bill. The doorbell retails fo $44.95 and has a one-year parts an labor factory guarantee. It is sel contained and can be hooked up to back door too.

Send a letter—or a singing tel gram—to Contemporary Marketin Inc., Dept. IEA, 790 Maple Lan Bensenville, Illinois, 60106, fo more information.

Potty Planter—A Real Goer

If your bathroom is like 20 million others in the nation, the top of your toilet tank is probably a catch-all for soap chips, old bottles and tissue boxes, among other things. We have found a practical new product that clears the clutter and beautifies the bathroom at the same time!

The Potty Planter is a self-watering planter box that fits on the toilet water tank. Simply replace the standard lid, plant your favorite greenery and leave the rest to Potty Planter.

Its specially designed wicks absorb water from the tank and keep the soil moist. You can grow beautiful plants in the bathroom with no maintenance! And satisfy your environmental responsibilities by using a natural, untapped source of water!

The Potty Planter is an item that will sell itself in bath boutiques, department stores or plant shops.

Recently, a super-market listed it in their food advertising and **sold out** within the first two hours of the shopping day! It is an unusual gift item for the home gardener with everything. And it will dress up restaurants with standard fixtures in the restrooms. Plants are generally not included, but could be added for increased profits.

The unit is made of a sturdy molded plastic similar to that used in making telephones. It will withstand years of planting without corrosion or cracking. And the manufacturer informed us that bowl cleaners will not affect either the plants or the unit!

The Potty Planter has a wholesale price of approximately $6 with discounts for quantity or cash orders. It currently retails for $11.95.

Contact: On Target, Dept. IEA, 4163 W. 5th St., Los Angeles, California 90020.

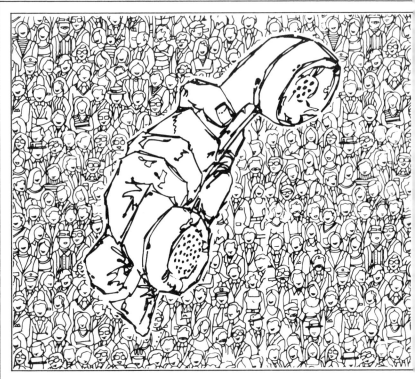

Dialing For Knowledge

How would you like to order your favorite magazine by telephone and have it "delivered" to your home television screen? This is known as computer data retrieval and may sound like future world technology. But it's happening right now in England and should be available in the States within the next few years.

The Prestel system is operated by the British Post Office which also runs the telephone system. It provides weather reports, stock market and race track results, as well as mail-order previews and sports information.

Capable of holding 250,000 pages of information at any time, it is considered a forerunner of the "electronic encyclopedia." The price for installation of the screen is now about twice that of a television set, but will drop as the demand grows.

Computer hardware stores are springing up across the U.S. and we can expect floor samples of a system similar to Prestel before long. We visualize all the daily newspapers being transmitted rather than delivered. And as you monitor the receiving unit, you can "read all about it" without getting sore arms or newsprint hands.

The system is an invaluable service to shut-ins, who can order any item from food to large appliances by phone. The charges are billed directly on the phone bill as is the cost for the initial call to the computer. Each page retrieved has a set fee—currently 3 cents a sheet—which also appears on monthly billing.

It won't be long before the kids call a computer for homework assistance, leaving the adults to compete for equal time. Just like the old days!

Space Age Sink On The Beam

If you wake up in the morning too tired to move, and it's an effort to flick on the electric toothbrush—here's a brand new labor-saving device you are sure to love. You can wash your hands without even turning on a faucet!

Aquatron is an electric eye beam sink control that triggers a flow of water as soon as your hands break the invisible beam. When you remove your hands, the water flow stops. Water temperature and pressure are preselected to your specifications, from ice cold to tepid to boiling hot.

Leisure-crazy Americans are sure to pick up on this idea in the mass market, but the device has many legitimate and practical uses—particularly in hospitals, where contaminated fixtures are a real problem. Without constant buffing and polishing, fixtures become laden with viral bacteria. Surgical rooms, nurseries and isolation wards are just a few places where the Aquatron will fit in nicely.

There are many other applications. Dentists' or doctors' offices all over the country should have them. Schools, hotels and public restrooms are also potential customers, as well as commercial or industrial buildings.

In addition to improved sanitary conditions, Aquatron cuts water usage and reduces energy bills, because there's no warm-up time. It can be installed easily by a handyman on any existing sink. Only the eye beams and fittings are countermounted. A 12-volt power supply and controls are housed under or behind the sink.

The unit sells for $155 with a one-year guarantee. And the manufacturer is looking for dealers.

Write: Qualco, Dept. IEA, 1 First St., Los Altos, California, 94022. Attn: J.C. Meyer.

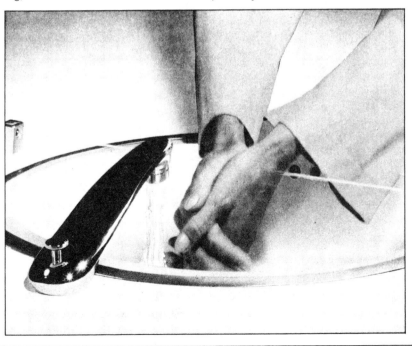

A Case For Security

Important business meetings are often conducted in private offices or conference rooms. If they are of highly confidential matters, they may call for security measures. But hiring guards is time-consuming and expensive.

The next best thing is the *Protector 501*—an effective security system in a case. Four infrared sensors detect the presence of an unwanted visitor and trigger an alarm transmitter up to 260 feet away.

The unit should prove invaluable to travelers and business people who stay in hotels. Money, jewels and secret documents will be safe if a Protector 501 is placed at the entry point of a room. And the four separate sensors can be placed at four different points for maximum security.

The device operates for 24 hours following a 15-minute charge-up in any 110 volt outlet. The alarm transmitter is powered by a standard replaceable dry cell battery.

Profitable response to this item at security and law enforcement shows is guaranteed. It is perfect for diplomatic attaches, who often carry top-secret papers from country to country. And anyone who transports gemstones or securities and bonds will find it a worthwhile investment.

The Protector 501 is housed in a compact briefcase and weighs 40 pounds. It can easily be carried as hand luggage on planes and trains. The manufacturer invites dealer inquiries. Write to Protect, Ltd., c/o Bob Wescott, Dept. IEA, P.O. Box 292, St. Helier, Jersey C1, England for information.

Night Light For Fido

Ever walked your dog at night and wound up dodging more cars than trees? Now there's an innovative new product that will protect you from being struck by inattentive motorists on country roads or dark city streets. **Luma-Leash,** the ultimate in doggie accessories, is a battery operated device that will keep a pleasant stroll or pre-dawn patrol from becoming a Kamikaze mission!

Dog owners are sure to eat up this latest product to hit the $5 billion pet industry—and it's sure to make Fido the first on the block, trend-setter if you will, and envy of all the other critters.

Whether displayed in pet shops, grooming parlors, or clinics, the Luma-Leash is sure to be an attention getter, and the retail price of $6.95 makes it well within the reach of the average pet owner, who spends about $300 per capita.

Luma Leash is made of sturdy vinyl in a variety of colors to suit the fashion conscious, and is packaged in a tiny dog house suitable as a gift for the pet with everything.

Write Protect-a-Pet Industries, Inc., Dept. IEA P.O. Box 412, Pompano Beach, Florida 33061 for information about dealer/distributorships.

8-Track Cassette Player

What do you do if you have an 8-track tape player and you just received 15 new cassettes for your birthday? Buy a new tape deck? Sell the cassettes? Trade with a friend? These solutions are inconvenient.

We've found a new product that will let you enjoy both types of tapes. The *MK-703SR Stereo Cassette Adapter* allows you to play your cassettes in any standard 8-track player. And it promises to be a hit as sales of cassettes continue to skyrocket.

Many American cars are now being manufactured with cassette players, but older models generally have owner-installed 8-track players. The minimal storage space taken up by cassettes is making them increasingly popular and the introduction of the MK-703SR converter should boost sales measurably.

Stereo outlets, auto parts stores and record shops are prime targets for the converter. It is easy to demonstrate. Simply place a cassette in the unit and slip it into an 8-track player. It has independent stop, play and rewind controls so you can hear exactly what you want.

The MK-703SR is the same width and 1/75th of an inch longer than a standard 8-track cartridge so it can be stored in a tape case or a glove compartment with no difficulty. Cars, campers, portable tape decks and elaborate home stereo systems with 8-track will now be capable of handling a greater choice of cassettes.

The unit wholesales for $32.95 and is guaranteed for 90 days. The manufacturer is currently looking for distributors for the MK703SR. For more information, write to Richard Harvey, Marketing Director, Dept. IEA, P.O. Box 1702, Costa Mesa, CA 92626.

Back On The Job

Job-related back injuries fell thousands of construction workers each year. One of the major causes of these incidents is carrying and laying heavy flagstone or concrete slabs for driveways and sidewalks. It's a job that generally requires two men and takes up valuable time.

Now a company in Denmark is manufacturing a new product that will save time, labor cost and will take the danger out of moving and laying flagstone. It is called the *Ponny Hydraulic Flagging Machine*.

The Ponny is sure to gain favorable response from contractors and construction workers. And with more and more people opting to build their own homes, the device will prove invaluable to them for moving slabs.

It can be operated by one person and will increase efficiency in the completion time of jobs. And it can be adjusted to any working height to eliminate arm or back strain. An innovative hydraulic grip feature on the Ponny holds and elevates flagstones for easy movement on the site. A handle releases to lower the flag stone accurately into position.

Pricing information was not available at press time as the Ponny just went into production. It should do well in hardware and builder supply stores although it seems to lend itself to on-site demonstration by a distributor.

Inquiries by interested parties are invited. Write to Oxbol Maskinfabrik, Thuesvej 4, DK-6840, Dept. IEA, Oxbol, Denmark for further and updated information.

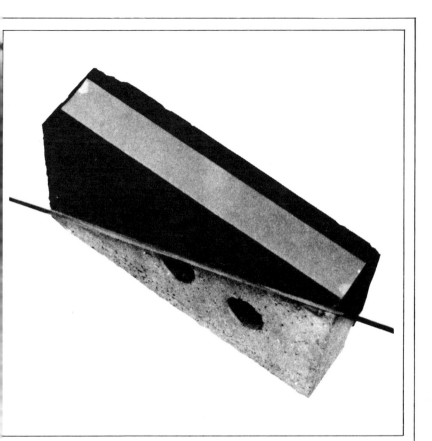

This Is A Stick-Up

Getting tape to stick to an unusual surface is like putting a square peg in a round hole. The W.H. Brady Company recognized the problem and has developed Bradyfoam. A double-faced mounting tape that will adhere to almost any clean surface.

Bradyfoam will please anyone with the need of a high-strength tape. Carpenters, hobby enthusiasts and painters will find it extremely helpful for holding things like parts or dropcloths in place.

It will do well in paint or hardware shops and auto supply stores. Artists and home decorators will find it a handy item for hanging fabric, posters or unframed canvases.

Bradyfoam is made of a specially designed polyethylene and has a tack-rubber-base adhesive coating. It will stick to any smooth clean surface, whether it is flat, curved or a totally irregular shape. And, as the photo illustrates, it is extremely strong. In this example a brick is attached upside-down to a pane of glass. Resistance to water, petroleum-based oils and alcohol is excellent.

It comes in two thicknesses: 1/32-inch and 1/16-inch, and is one inch wide. The only color currently available is white. So, if you see Bradyfoam as an item you could get attached to, write to James Steinman, W.H. Brady Co., Dept. IEA, 2223 W. Camden Road, P.O. Box 2131, Milwaukee, Wisconsin, 53201 for more information.

When Dinosaurs Ruled The World

The dinosaurs have returned. Thousands of tyrannosaurs and brontosaurs will be invading homes in the near future. And there's no way to escape!

This may sound like an advertisement for a sci-fi movie, but it isn't. It's a fact! A new interest in these prehistoric creatures has spawned an innovative new product: *Dinosaur Kits!* They're scaled-down models made of high-quality balsa wood and are guaranteed to create hours of fun.

Children—and adults—are sure to want at least one model. We found an executive who works on his tricerotops for relaxation at the office. It is also a great conversation piece.

The kits will do well in toy shops, hobby shops and gift boutiques. And they are a natural for zoo or museum stores. In fact, the Smithsonian Institute in Washington, D.C., has set up a display using the model dinosaurs in a miniature habitat.

Each piece is stamped and punched with top-quality, razor-sharp die cutting equipment, so there are no ragged edges. Corresponding numbers on the pieces and the "backbone" base of each model make for easy construction.

There are 15 models to choose from; eight small, three medium and four large sizes. The line currently includes nine different dinosaurs and more are in the development stage. Wholesale prices range from $1.35 for a six-inch tall tyrannosaur to $22.50 for a three-foot long plesiosaur.

Each kit includes an instruction sheet and a brief description of the dinosaur. Exclusive distribution is held by Small World Toys.

Write Small World Toys, Dept IEA, P.O. Box 5291, Beverly Hills, California 90210.

The bells are ringing, for me and my gal
The birds are singing, for me and my gal
Everybody's been knowin,' to a wedding
    they're going
And for weeks they've been sewing,
    every Susie and Sal.
They're congregating for me and my gal
The Parson's waiting for me and my gal.
And some day I'm going to build a little
    home for two,
For three, or four or more
In loveland, for me and my gal.

FOR ME AND MY GAL

Shower Serenade

If you have a secret desire to be a famous singer, it's likely you "practice" in the safety of the shower. We've found a duet of products that will add a touch of reality to every bathroom balladeer's fantasy.

Shower Songs are waterproof cards printed with the words to immortal favorites from "Clementine" to "Give My Regards To Broadway." They stick to the wall of the shower with a suction cup and turn an ordinary shower into Carnegie Hall.

Many crooners like to use a microphone—especially in the shower when it's difficult to hear yourself over the sound of the water. *Showermike* is the perfect accompaniment. It's a unique microphone-shaped soap that comes packaged complete with an owner's manual and heavy cord to hang it up until the next concert.

These two are natural gift items and can be sold separately or in combination. Gift shops, bath boutiques, drug stores and novelty shops will clean up with them on the shelves. They are a great promotional item for bathroom remodelers or hot tub manufacturers and installers.

Shower Songs wholesale at $2.00 for a unit of eight lyric cards and a suction cup. Orders are shipped with a supply of Shower Songs pins and posters. Write to Rose Garden, Inc., Dept. IEA, 520 W. Seventh Street, Los Angeles, CA 90014.

The Showermike wholesales for $2.50. It is guaranteed by the manufacturer to produce "an incredibly clean sound." Write to Rowe and Associates, Inc., Dept. IEA, 745 Fort Street, Suite 204, Honolulu, HI 96813 for details.

Take This Cure!

Are you tired? Sluggish? Irritable all the time? Maybe you should try *trepanning!* It's not a new patent medicine—it's a medical procedure that's been in the books for centuries.

All you do is have a hole drilled in your skull! Guaranteed to let plenty of oxygen in and all the "bad spirits" out, the oxygen gives you a permanent legal high. Two Londoners who've revived the fad claim to have achieved *eternal childhood!*

We've discovered that in ancient Tibet, yogis developed such holes after a lifetime of intense meditation. For the yogis, the hole represented a passageway for the soul to escape at death. Why wait?

If the budding fad catches on in trendy Europe, there are sure to be ample opportunities to capitalize on it. What about a color coordinated line of removable plugs? Then businessmen and others who stay quiet and reserved during the day can really "pull the plug" at five o'clock!

Every Man His Own Astronaut

Tired of rush hour traffic? You can thumb your nose at the exhaust-eaters down below from your very own rocket ship! We bet you thought all those fancy Buck Rogers' outfits were just for the government, or movie special effects wizards.

We found a new product hovering on the horizon that'll make every man an astronaut. Called Space Ranger, it's a propane-powered whatchamacallit that goes forwards, backwards, sideways, hovers like a helicopter, and probably leaps tall buildings with a single bound!

Made of stainless steel and aluminum, the platform will fly to a height of 5,000 feet, and has a cruising range of up to 10 miles, and speed of 40 miles per hour, depending on load weight and wind conditions. It will land and take off in a space as small as nine square feet. Payload limit is 270 pounds.

Of course the manufacturers recommend a ceiling for flying of 200 feet for maximum safety, and a maximum flying time of 10 minutes, for the same reasons. Plans call for an optional self-inflating parachute to be added soon, for protection of pilot and craft.

The 250-pound flying platform is offered as a do-it-yourself kit with all parts and plans for $5,795. You can obtain blueprints and plans for only $97.50. Welding skill and equipment, as well as simple workshop tools, are all you need to join forces with Buck Rogers, Luke Skywalker, and all the other outer space jet jockeys you've dreamt about!

As a home-built aircraft kit, the Federal Aviation Administration will inspect each stage of construction, prior to certifying it airworthy. And the pilot will need to be licensed.

Write to Space Ranger Corp., No. 119 Terminal Bldg., Dept IEA, King County International Airport, Boeing Field, Seattle, Washington 98108 for further details. We're betting that a smart designer could modify what they've done, using available technology, and make this item into an incredible attraction for fairs and amusement parks. Who wouldn't pay to go for a ride in one?

New "Car" Makes Honda Look Big!

As the price of gasoline goes up, the size of the car goes down. Somewhere there's a limit on how much a gallon of gas can cost, so there must be a limit on how small a car can be. With the Veloto, a French equivalent of a four-wheel moped, it looks like the limit has been reached!

The tiny two-place Veloto is designed to provide cheap, safe transportation for those who don't want to balance on a two-wheeler, or fork over thousands of dollars for a full-size auto.

It's sure to appeal to those who aren't in any hurry—especially old-sters who dwell in slow-paced retirement communities. Veloto is also sure to be a success on the college campus, where budget-strapped students always appreciate an atten-tion-getting way to get around.

The cleverly designed little car features a metal chassis, laminated polyester body, floorboard, water-proof linen top and zippered side doors. The standard Veloto comes with a manual windscreen wiper,

heavily paddded bench seat, rack steering, a hand brake and acceler-ator, parking brake, full lighting sys-tem, and inflated motorbike tires.

It weighs 209 lbs. and measures 6 feet 9 inches in width, and 5 feet in height. It's fueled by a gasoline and oil mixture.

Veloto is available in two models. Type A is pedal-started; Type BL is electric-started and comes with a 12-volt battery, brake light, spring suspension, chrome-plated bumpers, electric windshield wipers, odom-eter, and speedometer. Both models are available in sky blue, orange, mustard yellow, white and green.

The price FOB France is $1,127 for the Type A, and $1,424 for the Type BL. The manufacturer wel-comes dealer and distributor in-quiries.

Veloto should sell well wherever motorcycles, mopeds, and even bi-cycles are sold. Write Bel-Motors In-ternational, Rue De La Petite Gar-liere, B.P. 217, Dept IEA, 85103 Les Sables—D'Olonne, France, for fur-ther details.

Your Own Power Company

The answer to your heating problems may be sitting in your garage! Italian engineers have modified a car engine that will heat your home, and turn your basement into an electric utility!

The Total Energy Module, or "Totem," can save five tons of heating oil per year per unit, and can pay for itself! In fact, apartment owners with several units can even sell excess power to their local utility!

It's a standard 903 cc, four cylinder Fiat engine, modified to run on methane, or even coal gas. It drives a 15 kw alternator at a constant 3,500 rpm, so combustion is almost complete and emissions are low.

A pump circulates water for the home's space-heat radiators through four heat exchangers. These are piped together in series, to recover most of the waste heat from the generator, engine coolant, oil and exhaust system.

The engine is controlled by a thermostat which turns it on and off as heat is needed. The house draws current from an outside grid so there's no power break when the unit shuts off.

The Totem loses only 10 percent of its energy, whereas a conventional furnace can lose up to 40 percent. One Totem can heat a fourplex with up to 3,600 square feet. Two or more engines in a larger building can generate excess electricity, which the customer can sell back to the utility at the going kilowatt-hour rate!

The Totem is based upon established technology and mass-produced parts, so it can be engineered on a large scale. Purchase price and servicing are more expensive than on conventional oil-burning furnaces, but Fiat says the customer should break even in a few years of use.

The Module is still being tested in Italy, but this energy-saving device is certain to become a red hot item in a year or two! There may come a day when customers will be billing their electric companies—then who will want a rate increase? For more information, contact FIAT Motor Company, Dept. IEA, A-6; Corso Marconi, Turin, Italy.

Leap Into Profits With Ballet School

When Americans fell in love with the movie "Turning Point" they didn't just go home and talk about it—they went out and took dancing classes! This has vaulted the faltering dance school industry into a highly profitable business again. Some schools have doubled their tuition fees.

This can be an opportunity for you to leap into profits by starting your own dance school. One Chicago school says their beginning ballet enrollment would jump by 2,000 students, if they only had the space.

If each student paid only $5 per class, that would amount to $10,000 month gross! Parents are even sending their toddlers to ballet school, from age three, in record numbers.

You don't have to know much about dance to open this business. Major cities have many competent dance instructors willing to teach part- or full-time for a very reasonable salary, especially if they are "between shows."

If you can find enough space at reasonable rent, you really don't need much else except a few practice bars and some mirrors. Some other classes that are usually offered at dance schools are modern dance, exercise dance, gymnastics, jazz ballet, ballroom, and disco dancing.

The popularity of the movie "Saturday Night Fever" has caused considerable interest in disco dance lessons, and couples are willing to pay up to $18.50 per hour for a single semi-private lesson!

Your school can be promoted at nearby public and private schools, or you can have your instructors give free demonstrations at shopping centers.

Say It With Fake Flowers

A Philadelphia specialty shop has built a booming business from phony floral arrangements! Not the cheap plastic kind from dime stores, but imported silk blossoms elegantly displayed in glass-and-brass cases.

Made in Germany and France, the flowers are incredibly real-looking, and are combined with heart-shaped gingham pillows trimmed with lace for the traditional "hearts and flowers" look.

The hearts sell for $5 to $30, and the lovely blooms go for up to $25 apiece! A case will add $16 to $28 to the total price for the custom posies. At these prices, a business like this is certain to blossom into a healthy affair with the bank!

The Crimson Daisy, run like a typical flower shop, has another exciting specialty: For $10 to $15, the owner will preserve a customer's bouquet or arrangement, so that the memory of the special event will last forever under glass. Wedding bouquets alone should keep a similar shop in any metropolitan area busy. And what a great gimmick for a traditional florist!

To preserve the flowers, arrangements are dismantled and immersed in silica gel, a granular chemical. After two weeks, the flowers are removed and rearranged. The chemical is reusable—just bake it in any oven for three hours at 325 degrees Fahrenheit. Flower-dri brand silica gel is available from wholesale florist supply firms or Plantabs, Inc., the maker located in Timonium, Maryland, 21093, Dept. IEA.

A high class antique/boutique area would be best for location, and the more nostalgic romance you can pack into decor the better. Advertise in slick city magazines, bride's magazines, or even direct mail to marriage license lists, for plenty of retail trade. Interior designers are one of several other markets you can tap.

Chatty Cheerleader

"Barbie" is still America's favorite doll, but now she's hotter than ever, with the campus crowds! Decked out in campus colors, as a "talking" cheerleader, Barbie is making a few smart operators do handstands!

An Arkansas bank used the cheerleader doll as a promotional gimmick, and subsequently gained 5,000 new accounts and $12 million in deposits! The doll was dressed in an authentic University of Arkansas cheerleading outfit. A string-pull in the back produced official Razorback cheers. The company now offers a doll for Nebraska and Oklahoma as well.

Mattel, Inc. in Hawthorne, California, manufactures the dolls to order, but we've found that you have to buy in quantities of at least 25,000 at $4 to $5 apiece. And it take the company at least six to eight months lead time to produce the dolls.

We're sure a creative entrepreneur could locate a doll manufacturer in a major city to make these items in smaller quantities. She needn't look like "Barbie;" what's important is the proper outfit and the ability to recite the proper cheers.

Contact Mattel Special Projects, Attn: Jim Walsh, Dept. IEA, 5150 W. Rosecrans, Hawthorne, California.

The Way We Were

Nostalgia is as hot as ever—and we've discovered a new way you get in on the "memories" craze for "nifty" profits! Package old time movies, magazines, newspapers, radio tapes, antique car pictures and greeting cards for sale as Memory Kits!

Everybody has a favorite year. A smart nostalgia merchant can gather together old photos, newspapers, cards and tapes from each year.

Most of these memory kits would not need originals—replicas can be inexpensively reproduced to look like the real thing. You can even use tape to duplicate old records or radio broadcasts.

The Time of Your Life Company, Dept. IEA, 1349 First Street, Northbrook, Illinois 60062 has a storehouse of original old time newspapers, magazines, catalogues, etc., dating back to the 1870's. Cost depends on date and quantity, running from $2.50 to $6 per page. Start collecting your own memories, package them, and market them to antique stores or gift shops. These should sell especially well at fairs, swap meets, and even in tourist areas.

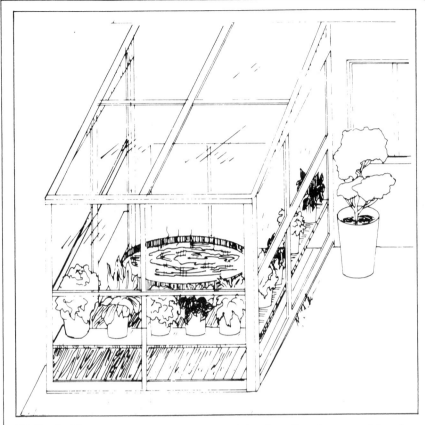

Pick A Craze,
Any Craze . . .

We've found a way any smart marketer can cash in on not one—but three of the nation's biggest crazes! Homeowners can now combine a sauna, hot tub, and greenhouse into one energy-saving solar unit!

Solar Sauna, a New Hampshire company, has plans for a solar greenhouse, solarium, hot tub, sauna and deck space in one compact unit 12 feet wide and 24 feet long. It attaches to the solar side of the house and wraps around sliding glass doors.

The sauna can be added after the unit is built, and the greenhouse deck area can be expanded in 4-foot increments. The unit's design allows the sun's heat to be magnified and retained, so there's no need for electrical heating.

Plans can be turned into kits that would sell well through home improvement centers and hardware stores. As do-it-yourself items are "hot," they can be marketed directly through regional advertising in slick city magazines or home sections of daily newspapers.

Another way to market units like this is through tie-ins with home improvement companies, which will build them for you. Promotions include demonstration models at home shows, energy and do-it-yourself fairs.

The cost estimates, construction plans and materials lists for the module you can use is available from **Solar Sauna, Dept. IEA, Box 466, Hollis, New Hampshire 03049 for $7.50.**

Instant Office

First there were secretarial services, then answering services and 24-hour paging devices. The latest convenience for aspiring businessmen has popped up in Canada—an "instant office."

Rather than spending countless hours searching for space, and negotiating on your own, for a fee of $300 to $700 a month you can rent all you need in one package.

Within hours of your call to one of the more than two dozen instant office companies across Canada, you can be doing business in a private, air conditioned office completely equipped with answering service, secretarial help, photocopying and teletype facilities.

Small businessmen and larger companies trying to quickly setup a branch office without losing precious time or spending too much on set up should welcome the opportunity to be "up and running" easily.

And we bet there are plenty of salesmen who are tired of working out of the back of their car or a cold motel room.

Contact Service Office Systems Ltd., Dept. IEA, 1867 Yonge, Toronto, Ontario, Canada.

Crime-Stopping Music

Last year retailers lost more than $2 billion to shoplifters and light-fingered employees. Soon, owners plagued with high "shrinkage" rates may be able to "suggest losses away."

East coast scientists are experimenting with anti-shoplifting Muzak for stores, as part of research conducted on behalf of the ever-present piped-music people. If it works, producers of this "message Muzak" will create their own "top ten" hits!

The new theft deterrent subtly weaves phrases like "I will not steal" into store music. The message is buried in the background so that the conscious mind cannot quite hear it. It is designed to work like a post-hyponotic "conscience" whispering in your ear, telling you to be honest!

"Message Muzak" could be an excellent ways to steal a piece of the $6 billion store security market. When proven, the service would be easy to sell to retailers as an alternative to costly TV monitors or sleepy guards.

And there's no need to let the Muzak people be the only ones doing it! While they pipe the music in, the concept should work equally well on any self-contained in-store sound system. So you could sell pre-recorded music tapes to almost anyone, or offer to install systems free as part of a monthly service plan.

With a psychologist's help, you could use rented time in a recording studio to add the "whisper voices" to any existing music tapes by mixing or overdubbing as necessary. The psychologist will tell you what words to use and the proper voice levels.

A logical spinoff after you've demonstrated results is to offer customers the opportunity to *advertise* to a buyer's subconscious mind, with phrases like: "Buy another one of those," or "Aren't you getting just a little hungry?"

Be A Pet Private Eye!

Millions of devoted and lovable family pets are lost every year, never to be seen again. Distraught pet owners frequently offer rewards for the return of their furry friends.

Here's a way you can reap your own rewards—open a *pet protection service*. All it takes is a toll-free number, some direct mail advertising and identification tags!

There's only one company doing this, so the market is wide open. The National Pet Lost and Found Company registers pets and provides owners with special tags for $12 per year. The firm keeps a file on every pet registered, including breed, markings, color, name and owner's address.

The finder of a lost pet simply calls a toll-free number printed on the tag. The service contacts the owner, wherever he is, to make arrangements for return of the animal. Re-wards are optional.

You don't have to serve customers on a national basis. In fact, most pets are lost in their home city or neighborhood. So a local or regional service in an area with lots of pet owners could be equally successful.

Such a service could be started from the home, or be a dynamite addition to a pet-related business like a boarding or grooming service. Tie-ins with the local humane society are also possible.

Obviously, a large customer base is important, and there are a variety of ways to develop business. A simple brochure placed in all the pet stores, veterinary clinics, or shelters in the area is a start.

Another effective technique is direct mail to pet owners. Lists can be obtained from local licensing agencies. Consider addressing sales letters *to the pet* for excellent response.

Contact: IBAC, Dept. IEA, P.O. Box 28356, Tempe, Arizona 85282.

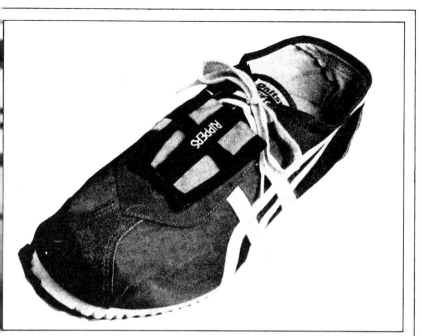

A Running Thing

Jogging has become the nation's favorite pastime, but most runners have a recurring problem—what to do with keys and emergency money when they're in action. Putting change in a pocket is risky and noisy, hanging keys on a chain is annoying and clenching things in your fist is impossible!

We've discovered an exciting cure for these athletic blues. The Ripper R-2 Shoe Pocket! This is an innovative lightweight pouch that wraps around the laces of your shoes. It stays securely fastened with a Velcro-type closure and holds a key, emergency money and a special ID card. It runs circles around any jerry-rigged wallet or pouch we've seen for joggers.

The Ripper R-2 is a long-awaited accessory that is destined to "take the country by foot" according to the manufacturer. And we don't doubt it! Joggers, as well as other athletes like soccer and baseball players, will leap for joy when they see it.

It's a natural for sports shops, shoe stores and department stores. And ice and roller-skating rental businesses can clean up by stocking this item. In fact, any sport from tennis to horseback riding requires that the participant carry some basic essentials without having them interfere with their activity.

The Ripper R-2 weighs less than an ounce when packed and can also be attached to a watch band or belt loop. With Christmas coming up, it is the perfect stocking (or running shoe) stuffer for everyone's favorite athlete.

It is available in several colors and is made of washable nylon, like that used in jogging shoes. A waterproof ID card, with room for name, address, phone number and doctor's name, is included. The wholesale price is $1.75 each. So if the Ripper R-2 Shoe Pocket jogs your interest, write to Rowe and Associates, Inc., 745 Fort Street, Dept. IEA, Honolulu, Hawaii, 96813 for further details.

Keeping Cows Contented With Antifreeze Lotion

Sometimes it gets pretty cold around milking time, and those icy fingers running up and down can get a mite uncomfortable. Not to say downright freezing!

It only takes a sudden chill wind to affect a cow's milk output, and not just any old thing will do to keep their udders "squeezably soft."

Now there's a product called Udder Frost Guard which acts like an invisible glove, to insulate udders from the cold morning air and ensure good milking through the winter.

Chemically, it's the same blue goo that skiers and football players use to keep warm, although it is sold under a different brand name.

With millions of cows across the country herding together to keep warm, and thousands of dairymen with warm hearts (but cold hands) there should be a ready market for the new product. It comes in four- and eight-pound tubes at $13.50 and $25.50 respectively.

Contact Reynes Products, Inc., Dept. IEA, P.O. Box 1203, Sonoma, California 95476.

Turn Pro With A Golfer's Girdle

For the average "hacker," the toughest part of the game of golf is mastering a consistent swing. Even the pros sometimes have trouble "getting it together," what with the need for a smooth take-away, down swing and follow-through.

Now an amazingly simple new product called the "Golf Swing Instructor" promises to be of great help to pro and "duffer" alike. Over 22 million people are hooked on the game in the United States alone, and only about 5 percent of them have **ever** played a round under 90.

The Golf Swing Instructor is an ordinary black elastic band with a velcro closure that wraps around a golfer's chest and holds his upper arm tight to his side.

The magic of the device is that it actually forces a golfer to keep proper distance from the ball, keep his arms straight, and elbows in— maintaining a proper "plane" with the ball, and actually uncoiling with power and authority every time.

Exclusive rights to the item are held by American Visuals, Inc., and it is set to retail at a whopping $12.95 to avid golfers in pro shops, driving ranges, sporting goods stores, and the like.

Marketing aids include a cassette film showing the "girdle" in use, tied in with a graphic point-of-purchase display. American Visuals is actively seeking qualified distributors for their promising new product.

American Visuals, Inc., Dept. IEA, 222 Columbus Ave., San Francisco, California 94133.

Dollars Down In The Boondocks

Smog-choked city slickers are spending as much as $100 a day to "get away from it all." And smart tour operators are making a bundle by providing out-of-the-way trips for outdoor enthusiasts. One thing we haven't seen is tours designed for "greenhorns."

But we've found one firm that takes ordinary tourists into the rugged outback of Australia in the comfort of a motorhome! Bill King's safari buses hold enough fuel for several weeks of wallaby-watching.

We think a smart tour company could offer a similar service here in the States, and "clean-up" in the wilderness! Most states have remote natural wonders that can be a part of the tour package, used to capitalize on the booming outdoor craze.

Why not offer bus-canoe-backpack tours, just like the fly-drive vacations common now? Tourists could be bused part of the way, taken to the "high lonesome" on horseback, and perhaps canoe back to civilization.

You should be able to build business by advertising in travel magazines and travel sections of newspapers. Brochures should be sent to travel agents, who will send you customers on commission.

Local universities or clubs can be offered tours at reduced rates—students could even get college credit for the excursion. It's vital that tours be truly unique, offering the customers something they've never done before.

Look Here, See There

Now there's a way you can lie flat on your back at the beach and *still* watch the girls go by. Or read in bed without propping yourself up with rock-hard pillows. Ben Franklin would've loved it!

"Bed Specs" allow you to do either by using cleverly designed high-quality glass prisms to bend light rays without distortion. One size fits all, and they can be worn over regular glasses if necessary.

Aside from the gimmicky angles, there's a real need for "Bed Specs" among people with neck or back problems who find it uncomfortable to be propped up in bed, but would still like to be able to read or watch TV comfortably.

Using these new glasses, such people can lie flat on their backs, as recommended by most orthopedic specialists, and maintain a relaxed back and neck, to avoid undue strain.

The glasses are being sold by mail for $19.95 and are said to be recommended by opthalmologists as a means to avoid eye strain as well. They should also sell well in gift shops, or eyeglass specialty shops too. And would make a great promotional gimmick for anyone selling beds, TVs, or even books.

For further information, write Henniker's, Dept. IEA, 779 Bush St., San Francisco, California 94102.

Fitness Clock Tells When You're Tired

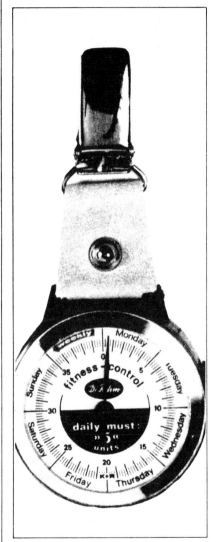

Do you know when you've had enough exercise to meet daily fitness requirements? Short of dropping from exhaustion, it's generally difficult to measure exercise. But not anymore!

Simply attach a Fitness Control Meter to your belt, pocket or a chain near your waist and gauge every move you make. A pendulum-controlled hand advances one unit on the clock-like face for every 2,000 movements.

Think of the market! All the joggers, tennis players and hikers would really get a kick out of this item. And it's a natural for people who need to exercise because of weight or health problems. In fact, its inventor, Siegried Rihm, a West German engineer, originally developed the Fitness Control Meter for recooperating heart patients.

Over 50,000 were sold in Europe during the first six months it was made available. Although a number of people bought them on a doctor's recommendation, a majority were healthy, but curious, exercise or sports participants!

The device can be used as a motivating factor for "lazy" exercisers by setting a goal of, say, 10 units daily. Five units or 10,000 movements are considered adequate exercise for people between the ages of 45 and 60. The amount increases according to age and health of the wearer.

Every little movement truly has a meaning of its own with the Fitness Control Meter. And you can make the move to healthy profits by demonstrating and selling it at home and recreation shows, health fairs, swap meets and medical conventions. It is also an ideal mail-order item. It should sell well to anyone who is health-conscious.

The device sells for about $20 and is no larger than a wrist-watch. Instructions and health-improving ideas are included with each package. Send a letter to Cooper Enterprises, Inc., Dept. IEA, 605 Avocado Street, P.O. Box 892, St. Cloud, Florida, 32769, for more information

Get The Bugs Out!

If you're holding the secret to nuclear armament or you're bugged because you suspect your neighbor is a spy, there's a device on the market that will set your mind at ease. The Bug Alert EJ7 is a pocket-sized detector that warns you of the presence of a transmitter or "bug" on visitors or in the room.

A tiny signal light on this nine-volt battery-operated device lets you know who your friends really are. The signal can be set on momentary control for instant warning or on memory control if it becomes necessary to step away from the person in question.

Holding it in your hand will enable you to pick up an invasion of "bugs" on your telephone. Why be the last to know! Bug Alert EJ7 assures you of privacy and keeps your business and personal contacts honest. Take the "ear" out of fear of conversing and speak freely.

It is encased in a durable phenoliccoated box, which will not interfere with close-range signals. The signal light is controlled by a simple latch switch that turns the device on and off. Bug Alert EJ7 is ideal for demonstration at law enforcement and security conventions. Politicians, executives and anyone seeking confidentiality are potential customers. The unit sells for $550 and is worth its weight in plutonium to those needing secrecy.

The manufacturer, Communication Control Systems, Inc., has been responsible for many innovations in voice stress analyzers and surveillance equipment. Well-known in the field of security, they are currently looking for Bug Alert EJ7 dealers.

Skin Your Car!

With new car prices fast approaching what homes used to cost, it makes more sense to treat your car as a long-term investment. That means keeping it as clean as possible.

The most frequent cause of body "dings"—expecially in rural areas—is stones, pebbles and sticks thrown up by tires against fenders and doors. Such blemishes are unsightly, and can actually lower the resale value.

Now you can prevent nicks, scratches and lower car values by "skinning" your car with Chip/Gard. It's a 10 millimeter clear plastic film with its own adhesive. Gravel, stones and sticks bounce off without chipping paint, and road tar wipes off using only solvent.

It works on any spot exposed to road gravel. So if you're a frequent traveler of dirt roads, you could theoretically "skin" your entire car, truck or offroad vehicle.

Chip/Gard is removed simply by peeling it off. It won't hurt the paint. A sheet 12½ inches wide by 12 feet long sells for $15.

This is a product which would sell well through auto supply houses, hardware stores, car washes, auto body repair shops and service stations. For further information write **Carlson Products, Dept. IEA, 312 South Third Street, Minneapolis, Minnesota 55414.**

Oriental Folding Bed

Now you can turn your van or RV camper into a veritable Geisha House—with the folding space-saver Futon bed from Japan. It doubles as a comfortable bench seat during the day, and becomes a comfortable bed at night.

The bed was developed in Japan, where living conditions make every square foot of living space precious. The Futon bed is ripe for exposure to home owners and apartment dwellers here as well.

The Futon bed, now being manufactured by the Futon Bedding Company, alleviates crowding in even the tiniest of apartments by folding into a sofa, ottoman or love seat. They're available in single, double and king sizes.

The company also manufactures other types of folding mattresses, cotton mattresses and colorful Japanese Futon comforters. In addition, the company carries a wide variety of tatami platform beds, shoji screens shoji lanterns and other exotic Japanese home furnishing.

All of these items would sell well in furniture stores, department stores, home decorator boutiques and even by direct mail. The company is looking for distributors for national sales.

For further information contact Futon Bedding Co., Dept. IEA, 415 Washington St., Marina Del Rey Calif. 90291 c/o Bill Shoichilto.

Signal When Ready

Farmers and zoo-keepers know that ten to fifteen percent of all their unattended stock animal births result in death to the newborn. With some 57 million cows giving birth each year in this country, it is easy to understand the problem. And that doesn't take other livestock, like horses, sheep and pigs, into account.

Professional dog and cat breeders also lose valuable stock on occasion because of breech births. The deaths occur partially because it is virtually impossible in many cases to predict the exact time of birth or to maintain round-the-clock watch of an expectant animal.

In addition, many animals, particularly cows and horses, don't always take care of their newborns or protect them from predators. In fact, some wild zoo animals kill their offspring before attendants can get to them.

But now, an electronic birth alarm—for animals—has been invented by scientists at the University of Arizona. It has a small transmitter which is attached with adhesive to the expectant animal that signals when the cervix dilates just before giving birth. A receiver is carried by the human birth attendant that picks up the signal as far as 15 miles away.

The reusable device will be produced by Vita-Vet of Arizona as soon as the Federal Communications Commission passes final approval. Its introduction indicates the possibility of additional development of devices to insure safe animal births. A person with an interest in electronic gadgetry would be able to duplicate the same type of item with relative ease. Talking with veterinarians would be the first step in order to understand the intricacies of animal births.

This idea will revolutionize economy and ecology in the nation. Not only will farmers be able to reach full utilization of grazing lands, escalating meat prices will drop as the supply meets the demand. And animals on the verge of extinction will be bred and monitored carefully to guarantee continuation of the species.

New Cat-House Door

A new magnetic cat door now on the market promises to please both cat and cat owner. Only the cat, while wearing a small magnet on its collar, has in and out privileges through this magnetically operated door. Strays and other small animals are kept out.

The 10 inch long, by 10½ inch wide, by 10¾ inch high pet door comes assembled for do-it-yourself installation in door, wall or window.

It's actually a two-door system. The cat first enters through a flexible plastic iris, and the collar-magnet passes over a "read" switch, which activates a solenoid-operated latch on the inner door.

As the cat enters, the door rides over its back and locks as it closes. The cat can exit at will, unless the door is locked for the night.

The manufacturer is working on a larger model for dogs. Wholesale price for the magnetic cat door is $47.70, with a suggested retail price of $79.50.

It's a product which can be sold in any pet-related business, department store, hardware store and home improvement center. For information on dealer/distributorships, **write Dept. IEA, Aladdin Pet Products, 110 Freelon Street, San Francisco, California 94107.**

Miracle Sponge Rubs Out Stains

Here's a new cleaner that'll even give Mr. Clean a run for his money! Even if your kitchen sink looks like an artist's palette, stubborn paint stains can be removed instantly with this new sponge-like cleaner.

The Tyrolit-Elastic grinding cleaner was developed in Austria for home and workshop use. The Tyfix, as it is called, consists of "elastomer synthetic resin compound" grinding granules. The blue bar comes in a sponge-like form for consumer use, and in ten types for industrial users.

The Tyfix will clean metals, wood, plastic, glass, enamel, ceramic and natural stone. It can smooth chafe marks and scratches invisibly, and refinish the area. It produces a matte finish on aluminum and stainless steel surfaces easily. You can use it to roughen wood, leather and plastic surfaces to allow for easier gluing.

This eraser can make old, scratched tools look like new, as well as clean up rusted chrome without leaving scratches. It has a variety of uses in the kitchen and bathroom, especially on ceramic tile.

Consumer markets for this product haven't been touched yet. It can be sold through hardware, grocery, variety stores, mini-marts, and through mail order. A good promotion for this item would be kitchen demonstrations in department stores or on an old rusted car in a busy parking lot. For more information, contact **Tyrolit Schleifmittelwerke, Dept. IEA, Swarowski KG A-6130 Schwaz, Austria. They are seeking dealer/distributors in the U.S.**

Stairway to the Stars!

Romantic spiral staircases are as hot as ever in the marketplace, and remain one of the most popular ways to get from one floor to another! We've found an easy-to-assemble kit that'll make a handyman step lively.

Mylen Industries has developed a spiral staircase kit that two people can snap together in a couple of hours. Priced at $295 and up (retail), depending on specifications, they're much less expensive than traditional construction methods which start at $1,000!

These stairways come in a variety of styles, with simple instructions. You set up the pole in two sections, and just snap the steps on the pole. A snap-on railing is added next.

An ideal market for these kits would be retail home impovement centers, or remodelers looking for ways to spruce up older homes. They make great-looking fire escapes, too—as an alternative to the usual ugly add-on kind.

You should be able to develop a business specializing in spiral staircases. Any major metropolitan area will have enough homeowners, builders, architects, and renovating firms to keep a crew of two hopping.

Mylen is looking for dealers and distributors.

Mylen Industries, Dept. IEA, 650 Washington St. Peeksill, N.Y. 10566.

Want A Mickey Mouse Job?

Ever since "Steamboat Round the Bend," the first Walt Disney cartoon featuring Mickey Mouse, the animated superstar has been the best loved and most easily recognized cartoon character in the world.

Mickey's likeness is over 50 years old now, and in that time his grinning mug has appeared on thousands of products, from piggybanks to telephones. Walt Disney Productions, Inc., has always been very careful about the quality, licensing, and distribution of products featuring Mickey, in order to maintain his "white glove" image.

Interest in the squeaky-voiced little guy is as strong as ever in the marketplace, and over 100 licensees are producing items in his image. Now there's even a store in New York City.

Owner Russ Phelan claims "Old Friends" is the only store in the world that carries characters from Disney exclusively, including Mickey's pals Goofy, Pluto, Donald Duck and the rest of the gang. The merchandise is of great interest to collectors, nostalgia nuts, and plain ordinary fans.

There's no reason why a similar store can't be equally successful in other major metropolitan areas distant from Disney parks. The key is, of course, obtaining as much Disney-character merchandise as possible, both current lines and items out of production, which will attract the "hard core" nostalgia buffs.

Walt Disney Productions, Inc., maintains two Character Merchandising Division offices, to which you can write for a list of their licensees. The New York City address is Dept. IEA, 477 Madison Ave., New York 10022. On the West Coast, write them at Dept. IEA, 500 S. Buena Vista, Burbank, California.

Using the list of manufacturers Disney will provide, contact their distributors for complete pricing and item information. Disney does no manufacturing or direct sales of merchandise itself.

The nostalgia angle is important, in a store like this, as well as a "clean cut" image. Most of your business day to day, however, will still come from toy sales.

For this reason, you should locate in a heavy foot-traffic location with a high percentage of female passersby. Almost all toys are bought for children by female relatives.

With an exclusive identity in the local market, you should get plenty of exposure in the media, and be able to offer merchandise that isn't readily available outside Disney parks.

© Walt Disney Productions

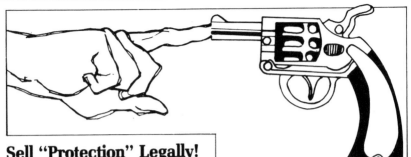

Sell "Protection" Legally!

Here's a way that crime *will* pay. Rising crime rates, overworked policemen, lenient judges, and a growing tendency to ignore illegal acts are getting headlines all over the country.

As a result, honest citizens are arming themselves to the teeth with guard dogs, firearms, and sophisticated electronic hardware. The counterattack is beginning, and these protection tools are creating an excellent business opportunity.

At the Protection Center, in Philadelphia, customers of this innovative new shop can buy anything from a 50-cent auto burglar alarm to an amazing $1,000 system that detects intruders and notifies the police.

This ground floor idea—a store crammed with hundreds of protection devices that anyone can legally use—should be workable in any major metropolitan area, where crime is most severe.

Of course, the home and personal protection market is nothing new, but until now, most of the devices needed have been sold by mail, in "gadget" sections of department or hardware stores, or by specialized (and often expensive) professional companies.

But this store is a place where concerned citizens can browse among locks that are opened by a special magnet instead of a key; tiny pushbutton devices that can activate an emergency telephone recording; a small wall safe that looks like an electrical outlet; tear gas (not legal for private possession in some states), and other protection paraphernalia.

One advantage of such a one-stop protection center is that patrons often make "impulse" purchases of items that they may never have heard of or thought about before. Of course, you'd want to stock the "big sellers" as well as impulse items.

Most of the Protection Center's sales seem to be in "reassurance" items, like jimmy-resistant deadbolt locks, heat and smoke detectors, and several signalling devices, for the homeowner. But personal protection equipment, self-defense manuals, anti-rape whistles and the like should also be carried, especially items for women.

Demonstrations of the products would be an excellent selling device. Cheap gimmicks that are unreliable have no place in such a store.

Build your reputation on the real value of the merchandise as well as your ability to help customers choose the equipment best suited to their individual needs.

Advertising and promotional potential for a store like this in most cities is tremendous. Co-sponsoring a "hot-line" for rape victims, or classes on protection against prowlers are just two ways to build awareness and sales.

Write: Protection Center, Dept. IEA, 403 W. Cheltenham Ave., Melrose Park, Pennsylvania.

Sticky Sun Screen

Ever since ancient Egyptians worshipped the sun, man has been awed by his closest star. But when you're driving down the highway at sunset, the sun's glare is more likely to blind than bedazzle! Now there's a sun shade that can cut glare anywhere: *Sun Dot.*

Sun Dot is a magic moveable 5-inch sun-shade that sticks to any windshield or window. The translucent plastic spot filters out 75 percent of the sun's glare, and can be moved to any position desired. Unlike standard visors, which never seem to be in the right place and cut visibility, the *Sun Dot* allows you to see where you are going.

It enables you to see a traffic control signal or road sign in bright sunlight, preventing accident hazards. It can prevent annoying glare you get from side windows, which can't be covered at all by the windshield visor.

The *Sun Dot* can be especially effective when used on long trips, when the sun hangs low for hours. Passengers will appreciate the shade on their side because they are also protected from irritating glare.

This item retails for $2.49 for a set of three, and wholesales for about $1.25 per set. At that price, car owners can't afford to be without one!

The *Sun Dot* would sell well in car accessory and even windshield repair shops. They can also be sold at tourist attractions and roadside shops.

They can be given away as a promotional item by auto body shops, auto insurance agencies, auto clubs, and auto dealers, as a business builder.

Yorkshire International, Dept. IEA, 220 Yorknolls Dr., Washington, D.C. 20027.

Your Own Mountain Stream!

You can carry a mountain stream in your back pocket! Terrible-tasting tap water in many parts of the country is getting headlines. We've all seen bottled water and tap attachments. Record sales of bottled water attest to the large market.

The Filbrook Filter from P.B. Enterprises can wipe out that "chemical" flavor without chemicals or tap attachments. It comes with a decanter and can filter up to two quarts of water in minutes.

Since the filter element is separate and portable, you can take your "spring water" with you and use it with any container. So, campers and hikers would provide a fantastic market. All you need to do is sell the filter element separately!

Activated carbon removes chlorine, DDT, sulphur, and all organic tastes and odors. The cellulose filter takes out rust and discoloration.

Each replaceable filter will last several months. The filter-decanter set retails for $6.95, which includes four extra filter discs.

While this product is sold through the mail now, there are many other

markets for it. The filter can be sold through grocery or department stores, even camping centers.

Dept. IEA, Filbrook Filter, P.B. Enterprises, Dept. CT6, Worth Promfret, Virginia 05052.

New Gun Lock Can Save Lives

Every year, headlines scream about children killed or injured playing with handguns found in the home and tragically treated as toys, by unsuspecting tots. A new gun lock promises to help make family handgun ownership safer.

This **keyless** gunlock fits all double-action revolvers with a standard trigger and can only be removed by an adult. Kids don't have the strength to remove the lock, which operates on the same principle as "adults-only" medicine bottles, using a heavy-duty spring action.

With the massive increase in interest in self-defense and protection, sales of handguns show no sign of a slowup, and this item should be an excellent one for gun shops and other places where pistols and ammunition are sold. Law enforcement agencies are the primary market orientation now, so market exposure has been limited.

The gun lock sells retail for $7.95 and wholesales for $4.77 with a minimum order of six units. You can send for a sample and dealership information to Safariland, Ltd., Dept. IEA, 1941 S. Walker Ave., Monrovia, California 91016.

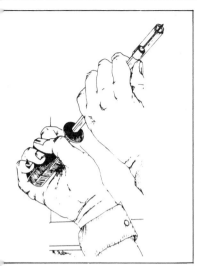

Hammer Away!

You can be a steel-driving man just like John Henry—in the tightest of corners—with the *Sharpshooter* nail driver. Like a hammer, the 23-inch tool drives home everything from a two-penny nail to a 20-one.

It's especially handy in tight spots, where there's no room to swing a hammer.

This new product is of particular value to cabinet makers, furniture builders, handymen and do-it-yourself home repair buffs. *Sharpshooter* not only eliminates the danger of damaging costly construction materials, but it's virtually impossible to smash your thumb!

The tool consists of a solid steel driver handgrip, a hand guard, 9/16-inch drive piston, case hardened tip and ½-inch barrel. *Sharpshooter* sells for $12.95 and carries a full money-back guarantee.

It should sell well in hardware stores, home improvement centers, department stores and lumber yards or by mail. For further information, write the Maverick Manufacturing Company, Dept IEA, 919 Lincoln Avenue, Alameda, California 94501. Dealer/distributor inquiries are invited.

Divorce In A Word

People love to send each other cards. Any occasion from birthdays to buying a new car is a good excuse. And now there are even *divorce* cards to notify friends of your new status and remind your ex-partner of the way it was! With the upsurge in divorces in this country, you can turn a way with words into a lucrative second income as a voice for those who have trouble expressing their feelings.

The market is there—and untapped. It won't be difficult to get one of the major card manufacturers to buy tastefully written divorce messages. They generally pay between $15 and $35 per message and are constantly looking for new material.

Check at the library for a publication called *Writer's Market* which lists manufacturers and their requirements. In most cases, they will retain the rights to use your words as they want, so try to get the best price.

If you want to create your own line of divorce cards, there are many printers who will give you design and printing cost estimates. You can hire a freelance photographer or artist to provide photographs or drawings to accompany your words. The printer will help you arrange a layout.

Carry your cards to stationery and gift shops in your area. Independent shops should be willing to stock them; larger chains may require you to deal through their main headquarters. Either way, once you are established, you will have no problem with distribution. So if you're looking for a way to separate yourself from the day-to-day routine, divorce cards could be the answer.

Makes Faucets Into Fountains

With summer here, and plenty of hot weather coming along, every household can expect to be using a lot more water for drinking. The usual method is to grab a glass, fill it with water, and stick the once-used vessel into the dishwasher.

Some people use the same glass over and over, making it a perfect breeding place for what the advertising writers love to call "household" germs. While many people have solved the glass/germ problem by using disposable paper cups the price of these paper or plastic cups is going up faster than the temperature.

The answer, as we found out one hot, dry day is to turn kitchen and bathroom faucets into fountains. And then be able to turn them back into faucets with a flick of the finger. We found the answer, by the way, out in Oklahoma, where it's known to get a mite hot in the summer.

Called, not surprisingly, "Faucet Fountain," this device simply screws right on the end of an existing faucet without the need for tools. Turn the finger-tip control one way, and you have a faucet. Flip it the other way and you have a fountain. The unit is of anti-splash design, chrome-plated equiped with aerator and comes with unconditional guarantee. The low retail price of $3.98 each, two for $6.98, should make Faucet Fountain an easy-seller.

Write Abbotts Faucet Fountain Co., Ltd., Dept. IEA, 858 Brookwood Dr., Box 103, Oklahoma City, Oklahoma 73139 for further information.

Life Saving Airfoil To Aid Stricken Boaters And Pilot

We've seen many devices used to aid stricken craft and make it easier to attract the attention of rescuers. Radio communication gear doesn't always work, and many pilots or boaters cannot pinpoint their exact location anyway, in an emergency.

Now there's an airfoil that will fly over your disabled boat or plane, putting you immediately on radar. As an airfoil, not a balloon, it is designed to stay in the air indefinitely, even when there is no wind. And as they approach the distress site, rescuers can't help but spot the bright orange device floating overhead. It stays with the survivors, not the craft.

Natural markets for the new patent-pending item, called the "Hembree Air/Sea Rescue Device" are the millions of private aircraft and boat owners in the country.

The device is expected to retail for $289.50, with a wholesale cost of only $90, so you can see that the profit margin in this product is sky-high too.

Write to C. A. Higgins & Associates, Dept. IEA, 2933 Briand, San Diego, California 92122 for further information. They are looking for a manufacturer to purchase exclusive distribution rights for the product.

Beep For Phillip Morris

Remember the bellhop that would "Call for Phillip Morris?" Nowadays, the renowned Mr. Morris is likely to hear a few beeps on an electronic paging device attached to his belt.

For years, doctors, executives, and service personnel "on call" would be summoned to the phone this way. Now the "beepers" seem to be everywhere. Because they can be set off manually, salesmen are even using them deliberately at key times in sales interviews.

Page America, one manufacturer of these devices, has come out with a specially designed unit for rental to hotel and motel guests. And they've signed up 70 hotels across the country for "Rent-a-Beep" programs.

Guests pay $5 per day for the tiny receivers, and as long as they are within 50 miles of their hotel, they can be "beeped" for messages. In addition to the convenience, there's a certain amount of "snob appeal" in having a beeper sound off at poolside. A lobby display does the job.

There are many hotels and motels that could use a service like this across the country, and there should be plenty of opportunity for a bright entrepreneur to get a piece of the action.

Service-oriented hostelries should jump at the chance. Of course, the larger hotels, with the higher occupancy rates and turnover, are the best prospects for a service like this, which could be tied into the hotel switchboard or a cooperative local answering service.

Another huge market that hasn't been touched yet is trade shows and conventions. Many of them across the country attract huge numbers of people from out of town, who need to stay in contact with their home office, or others at the shows—for sales development purposes, or even job interviews.

Every one of the shows that we've been to has a "message center" of some kind for this purpose, where beepers could be rented to exhibitors, attendees, or convention officials. Our experience has been that the message centers at most shows could stand a lot of improvement, and this is a profitable way to do so.

Convention hotels and municipal convention centers in major cities know well in advance what their bookings will be. Contact them for the names of show officials, who should welcome this new service, if only as a way to keep themselves organized.

Contact Page America, Dept. IEA, 150 E. 58th St., New York, New York 10022.

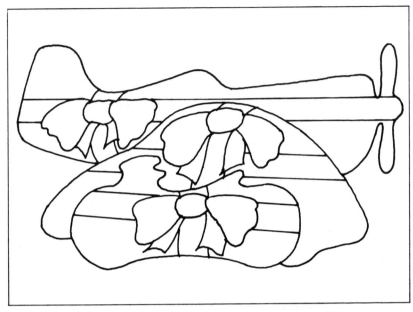

Wrap Up This Idea

A nicely wrapped gift that looks "too pretty to open" is always appreciated, and says something "extra" about the giver. But most of us are "all thumbs" at fancy gift wrapping, or don't have the time it takes to do the job right.

Not too many stores offer gift-wrapping for free any more—and in some it's a chore just to get a box that fits the item purchased. Even larger stores that will gift wrap use inexpensive, look-alike commercial wrapping.

We've found a few gift wrapping services that operate out of the home, stressing luxury wrappings and personalized work. Why not take the idea one step further and set up a kiosk in a large regional shopping mall?

Anyone with some artistic ability could offer fancy gift wrapping paper and those nifty custom bows (hand-made) as a clear step up from the stick-on kind we usually have to settle for. Personalizing the wrapping to the occasion—and the recipient—would be vital.

Custom packaging and wrapping of oddly shaped items should be a specialty. Ever try to wrap a record album or bicycle in a way that made the gift a surprise? Of course, you would charge extra for this type of service.

A service like this, perhaps called "The Wrapper" and stressing custom work with creativity, should get plenty of business in a high traffic mall, especially around the holidays. The "We Wrap Anything" angle should be worth some free publicity from the media. Send them good photos of your most unusual creations.

A spin-off idea is to tie the service together with a "drop off" service for mall shoppers, who tire of lugging purchases and packages around with them during a day's browsing. A simple "hat check" system would be sufficient, and a reasonable charge will minimize abuses. Of course, it offers salespeople the chance to ask if any of the items need wrapping as gifts.

New Valve Cap Tells Tire Pressure

One thing most people don't do is check their cars before they zoom off. A pilot may spend an hour preflighting his airplane, but the average car driver probably wouldn't notice whether his headlights were missing! We're guilty of this pre-driving negligence, too—and that's why Tire Pressure Controllers attracted our new-product eye.

Tires often have a habit of losing air gradually, causing increased wear and poor gas mileage. When you finally notice a low tire, it may have already been damaged by driving on it. An occasional glance at the simple Tire Pressure Controller can warn you of a slow leak in plenty of time.

The device simply screws over the regular valve stem of each tire. After the tire is filled to the proper pressure, the adjusting cap on the Tire Pressure Controller is turned until it is flush with the piston. This is the correct position for the tire pressure you have selected.

A hollow, or sunken spot, in the adjusting cap will tell you, before you can see it in the tire itself, that the tire has lost pressure. After you have checked the origin of the decreased pressure and corrected the situation, you merely reset the Tire Pressure Controller for future use.

This handy product would seem to have a market among car buffs, housewives who can avoid being stranded by a flat tire, and anyone who wants to spot-check for slow leaks. Wholesale price is $2 Canadian, suggested retail $2.89. Duty and transportation extra.

Write Versailles Ltd., Dept. IEA, 620 Notre Dame St. West, Montreal, Quebec, Canada, for further details.

Grow Your Own Sponges

You can get money to grow on trees. Just raise a crop of loofah sponges in your backyard, and sell them as pot scrubbers or back-scratchers.

Anyone that can grow cucumbers can raise a bumper crop of loofah (Luffa Cylindrica), a close relative of melons and squash which are also in the gourd family. You grow them the same way, in rich soil with plenty of water.

The loofah will grow on vines as long as 20 feet, and bear prolifically. Each vine will yield from 25 to 50 large fruits. What you need is a large trellis for the vines to climb, and a bit of a "green thumb."

The gourds are dark green and 12 to 24 inches long. When yellow, they are ready to harvest. All you do then is soak in water to remove the outer peel, let them dry, and you have a large inventory of natural sponges to sell. You can bleach the sponges in a solution of chlorine before drying, for a better appearance—or experiment with dyeing them different colors.

Loofah gourds are sometimes called luffa, dishcloth gourds, or vegetable sponge depending on the geographical area of the country. If you can't find seeds or young plants in a nursery or garden shop, seeds can be ordered from Nichols Garden Nursery, Dept. IEA, 1190 N. Pacific Highway, Albany, Oregon 97321, or Park Seed Co., Dept. IEA, Box 31, Greenwood, South Carolina 29647. Planting and care instructions on the packet should be followed carefully.

We think this is a great low investment business, with little risk, and the sponges should sell quite well at craft fairs, flea markets or other outlets where "natural" products sell best.

Drill A 'Hole' Lot Better!

Years ago the portable electric drill replaced the tiresome hand drill. Now any hand-held electric drill can be a drill press as well! It's all made possible with the Portalign Precision Drill Guide, which permits even hand-held 90 degree angle drilling.

The availability of the new drill guide enables cabinet makers, finish carpenters, machine shops, furniture makers and handymen to even do precision angle drilling by hand on round stock such as doweling and metal rods—at a uniform depth!

The drill guide wholesales for $10, with a suggested retail price of $19.95. It attaches to most 1/4 inch and 3/8 inch portable electric drills.

The basic function of the new device is to perform accurate 90 degree to surface drilling. By extending the guide rods through the drill guide's base plate, precise angle drilling is possible. The depth stop attachment enables holes to be drilled to a uniform depth.

Centering on large round stock and on flat edges is done by extending the guide rods through the base plate, placing the base plate against the stock, and tightening the guide rods against the sides of the stock.

With the proper bits, the drill guide can also be used for hand-held sanding, sawing, shaping and routing. The drill guide can be mounted underneath work benches in a stationary position for edge sanding and shaping.

The device should sell well in hardware stores, home improvement centers, do-it-yourself shops and department stores.

For further information, contact: Portalign Tool Corp., Dept. IEA, 4903 Pacific Highway, San Diego, Ca. 92110.

Be A Living Doll

The next time you make a snide remark about the clothes hanging on a mannequin don't be shocked if it gives you a small "Humph!" and turns the other cheek!

Beverly Kadow may be a warm-hearted person at home in Portland but at work she's just another dummy. And she would probably take that as the nicest compliment a "freeze" or "robot" model could get.

Working alongside regular mannequins and holding a pose forty minutes or more, Beverly has made **freeze modeling her specialty**, to the amazement of browsing shoppers.

We've seen this idea in several major metropolitan areas but it has great potential anywhere as a venture of your own. The first thing to do is contact all the local retailers, boutiques, department stores and bargain shops. Offer them your services as a freeze model and highlight the promotional aspects.

If they seem hesitant suggest they add a special "Test the Dummy" game during a regular sale day. The first shopper to make the live mannequin smile or break a pose without touching wins an outfit similar in price to the one you model.

On quieter days stir things up by giving a little wink to unsuspecting shoppers. Or shift poses slightly to earn quick double-takes. Couples will argue on end whether you're real or not, and normally subdued patrons will often go through antics usually reserved for palace guards.

Word will spread of the store's "live dummy" in the window. Traffic and sales should increase from the curious and offset your modest fees.

Plants Love Mystery Spray

Incredible increases in crop production are being reported by users of Bio-Cat Sure Grow. Tests run by university agriculture departments verify that the wonder spray actually expands production by 20 percent to 50 percent!

How it works is a closely guarded secret. We were able to find out that the spray contains some zinc and magnesium. And that it's a biocatalytic, inorganic compound which is non-polluting. The rest is a secret. And no attempt has been made to patent the mystery product, lest the secret be made known.

Bio-Cat is not a fertilizer. It's a soil conditioner which acts as a catalyst when it comes in contact with the soil, breaking it down and releasing trapped nutrients. Its effect is dramatic in salt-stressed and high alkaline soils.

It's been tested on produce, hay crops, small grain crops, citrus, other fruit growing trees, house plants and row crops. Sprayed from an airplane, a half-gallon of it diluted with water will take care of an acre of farmland.

The manufacturer is seeking distributors for Bio-Cat, which is available in eight-ounce, quart and gallon sizes. Wholesale prices are $1.02, $2.25 and $6.71; suggested retail prices are $2.25, $4.99 and $14.95, respectively.

Contact: BioCatalytic Corp., Dept. IEA, Suite 1810, Fort Worth National Bank Bldg., Fort Worth, Texas 76102.

Punch A Computer Instead Of A Clock

Punching a time clock is one of the things people try to get away from when they join IEA. But millions of workers across the country still have to do it.

Now there's a replacement for the time clock and the whole manual payroll system that's grown around it. The computerized CHI 4111 Clok uses a plastic employee identification card badge, or an IBM-type card to identify the employee, record the time—and prepare the data for input directly onto a computer.

All information is taped on a cassette, which can be fed into a computer at any time. Daily reports on overtime, tardiness, and other personnel statistics can be prepared without manual auditing or clerical work.

The CHI 4111 Clok costs only $19.95 and is completely self-contained, requiring no special wiring. It uses standard 110-volt power from any convenient outlet. The information it generates can be analyzed on site, or transmitted over phone lines to a remote central computer if necessary. The CHI Clok manufacturer makes software programs and companion minicomputers available at extra cost.

Large companies employing many people will be the primary purchasers of this new timekeeping/analysis system, as a means of avoiding the labor cost involved in maintaining payroll records the traditional way. Side benefits include the companion identification card program, and the ability to monitor work done on particular projects, as the card employees use can be coded.

If you think it is time to look into using or selling a system like this innovative new one, write to Computer Hardware, Inc., Dept. IEA, 4111 N. Freeway Blvd., Sacramento, California 95834.

Help! It Means What It Says!

Being stranded on the side of the road due to auto malfunction can be risky—especially for lone women on deserted highways. Recent newspaper headlines describing stranded motorists accidentally run down, or purposely violated, attest to these dangers.

And factory-installed flashing hazard signals have lost most of their impact; drivers frequently turn these on when they pull over to the side of the road for a nap, cup of coffee, or smoke.

But a new Flashing Help Sign makes it clear you're in trouble. And it can save lives! Accepted by the National Safety Council, the device hooks to any car window and alerts drivers from both directions of traffic to your plight.

The Flashing Help Sign is made of acrylic plastic, has an on-off button, and measures 11½ inches long by 4½ inches high by 2¾ inches wide.

The distress signal should sell well in auto supply shops, department stores, hardware stores, car washes, service stations, roadside cafes, and wherever auto accessories are sold.

The Flashing Help Sign is manufactured in Japan and comes in a handsome vinyl bag, which fits in the glove compartment. The suggested retail price is $10.95. The product wholesales for $9.31 for quantities of 25 to 50; $8.76 for quantities of 50 to 100; and $8.22 for quantities over 100.

Henniker's, Box 7584, Dept. IEA, 299 Bush St., San Francisco, California 94102.

Do-It-Yourself High Fashion

You might not know it by the plethora of blue jeans and "po' boy" clothes that people are wearing these days, but there's still plenty of call for high-fashion ladies' dresses, blouses, and jackets. And when Dior and Saint Laurent come up with an exclusive original, you can bet some outfit is standing by with a close copy.

The catch is that high fashion clothing "inspired" by Paris designs is still pretty expensive, and beyond the reach of many women who'd buy it if their pocketbooks didn't tell them not to.

We've found a company called Canned Couture, New York City brainchild of two former fashion models, that packages Paris-inspired design in kits, selling for $14 to $30, that milady herself can stitch into a first-class example of haute-couture in two hours or less at home.

With a batch of kits, any woman sitting in front of a Singer can whip up a 10-piece designer wardrobe for less than $200, that will carry her from morning till night.

The carton-couture kits come with precut fabrics and notions, a front-view color photo and back-view drawing, instructions for sewing and color coordination of accessories.

The kits should sell well in almost any city of decent size, or even through the mail. Existing sewing centers are a natural retail outlet. It wouldn't take much to copy the copiers with your own line of Paris fashion "originals."

You could promote the outfits at ladies' clubs, fashion shows and even at better restaurants during luncheon hours. Put two look-alike dresses in store windows, one an original and the other a copy, with a sign asking "Which One is the Original?"

Write: Minnesota Fabrics, Dept. IEA, North Avenue, Elmbrook Plaza, Milwaukee, Wisconsin.

Strike Three—You're Rich

There's nothing more frustrating to an avid fan than having to miss a favorite team's game. And, if the fan is, for example, a traveling salesperson, it's likely that the majority of the team's home games will not be broadcast in other cities and towns.

We found a sharp operator who has taken this problem and turned it into an extremely profitable service business. Dan Grimland of Indianapolis started a company called Telesport that caters to the interests of loyal fans. It enables them to "order" a game in advance and listen to it as it happens via a patching system from a transmitting station and their telephone. They just sit back and listen.

The response to Telesport has been overwhelming. After placing a series of small ads—his only form of advertising—in the local newspaper last year, Grimland was flooded with 5,000 responses in three weeks. Many of the people had lost touch with home-town teams and loved the thought of getting the games over the phone.

This is an unpatentable idea that could be set up anywhere to serve the needs of the thousands of sports fans across the country. We were unable to find out the exact technology behind Telesport. Our investigators, however, discovered that one way would be to call someone in the transmitting station's range and have them put their phone next to the radio.

You would then have to patch your call through an answering service type trunk line so that the incoming caller would receive the broadcast over the phone. To avoid restricting transmission to only one incoming caller, it would be necessary to install heavy-duty equipment capable of handling sophisticated monitoring functions. Sales representatives of the major telephone companies should be contacted for in-depth research as to the best equipment to use.

Grimland charges 25 cents a minute, so you can imagine the revenues on an hour-and-a-half football game. So, gear up and go for a touchdown in a telephone sports service.

Write: Telesport, Dept. IEA, 1355 Jefferson Dr., Indianapolis, Indiana.

154

Growing Sandwich Business

Sally Nichols started making flowerpot sandwiches in her Atlanta kitchen as Christmas gifts several years ago. They became so popular, she has now opened a "flowerpot" restaurant to satisfy the appetites of her growing following.

This is an idea that could blossom into a healthy business for anyone who is looking for a way out of the kitchen. Although it can be operated from a home very successfully. And it won't be hard to find customers.

The flowerpot sandwiches can be sold to existing restaurant owners or caterers as a sideline attraction to their regular menu. And they're great for parties and picnics.

A good way to get the business is to hand-deliver a flowerpot sandwich to restaurant owners or organizers of church and social club picnics. Put a card into each one on a florist's greeting card pick.

The trick is to use unbaked bread dough and a filling that will not soak through the bread as it cooks. Dried vegetables, precooked meats and cheeses can be combined to serve the purpose tastefully.

Four-inch unglazed clay pots are the perfect size for a standard sandwich, however, larger ones can be made to accommodate lumberjack appetites. Pots, that are ordered without drainage holes, are best, but the sandwiches can be made in regular pots if a tiny cork is put into the hole on the bottom. Baking temperatures should not exceed 350 degrees.

It is important to remember to cook only in new pots. Ones that have been previously used for plants may be permeated with soil nutrients or vitamin additives which could alter the flavor of the sandwiches.

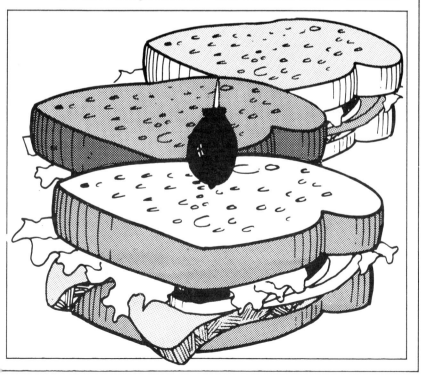

Little Houses

At a recent sale in London, Titiania's Palace was bought for $256,500 completely furnished with antiques dating from the time of Queen Mary. The catch? Titiana's Palace is a *doll house* built in 1907 for the 3-year-old daughter of Sir Neville Wilkinson.

Of course, not all doll houses are as lavish as that one, but it's an example of the booming interest worldwide in miniature mansions and the tiny furniture that goes inside them.

Antique doll houses are rare, commanding high prices from both male and female collectors. But demand for them has become so intense in the marketplace that *reproductions* are selling for as much as $500. And do-it-yourself kits with plans for gingerbread Victorian-style doll domiciles can go for as high as $200.

We've found a few shops that specialize *only* in doll houses and miniature furniture to decorate them. Business is booming and owners can't keep up with customer demand.

So the market is there for a bright operator who can capitalize on this mushrooming trend in a well-located specialty store in most major metropolitan areas.

As with most hobby-oriented shops, it's vital to locate in a large city in order to have enough of a customer base from which to draw. In addition, the few existing specialty stores are using national advertising in hobby magazines to build mail order business.

Repeat business comes from customers who return again and again for tiny furniture, pots and pans, silver tea sets and even scale hand-painted china table settings. Some of the furniture sells for as much as $50 to $100 an item, depending on accuracy of detail and quality. We've even seen tiny *operating* television sets!

There are many manufacturers of doll houses, furniture and accessories. Most are represented by distributors in major cities under the yellow pages heading "Toys & Hobbies—wholesale." You should be able to obtain all the new merchandise you need from them.

Highest profit margins will come from items you can sell to collectors. These can be found by rummaging through garage sales, flea markets and the like, or by advertising in such publications as the *Antique Trader.*

An important first step is to write the Hobby Industry Association of America for membership information. They maintain current directories of manufacturers, and conduct trade shows where vast numbers of new items are displayed by manufacturers "under one roof." Their address is: Dept. IEA, 319 E. 54th St., Elmwood Park, New Jersey 07407.

Peddle Picassos

A New Hampshire man is making a big bundle selling fine art to businessmen as decor items for the home or office. And as smarter investments than the stock market. You can easily do the same, and capitalize on the fact that most fine art dealers don't aggressively seek customers or use the investment angle.

Keith Ennis runs a company called "Only Originals" that does the shopping for busy executives who like art, but don't have time to browse through galleries to find just the right painting—at the right price.

Ennis represents over two dozen New England artists. He uses a slide show in the client's office or home to help customers choose art works that fit their taste, office or home decor, and financial objectives.

Paintings range in price from $10 to $2,000, with the average sale at about $200. Commissions for representing artists generally fall in the 20 percent to 50 percent range. He offers a money-back guarantee as well.

This is an easy-to-copy idea you can get into without an overwhelming art background. What's important is *the ability to prospect and sell.*

You should be able to get plenty of leads and contacts from architects and decorators, as Ennis did when he began. But "cold calling" at new office buildings and mailing handbills directly to office dwellers in the area can be effective as well.

Make contact with *quality* artists at local art shows and graduate schools of fine art. You can get the addresses of many artists through galleries, as well.

Write: Keith Ennis, Dept. IEA, Only Originals, Amhearst, New Hampshire.

Metal Sponge To Soak Up Hydrogen

Hydrogen is the most common chemical element in the entire universe. And it is an incredible untapped source of energy, because it burns with a hot, smokeless flame.

Trouble is, hydrogen has been difficult to store and handle safely and efficiently. Until now. Pilot studies have shown that the best way to store hydrogen is in a sort of metal "sponge" made of iron and titanium.

What happens is that under proper temperature and pressure, the iron-titanium alloys will soak up the hydrogen, forming a metal hydride compound. Lowering the pressure and temperature releases the hydrogen, so it percolates out as a gas. The iron-titanium mix can be used over and over again as a small storage bin.

This is a fantastic improvement over previous methods of storing hydrogen. As a gas, it takes up too much space and is super-volatile (remember the Graf Zeppelin?). As a liquid, it takes too much energy to maintain the low temperatures required for storage.

Using the iron-titanium alloy has other advantages. The amount of hydrogen that can be stored in it, in terms of density, is about 10 times greater than that of hydrogen gas at 100 atmospheres of pressure. So you can store a lot of hydrogen in a very small space, and it can be very portable.

In addition, iron and titanium are abundant minerals that are also inexpensive. And the hydrogen can be put in or taken out at room temperature.

It will be quite some time before hydrogen becomes a widespread alternative energy source, available commercially. But right now the Public Service Electric and Gas Company of New Jersey is using metal sponges like these to store power. Utilities are the first major market.

What they do is make the hydrogen with electricity during low-demand periods, and then "squeeze the sponge" when peak periods hit. The Daimler-Benz Company in Europe has built and tested an automobile that runs on it, with a small "sponge" in the trunk. One of these days, pulling into a service station to fill up may be a real gas!

Buy Land On Mars!

Have a desire to *really* get away for the weekend? We've found a land investment that's literally "out of sight!" You can buy a parcel of canal-front property on Mars or a mountain retreat in the highlands of Pluto for a mere $4!

United Planets Commission will sell you any amount of acreage you want on the planet, moon or star of your choice—Earth excepted. With real estate prices for earthlings skyrocketing, those with a sharp eye for a good investment are sure to see this opportunity as heaven-sent.

Two Southern California students launched UPC "on a wing and a prayer" and have a super-hero called Captain Uranus hawking the parcels as a gimmicky take-off on real estate sales schemes here on earth, complete with proposed recreational facilities and other standard come-ons.

Bob Manners and Richard Stellar receive over 100 responses a day to ads placed in campus newspapers promoting their "unreal" estate business, and are selling "stardeeds" at a fast pace. Imagine what aggressive marketing and promotion could accomplish with this idea!

With all the hoopla surrounding *Star Wars, Close Encounters* and the Sci-Fi binge the public is on right now, this should be a real mail-order winner It's a super promotional gimmick for realtors, or even theatres showing these movies. A booth in the lobby is all you'd need!

A tongue-in-cheek promotional package should be easy to develop with a little imagination. All that's left is printing some fancy deeds, which should be suitable for framing as gift items for all the *Star Wars* freaks.

Dressing Up With Stripes

Pinstriping is a great way to dress up a plain car. It can add a racy sleek look to even the oldest clunker. And it's possible to do your own pinstriping inexpensively using one-eighth inch colored striping tape sold by most auto supply stores.

No brushes, special paint or art degree are needed. The tools of the trade are tape and a good eye! Once you've pinstriped your own car why not stripe the town and go into business doing other cars. It won't be hard to convince people how terrific it looks if you've done a good job on your own 'demonstrator.' One enterprising operator we found made $30,000 last year, working out of the trunk of his car.

Visit used car dealers and tell them how a $15 to $25 pinstriping job could boost sales on slow movers. Stake out a car wash and offer to stripe owners' cars while they wait. What's 20 minutes when you're talk-ing about a touch of class!

Truck drivers and RV or van owners are always interested in sprucing up their chariots. A heavily populated highway restaurant would provide plenty of customers. While they eat or freshen up, their vehicle is being jazzed up. The parking lot pinstriper stripes again!

Striping tape has an adhesive backing and is easy to apply to a vehicle. It will not be affected by washing, but may tend to discolor after a year or so depending on weather conditions. One danger is that a small section may buckle if a car is hit. A 'repair kit' say, one foot of tape could be included in the deal, so customers can replace bad spots if needed.

This is a great sideline business for high school or college students to get into. A pinstriping job takes very little time. Once established, making $100 a day will provide a nice down payment on a new car in very little time.

160

Keep 'Em Down On The Farm

There are a lot of people—and we mean a *lot* who want to get away from today's world and return to the slower pace of yesterday. Of course, dude ranches and country vacations have been around a long time—along with their garishly lit tennis courts, swimming pools and cocktail bars. If that's "getting away from it all," we'd rather stay here!

But one working farmer has accidentally come up with what could be a real money-maker. Larry Mead runs a 265-acre farm near Watertown, New York. He needed some extra money, so last year he rented out spare bedrooms in his 11-room house.

Farmer Mead has found that he has a tourist business on his hands. But it's a tourist business with a difference—he hasn't changed his farm to suit the paying visitors. They live as he does, do as much or as little of the actual farm work as they wish and eat meals family style—with the Mead family. The food isn't fancy, but it's plentiful and wholesome.

Any farmer or rancher could make extra money without having to change his operation or physical layout. Even if you don't own a farm, you can still take advantage of this money-making new business by becoming the farmer's "booking" agent and adviser—or even a partner. He would provide the physical facilities and you would—for a predetermined fee or percentage—handle the arrangements.

In either case, the first step is to plan accommodations and meals. Next make sure you have the necessary insurance to cover any liability suits. Then it's simply a matter of advertising in tourist publications and big city newspapers. Also notify your state department of tourism, department of agriculture, chambers of commerce and the like. You might offer a free vacation to an editor or reporter of a big city newspaper in exchange for a publicity story.

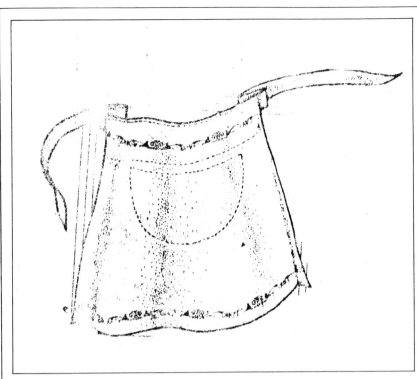

Tie Up The Apron Business

Remember the aprons your grandmother used to wear for different occasions? Pinafores for everyday and fancy little waist-huggers for special company dinners. Aprons have been pushed to the back of the drawer, but are now enjoying a big revival. You can get in on the fun—and profits—by opening an apron specialty shop.

A small storefront is all that's needed. A mall or "strip" shopping center location in the suburbs is ideal to attract foot traffic. The majority of your customers will be women, but unique window displays (perhaps a barbecue scene) will draw in men looking for new gift ideas.

We found one apron specialty shop that sidelines other kitchen items like oven mitts, chef's hats and toaster ovens. Even though they are located on a busy street with no immediate parking, the store is *always* crowded.

Manufacturers are selling more domestic aprons than they have for years *and* outfitting a store like this with a variety of styles will be a cinch in any major city. Another supply source is craft or sewing groups that can whip up a batch of custom models in a few days. All you do is supply the fabric and patterns. Offer to pay minimum wage or at least give a healthy donation to the group.

Flyers and mailers are the best advertising for your grand opening. A coupon for free gift wrapping is a good way to draw new customers. So wrap up the market in your town.

For further information, Aprons Only, Dept. IEA, 10636 Santa Monica Blvd., Los Angeles, California.

Rent-A-Dish

Millions of people from students to corporate employees rent furnished apartments for short periods of time. But in most cases, "furnished" does not include linens, dishes or any utensils. And this problem provides the base for a very profitable business. A housewares rental service.

We found one entrepreneur who started his business 10 months ago and has doubled his gross profits in the last six months. The housewares rental business is young and the market is wide open in major metropolitan areas with a large transient population.

Contacting apartment complex owners and managers is an excellent way to gauge the market in your area. Corporate personnel departments will also be able to give you an estimate of the number of employees housed temporarily for training programs or special assignments. Rental list companies and real estate offices are also good contacts. Consider a working relationship with furniture rental firms like Abbey Rents.

A minimum investment will get you started. At first, 10 to 20 basic apartment setups will be sufficient. This would include two sets of sheets, towels, pillow cases, a blanket, pots and pans, and dishes and silverware for four people. These can be purchased inexpensively as manufacturers' seconds or in closeouts and white sales at department stores. The package described will rent for about $40 per month.

As you become established, you can add extras like small appliances, vacuum cleaners, televisions and stereos to round out your inventory. But remember the portable aspect of this specialized business—you want to keep delivery, pickup and storage as easy as possible.

Flyers describing your service are an effective and inexpensive way to advertise. These can be left on counters and bulletin boards in many locations to attract potential customers. Also, get a display ad in the yellow pages for year-round exposure. A classified ad in local newspapers can be run cheaply on a continuous basis. There may be health regulations in your state requiring you to sanitize and steam clean items before renting again. Check with your local health department for information. The time is right to get in on the ground floor of a housewares rental business and climb rapidly to success.

Write: Homemaker Rentals, Dept. IEA, 4640 Admiralty Way, Marina Del Rey, California.

Space Age Johnny Appleseed

Plant lovers and gardeners are constantly on the lookout for innovative ways to increase their knowledge about things that grow! Greenhouses, elaborate watering systems and plant clinics are just a few of the many "extras" that are enjoying blossoming success among amateur botanists.

We have found a product that is guaranteed to send a green-thumb into ecstasy! The Infa-red Super Germinator is a compact unit that will allow flora fans to start from scratch, so to speak! Just put any plant, flower or vegetable seeds in the germinator and watch them sprout!

The Super Germinator is extremely useful for farmers, professional gardeners and nursery owners as well. These people depend on guaranteed growth results for their profits. Seeds that are germinated before planting or sowing will insure faster delivery of quality product or greenery.

Constructed of durable stainless steel, the 12-by-17-inch unit activates germination with an infra-red lamp. The temperature is controlled with an external switch that triggers an automatic on/off device to maintain consistency in heating.

The Super Germinator will help profits grow in plant shops, home and garden centers, farm supplies catalogs and nurseries. It has tremendous demonstration potential for county fairs and exhibitions and is a practical addition to any serious gardner's equipment.

Distribution inquiries are invited by the manufacturer. Write to Catros-Gerard, Dept. IEA, 31 Allees de Tourny, 33000, Bordeaux, France for details.

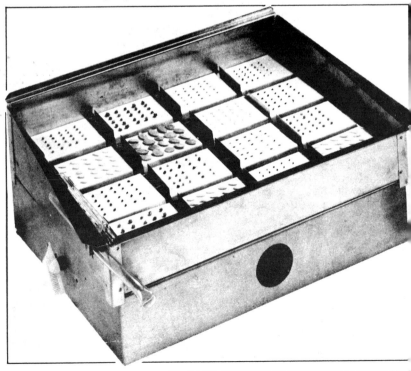

Bright Idea Beanie

Do you ever have trouble remembering someone's name—like your husband, wife or kids? Worse still, do you occasionally forget your **own** name? What you need is the Original Thinking Cap, a bright new gimmick guaranteed to turn you into a whiz kid!

The Thinking Cap is real! A battery-powered flashlight bulb actually lights up—giving people the

the employee with the best idea in the suggestion box. And what a great way to impress the boss! Just make sure he has a sense of humor.

A brochure included in the packaging suggests various "practical" uses for the Thinking Cap, like wearing it for jury duty, on job interviews and when taking exams!

Seriously though, the wholesale price for this great gimmick is $4.50. Joke shops, toy and gift stores will

impression that brilliant thoughts are zooming through your brain. It is possible, however, that these gems of wisdom will get pushed aside by all the laughter that you—and anyone who sees you wearing the cap—are going to be doing!

This illuminating item comes from Bright Ideas Designs, a company that has really dreamed up a good one! It's the perfect gift for young or old. It's a strong incentive prize for

attract a large portion of the market. It can be displayed and demonstrated anywhere —from department stores to home and gift shows and swap meets—to attract impulse buyers with a sense of humor.

Write to Bright Ideas Designs, Dept. IEA, 20292 Carlsbad Lane, Huntington Beach, Calif., 92646, for more information on lighting up your life!

It's A Dog's Life

Bowser may be your best friend, but how about making him your business partner? We've come up with a way that your pooch can help pay for his favorite biscuits. He supplies the hair and you spin it up in profits!

The big money comes from making the dog hair yarn into items, like sweaters, shoulder bags or pillows. We're not just spinning you a tale. Granny Lynn Toothman of Ohio has perfected the art of dog hair spinning. One of her hand-made sweaters costs $250 and a coat will run twice that much.

Obviously this is not a get-rich-quick business. Spinning takes a lot of patience and skill. But think of the dog owners who would love to have something made from the hair of their favorite pooch. Or, how about customized doggie jackets for the proud pup. These little numbers should bring upwards of $50 apiece and could be sold through pet and gift shops, or strictly by special order.

To get more hair than you can shake a stick at, contact the pet grooming salons in town and ask them to save the shavings. The best hair, according to Granny Toothman, is that from Samoyeds, Malamutes, Huskies, Keeshounds and Afghans. Their long hair is generally silky and easy to turn into good workable yarn for knitting or weaving..

The hair must be from a dog that has been carefully washed prior to being brushed or clipped. If not, the yarn will be dirty, probably greasy, and full of the odds-and-ends dog hair accumulates.

Put an ad in the local newspaper offering to make samples for $5 to show people how the hair will look made up. Distribute these with a batch of cards to stores who will carry your product or serve as a go-between. This is an doggone good way to make Fido worth his weight in gold —and biscuits.

A Planner For Success

Simple ideas can often be turned into big money-makers. We recently found one that offers tremendous potential with very little capital and almost no work involved.

The trip planner is a basic, yet extremely effective pre-printed list of necessities for travelers. As the items on the list are packed, they are systematically checked off. There is no danger of leaving home without a toothbrush.

This idea can be adapted to fit many situations, from parties and showers to camper or boating vacations. People are constantly looking for ways to organize their life and this is the perfect way. Plant lovers are a prime market for a specialized planner, as they often have many plants with different watering or care schedules. Another natural is a children's household chore planner broken down for a weekly schedule.

All that's needed to get into this business is a clearly typed 8½ by 11 inch sheet. The list should cover every peculiarity and necessity of the specific situation, like individual clothing items, special medication and personal effects for the traveller. Recruit friends and family members in order to compile the most complete list. Everyone is bound to remember several items they have forgotten to pack or prepare.

When the example sheet is perfect, take it to an instant print shop. They will make as many copies as requested and pad them to any specifications. One thousand printed sheets broken down to 50 sheets a pad, for example, will cost no more than $20 with prices varying slightly according to quantity and padding requirements.

The finished planners can be wholesale priced at about $2.50 for gift stores, supermarkets and speciality stores to attract the desired market. They also have great mail order potential, either on an individual basis or through a major distributor. Home shows and swap meets will draw the impulse buyers, who will want one even if they only need it for one event, like a shower or that special vacation.

Zero Population For Insects

We've heard of chastity belts for dogs and sterilization for hamsters. But now there's a way you can get rid of pesky bugs around the house—by using birth control for insects!

Millions of dollars are spent every year on preparations to kill flying, crawling and burrowing bugs. Now Albany International Corporation in New York has developed a way to nip the mating instincts of the little critters in the bud. And prevent a population explosion that could destroy plants and crops, not to mention a backyard barbecue party.

Synthetic pheronomes are chemicals that reproduce the mating scent of female insects. Albany's Conreal system releases these pheronomes into the air which confuses the males. If the male can't find the female, the mating cycle is interrupted.

The pheronomes can be developed to duplicate the mating scent of any specific insect. This should have an incredible impact on termite and other pest control businesses. The system uses hollow plastic fibers which release the pheronomes over a period of several weeks. Instead of calling for costly and repetitious spraying, it will only be necessary to stop by the hardware store or super market for a new supply.

An additional benefit is that pheronomes are made from natural chemicals so they are non-toxic and will not harm the environment. The first successful use of the system has been with pink bollworm, a nasty pest that destroys cotton fields. Although still in its infancy, the system should prove invaluable to farmers and commercial plant growers as well as homeowners.

Write: Albany International Corp. Dept. IEA, Sage Road, Menands New York.

Fireworks—
Business With A Bang!

"There's no business like show business" as the saying goes, with its lights, action and color. Not to mention the fireworks! And this is where anyone with a love for fireworks can get into show business with a bang. As a fireworks display specialist.

Everyone loves a fireworks display. The basic instincts, sight and sound, are satisfied as brilliant bursts of color and noise explode overhead to the "oohs" and "ahhs" of an enthusiastic audience. That's entertainment!

And there are booming profits—up to 45 percent gross before taxes for one display specialist we found—to be made in this business, as well. Don't think that the Fourth of July is the only time you'll be working. With a spark of advertising and promotion, one owner we found has become a blazing addition to parties and picnics sponsored by Elks Clubs, Boy Scouts and other civic groups, local baseball and soccer games and grand openings of major businesses. Year 'round!

There is no typical fireworks show. They run from three minutes as in a half-time college football show to 45 minutes for the special extravaganzas seen at large amusement parks. Fees to the display specialists can range from $1,000 to $15,000, depending on the magnitude of the show.

Prices for the explosives also vary, but we found that the material for a 5 minute show can be purchased direct from the manufacturer for about $550. This price, however, does not include the careful planning and choreography that goes into a good display. So, it is best to check the Yellow Pages under "Fireworks" for a distributor, as they will custom design a show based on the buyer's budget.

There are several American manufacturers of fireworks, like New York Pyrotechnic Products, Inc., in Bellport, N.Y. The favorite source, however, is the People's Republic of China which produces tons of fireworks every year for exporting. The Consumer Products Safety Commission in Washington, D.C. monitors safety standards.

The Chinese displays are extremely intricate and have been declared art works by several observers. The names, like "Moon Wooing Venus" and "Spring Prevails Over the Garden," are representative of the visual impact of these displays.

Before going into business as a display specialist, it is necessary to get a license from the Fire Marshall's office in your state. This generally involves a year or so of on-the-job training with a licensed handler, and a written test. Most display specialists and companies hire trainees on a part-time basis and this is the best way to learn the ups and downs of the business. A fireman is an excellent candidate, in terms of background.

Most cities now have specific ordinances about fireworks displays, in addition to licensing. Generally, the specialist is required to file for a permit 10 to 15 days prior to giving a display. Local fire departments have information about what is needed.

So, although it takes more than being able to light a match, the business is just getting off the ground, so to speak. The interest in fireworks displays as a promotional gimmick has sky-rocketed in the last few years. And specialists currently in the field just can't meet the demands!

Contact: New York Pyrotechnic Prods. Inc., Dept. IEA, Association Road, Bell Port, New York.

Rolling Rentals

Motor homes are luxurious rolling vehicles that spend three-quarters of their usable life sitting in a driveway—like big beached whales. Why not turn that slack time into a profitable rental business?

A company in Atlanta is doing just that—and moving along very well on the profits being generated. They sign up owners of motor homes on one hand and attract renters with the available selection on the other. This kind of service fills a need for everyone concerned. Owners are helping pay for their investment and renters have the use of a mobile home that they may not otherwise be able to afford, or enjoy.

You can capitalize on this idea in any area where people like to get away from it all for high-class camping. And you don't need a big fancy office or a lot of capital to do it! A telephone and the time to track down the mobile homes will get you started. RV dealers can probably provide names of recent purchasers.

A card file is important to keep records of owners' mobile home particulars like size, type, mileage, last servicing date and any restrictions, for example, about pets or children.

Profits are made by getting the two parties together. Fees can be a straight charge or based on the length of rental. Either one or the other party can be responsible for payment or separate initiation fees can be developed.

There are a lot of people out there with part-time "white elephants" on their hands (or in their driveways). Just as many people are willing to pay for the use of one of these home away-from-homes for a weekend or several weeks of vacation time.

A little bit of match-making will put you in the driver's seat. And turn a white elephant into a dark horse business overnight, with high riding profits.

When In Rome . . .

Anyone with a shower or bathtub owns 80 percent of a home steam bath. The other 20 percent needed to complete the luxury is the Roma Steam Unit! And with the high percentage of Americans interested in health and relaxation aids, Roma is the hottest business opportunity to come along since indoor plumbing.

The Roma Steam Unit converts any size enclosed shower or tub into a steam bath that would make a Roman drool. A compact appliance, it measures 14 inches wide by 27 inches long by 4 inches deep. It can be installed—by a handyman—in a closet, attic or wall within 20 feet of the stall.

The market is extensive. Not only homes or apartments, but motels, hotels, resorts, convalescent hospitals, resorts and clubs are likely candidates.

There are three residential models for enclosures of 85, 150 and 250 cubic feet. Commercial units convert areas of 300, 450 and 800 cubic feet. All units come with a variable timer and a unique polished-chrome steam head that can be filled with oil of perfume for an added "scents".

Roma has an innovative back-up system. A teflon-lined steel tank eliminates condensation and the danger of corrosion or rust. The steam is produced by electrodes so there are no wires, coils or water hook-ups. The unit is guaranteed for a year. Retail prices start at about $500 for the smallest residential enclosure unit and peak at about $1,800 for the largest commercial application.

The manufacturer is currently setting up dealerships. Energy Sales Co., Dept. IEA, P.O. Box 1224, Downey, CA 90241. Attn: Felix Wilson.

Dancing To The Bank

Several years ago, we predicted that the European discotheque would invade America. It has swept the nation and is the hottest thing since radio. The next wave we see on the horizon is *ballroom dancing*.

In Italy, for example, dancers are packing ballrooms and discotheques that play waltz, tango and polka music. The big band sound is enjoying a revival and vying with rock'n' roll contenders for top position on music charts in Europe.

Teenagers are *holding* their partners as they dance—a new if not unwelcome experience for many. The return of ballroom style dancing is, according to one expert, a nostalgic flight from the harsh realities affecting our modern world, like crime, terrorism, pollution and noise.

The profit potential of *ballo liscio* (smooth dancing) is evident. Dance halls are popping up like weeds, and sending the owners tap-dancing all the way to the bank. Six new 5,000 person capacity dance halls recently opened in two Italian cities and are sold out every weekend!

Orchestra leader, Raoul Casadi,

the king of Italian swing, built the $5 million Ballo Liscio House near Bologna. Cash registers there accompany the music to the tune of $2,000 to $3,000 a night. And in America, discotheques and dance clubs are constantly packed with new-breed traditional dancers. A whole new lifestyle has developed around the "new" style of dancing.

There is always room for another dance hall. Every city is susceptible to Saturday Night Fever—at any time during the week. And you can capitalize on the ballroom dancing craze. All you need is a hall or a renovated warehouse, a good band and some grand opening advertising. Word-of-mouth will soon make your presence known. The American Federation of Musicians has local union offices in every major city. They will help you locate musicians who specialize in the big band sound. There are also many non-union semi professional musicians.

Publicity is easy to arrange. Hand deliver free passes to the local press; they'll find their own stories. In no time at all you can be tripping-the-light-fantastic to the beat of a driving cash register.

Space Age Earrings End Ear Piercing

Women, from six to 60, love the pierced ear look. The process, though, can be extremely annoying. Infection and torn earlobes are often the price for being in vogue. Merchants often have to "induce" customers by giving free earrings with each ear piercing. We have a space age solution to the pierced ear dilemma. Cobalt!

Two tiny cobalt and salarium magnets are the secret to achieving the popular look of pierced without the fuss and bother! One on the inside of the lobe and an earring mounted to a matching magnet on the outside.

Virtually any style can be manufactured as magnetic earrings: decorative studs, gem stones or dangling hoops of all sizes. The real beauty, though, of these earrings is in the comfort. Once in place, they stay—secure and painless. None of the discomfort associated with clip-ons and no fear of wounded lobes.

Earmarked for success, magnetic earrings are selling for $5 to $15 in national department stores. Supplies of cobalt are at a premium and may be difficult for the small manufacturer to obtain. Salarium is abundant in the United States, but cobalt (which makes up 60 percent of each magnet) is extracted as a byproduct of copper—in Zaire. And being imported at $26 per pound.

Magnetic earrings wholesale for between $1 and $3, allowing a profitable edge for retailers. They are a natural adjunct to jewelry lines in clothing, gift or drug stores. As costume jewelry is largely an impulse-buy items, the earrings should do well at swap meets or flea markets. The teen-age buyer has more money for personal spending than ever before and is typically very fashion-conscious. This is an excellent market to explore.

The possibilities are limited only by public acceptance, and magnetic earrings seem destined for overwhelming popularity. When it comes to the pitfalls of piercing, magnetic earrings are just what the doctor ordered.

Hattie Carnegie Corp., Dept. IEA, 437 Fifth Ave., Manhattan, N.Y.

Clean Water With A Fishnet!

Our researchers have found an incredible new Austrian product that purifies water in aquariums, fish ponds, rivers and lakes through water aeration using what looks like a fish net.

Until now, expensive and largely ineffective chemical or mechanical aeration methods have been used to keep fresh water clean. So the potential of this product for commercial and environmental uses is fantastic.

The tested product is called *Oxynet*, and is coated with an electrically resistant lacquer, manufactured from semi-conducting plastics. Resting on the bottom of a pond, it creates oxygen by activating sediments, and pulling impurities down.

There are no chemicals or harmful metal ions involved in the process, which also inhibits growth of fungi. The effect of oxygen production actually *increases* with the impurity of the water. Enrichment of the water is molecular and there's no significant build-up of bubbles.

All you do is lay *Oxynet* on the bottom and weigh it down with stones, being careful not to bring the net in contact with metal. For best results,

there should be a layer of sediment above the net itself. *Oxynet* will last from one to three years before replacement, if properly used.

Because the net works without use of outside energy of any kind, and without outside control, it is far more economical for large-scale commercial use than any chemical or mechanical means now used by fisheries. Even with a high water temperature, fish ponds and even home aquariums equipped with *Oxynet* have an ample supply of oxygen.

Three fish-breeding organizations have used *Oxynet* in long-term tests with excellent results, including the Austrian Institute for Water Research and Fish Breeding in Scharfling, and Vollmer-Schippmann in West Germany. But the potential for this product, still waiting to be introduced in America, goes far beyond commercial fisheries.

If you can get your hands on this one early, it should prove to be a hot item in tropical fish stores, government or private environmental control projects, or even resort areas.

The price is about $4 per square meter, and samples are available for testing purposes from Eltac, Nagler & Daum K.G., Dept. IEA, Speckbacherstr. 29, A 6020 Innsbruck, Austria.

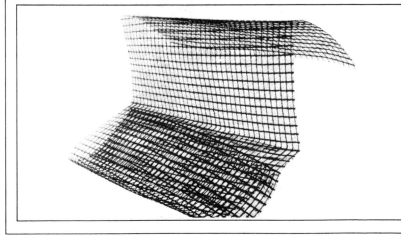

174

Grand Old Flag; Brand New Pole

It's a good patriotic habit to raise the flag on national holidays. But who wants a flagpole blocking the view the rest of the year? Certainly not the manufacturers of the three-sectioned Minuteman flagpole kit! There's no bother about digging holes—the Minuteman digs its own!

The tip of the bottom section is equipped with fine cutting teeth that dig into the ground as the pole is turned, about one inch with each revolution. A three-pronged stabilizer completely supports the pole once it has reached the desired depth. Not even the United States Cavalry could knock it over.

By adding the two additional sections, Old Glory sways in the breeze at about 15 feet high. The tapered steel pole is covered with a white electrostatic finish that will not chip, peel or discolor. And for that crowning glory, a gold-finished eagle.

Even Betsy Ross would be proud of the cotton bunting 50-star American flag that is included in the kit. Everything else is there—flag rope, swivel pulley and steel snaps—to bring honor back to Flag Day, Independence Day and Labor Day. But the Minuteman doesn't have to leave its post if year-round allegiance is preferred. The three sections are constructed to overlap so that no water or condensation can seep inside the pole.

The Minuteman flagpole kit is a terrific promotional advertising feature for hardware and home decorating stores. It lends itself to family-oriented drug stores and, at a retail price of $30, is an ideal mail-order product. And what an excellent raffle prize for a Kiwanis or Shriner's club event!

Do your patriotic duty and write to **Ajax Home Equipment Company, Dept. IEA, 3325 Ferguson Rd., Fort Wayne, Indiana, 46809,** for an all-American business opportunity.

Hot Shot Water Heater

These days everyone wants to save money on their heating and electric bills. Now there's a way you can reduce energy costs and still have the hottest shower in town.

Hot Shot, an exciting new product from Carrier Air Conditioning, is a reclaiming device that takes the heat created in air conditioning or pump systems and turns it into hot water. Waste heat is thereby put to good use.

Users get nine gallons of free hot water for every hour the air conditioner runs, by connecting *Hot Shot* to the in and outlet pipes of the water heater. Results are based on testing in a 36,000 BTU air conditioning system, and variations will occur depending on the air conditioner capacity.

Hot Shot should find an excellent market among home-improvement contractors, air conditioning firms and others going after the huge homeowner market, tied in with the energy conservation angle.

Hot Shot works because the water heater runs less when its 35 watts are doing the work. The heat from humid air serves as the generator for a refrigerant inside *Hot Shot*. When brought into contact with 60 degrees Fahrenheit water, it will heat to 140 degrees Fahrenheit and send hot water direct to the tank.

Only 5 inches wide by 18 inches deep, *Hot Shot* is mounted easily and quickly on the ceiling or wall near the hot water tank. One-half inch pipes connect air conditioner, water tanks, and *Hot Shot* together.

Carrier Air Conditioning is looking for dealer/distributors for their new product. Contact them at Department IEA, Carrier Parkway, Syracuse, New York 13221 for further information.

Life-Saving Neckwear

Seconds count for coronary patients and others who need immediate medical attention. And a heart attack can render someone helpless only a few feet from his home phone. Now help can be on the way at the push of a button!

Microlert is a matchbox-size transmitter that can be worn as a pendant around the neck—or a wrist bracelet. By pushing a button on the one-ounce device, a signal is sent up to 300 feet away to activate a sending unit hooked up to the phone lines.

The sending unit will automatically make up to 50 phone calls in sequence, to preselected numbers, and play a prerecorded message indicating the nature of the emergency. Calls can be to the emergency paramedic services, doctor's offices, or relatives and friends.

The device can't send out a false alarm, because it is designed with built-in "safeties" that prevent accidental triggering, even if a wearer rolls over in his sleep!

While designed with the needs of medical patients in mind, the product can be easily adapted for use by homeowners or businessmen to signal police or fire departments in the event these emergencies strike.

Microlert is available from Micro-Alert Systems International, to consumers at a monthly lease cost of $20. Its sending unit is FCC-approved for hookup to telephone lines nationwide. Connection is made using a standard jack installed by the local telephone utility.

A national program is being launched to make *Microlert* protection available at hotels and motels for travelers. MSI is looking for distributors. Write Micro Alert Systems Int'l., Dept. IEA, 3030 Empire Ave., Burbank, CA 91504.

My Plant Called Me A 'Pansy!'

Some days you just can't find anyone to carry on an intelligent conversation. Your wife's wrapped up in "girl talk," the kids are speaking some foreign language, and even your Siamese cat would rather sleep than talk to you. Don't despair. Now, thanks to a new and unique product we've (ahem!) unearthed, you can talk to your plants—and they can talk back.

It seems that many plant lovers really believe that a little pat in the right place and a few kind words can do wonders for the health of their little green friends. So, they talk to plants. But until now it's been a pretty one-sided conversation.

Future Plant will rectify that dull situation by allowing your plants to talk to you via bio-feedback. You attach the device to a plant, turn on the switch, and you supposedly can interpret the plant's reactions. A happy plant sets off a steady pulse on the device's light-emitting diode.

Blow some cigarette smoke in your plant's face, or hit it with cold water, and you get the equivalent of a cough or a shiver. The LED pulse stops. A lighted match or other threat of violence stops the LED pulse, too. But, says the manufacturer, if you caress your plant's leaves, the LED gives off a warm glow of well-being.

Prices were unavailable at press time, but there should be a ready market for this device among dedicated gimmick-lovers—or true believers. For further information, talk to the real live people at Advanced Marketing Concepts, Dept. IEA, Brentwood, Montana 63144.

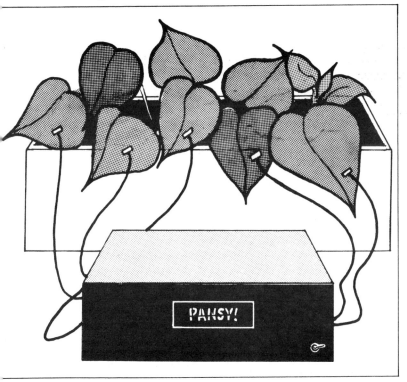

These 'Boots' Were Made For Stopping

The next time you get booted, don't leave town—check your glove compartment. It may be hiding long-forgotten parking tickets. Several cities across the nation are latching on to *The Boot*, an automobile immobilizer that leaves drivers stranded until they "pay up" overdue parking fines.

We see tremendous sales potential for *The Boot*. Law enforcement agencies are constantly looking for effective ways of collecting parking fine revenues. And some cities using the device are seeing a return of up to $5 million in revenues! The $250 cost of *The Boot* makes it well worth it.

So far the market is focused on police departments in major cities. This leaves the small town or county agencies open for business. New and used car dealers and antique automobile buffs are an excellent market. They are always intereste in new anti-theft devices. And th bright yellow Boot is a highly visib. deterrent to would-be car thieves joyriders!

It works like this—a clamp e circles the tire, holding the wheel ri between two steel jaws. A long ar is placed over the clamp and secure with a lock box and padlock.

It can be attached by one perso and fits all wheel and tire sizes fo domestic and foreign cars. And doesn't cause any damage—exce (for police applications) to th driver's wallet. There is no way *Th Boot* can be removed by force. Whe it's on, it's on until the person wh put it there takes it off!

Write Technology Transfer Grou Dept. IEA, 2020 Connecticut Av N.W., Washington, D.C. 20008, fe further information.

Green Mansions

As indoor plants continue to grow in popularity, even competing with dogs and cats in the hearts of their owners, it's to be expected that the leafy pets would need a home of their very own!

Philip Statlender, a Connecticut artist, has come out with a line of Gothic, leaded glass homes which are the last word in status for plants.

These green mansions are built using the copper-foil method of leaded-glass crafting. Floor plans range from three-bedroom models which measure 16 inches square to eight-bedroom estates which are 24 inches in height, width and depth.

The handcrafted plant homes range in price from $340 to $840; each is signed and dated. For an additional fee, Statlender will even do the planting and deliver within a limited area. Though the creations are generally one of a kind, they can be purchased in limited editions with a negotiated discount.

The display cases are made of double-strength clear glass, stained glass, copper foil, tin lead solder and brass. The artist applies a copper-colored finish to all metalwork and enclosed sections are accessible by means of hinged, latched doors.

The plant homes are mounted on adjustable, non-marring feet and come with contoured glass planters and instructions for case and plant care.

Plantless persons, as well as operators of gift shops, jewelry stores and specialty shops would welcome these creations as highly original display cases for valuable and beautiful items.

High prices for the glass houses reflect the labor and creativity invested in each of the artist's creations. But application of assembly line techniques should permit higher-quantity production, and our Manual #61, Stained Glass Window Manufacturing, will provide the details needed to adapt this idea to a business of your own.

Write Franklin Art Glass Studios, Dept. IEA, 222 East Sycamore St., Columbus, Ohio.

Catch A Falling Drip

A leaky water pipe can cause thousands of dollars damage if undetected. Now you can catch a trickle before it becomes a torrent with the new Hydro-Alarm 510. The new German device is a free-standing sphere that can be placed anywhere leakage is suspected.

Hydro-Alarm 510 can be used for industrial or household application where seepage or penetration of liquids is possible. Prime spots are areas where water heaters, storage tanks, washing machines, aquariums or water beds are located.

A sensor at the bottom detects electrically conductive liquids like water, milk, alcohol or juice. If contact is made, Hydro-Alarm 510 emits a shrill fluctuating signal, stopped by drying off the bottom of the unit.

The casing is made of a strong plastic that will float in the event of flooding. The monitoring system is operated by two 1½-volt batteries and is watertight to insure safety.

Hardware, appliance and home improvement stores will attract a pertinent market. Industrial trade shows and housewares exhibitions are a good way to demonstrate the unit's capabilities.

Price for the Hydro-Alarm 510 is $28 net F.O.B. Germany, excluding batteries. Discounts are available on quantity. Write to Volltronic, Columbus GMPH, Dept. IEA, P.O. Box 900 280, D-8000, Munchen 90, Germany, for further information.

Shape-ly Creation!

You don't have to be a magician to amaze your friends and family. You can transform a plant holder into a hat and back again at the flick of a wrist, with *Creataform!* They're selling like wildfire at craft fairs.

Use your imagination to create planters, headgear and decorative household items from an easy-to-copy honeycombed wood fiber shape. The flexible Creataform can be turned inside out for an alternative base shape.

Two Creataforms can be used to make a pedestal and planter or tray and fruit dish combination. As a hat, it expands to fit any size and can be decorated to suit individual taste. It comes in a natural brown tone that will blend with any color.

Plant stores and flower shops are an excellent market for sales using Creataform. It holds 2- to 8-inch pots snugly and will not be the slightest bit damaged by plant watering. Toy shops, too, can tickle the imagination of the younger crowd with this innovative product.

At a wholesale price of approximately $1.25, with discounts on quantity, it is a unique promotional idea for any new or expanding business. It comes attractively boxed with an illustrated instruction sheet showing different applications.

As we went to press, we learned that the manufacturer is in the process of changing their packaging. They may also rename the product, but write to Creataform Productions, Dept. IEA, 18900 La Montana Place, Tarzana, California, 91356, for further information.

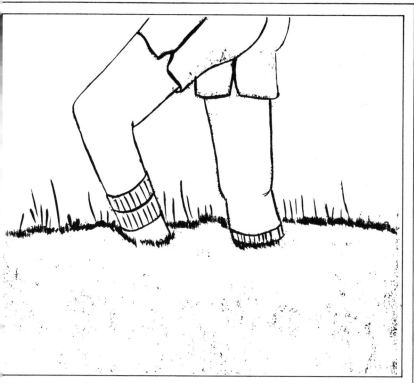

Here's Mud In Your Eye

If you just discovered that the 20 acres of "choice, water-fed" property you bought sight unseen is a swamp—don't despair! You can recoup your investment by turning that bog into a slogging course!

Mud slogging, a cross between sloshing and jogging, was invented by the Dutch and is destined to be the next sport to turn out health conscious Americans. The only thing you need is a field full of mud and some earthy advertising to draw attention.

Geert Jan de Weert, the organizer and guide of slogging excursions in Holland charges $3.50 per person for a two-and-a-half hour slog—the highlight of which is a Dutch-treat lunch on a mud island. He leads 120 sloggers across North Sea mud every Saturday from May to September. That's $420 clear, as he has absolutely no overhead, in one afternoon!

Slogging beats jogging in that it is strenuous and extremely good for the legs without the fear of bone spurs caused by running on hard surfaces. Walking (or sloshing) at a brisk pace in mud for half an hour will do as much for the circulation and muscles as one hour of jogging.

The obvious disadvantage is a sloppy layer of mud from toes to knees, although the therapeutic qualities of the mud will compensate for any discomfort.

You will want to advise your clientele to wear sneakers and shorts. Heavier footgear and long pant legs get mud-logged and slow sloggers down. You must not allow bare feet under any circumstances, as people could step on a submerged object and cut themselves.

Geert Jan de Weert, Dept. IEA, Kerkplein 2, Sierum (Friesland), Holland.

Home "Town" Views

What kid wouldn't want a Western-style town right in his or her own bedroom! Here's a way you can turn your child's fantasies into realities. And make good old Yankee bucks doing the same for every kid in the neighborhood!

Build child-size store facades to be placed in bedrooms and used as a "front" for toy and clothing storage or play areas. We found two kids whose bedroom is a miniature, old-fashioned Western village, complete with hotel, general store and toy shop. The walls are painted to depict an outdoor setting and cobblestone linoleum on the floor completes the scene.

Working on the "stage set" concept, their daddy—a kid-at-heart—built bunk beds into a scaled-down hotel facade, with swinging doors, curtained windows and a trap door from the top bunk to the bottom. The toy shop and general store houses—you guessed it—toys, games and books.

Building and installing "theme"

rooms offers tremendous potential to creative and/or handy persons. Once a basic shell pattern has been established, stores can be adapted to customer preference using pre-fab techniques. Western, French Provincial or modern facades are easily achieved with the addition of the proper accessories. General carpentry skills are required, however, to insure quality work.

The structures stand between 6 feet and 8 feet high and, except for the bunkbed hotel, are about 3 feet in width. Wall paneling and synthetic brick sheeting provide authentic looking store fronts; windows and signs are painted on or added separately.

The decorating boom in the nation will attract customers looking for something unique. Profits will build as rapidly as construction will allow. Grown-ups and children alike will clamor to have ownership of one store or a village in the privacy of their bedroom. Variations can be designed for use in family rooms and dens.

Miracle Seashells!

Researchers near Seattle, Washington have discovered that smelly piles of discarded seafood shells like crab, shrimp, lobster and other crustaceans, can yield a wealth of useable materials.

For example, one ton of waste crab shells can be broken down into separate components and result in 160 pounds of high-grade protein, 160 pounds of chitin and 128 pounds of chitosen.

Chitin, a cellulose-like material, is the structural basis of crustaceans, while chitosen is a derivative of chitin. The protein, which accounts for 25 to 40 percent of a shell's weight, is being tested for use in animal feed, and eventually, in food for humans.

Chitin has been found to be extremely effective as a healing salve for skin ulcers and protracted cases of psoriasis. The chitin-based compound also dramatically reduced swelling of rheumatoid arthritis. Surgical incisions reportedly healed twice as fast when a chitin-based powder was used. It is also a helpful additive to stomach antacids, as it has digestive qualities.

Chitosen has tremendous coagulant properties and has been tested in various industrial applications. It rapidly cleans polluted water and has been tried in hydraulic dredging operations with amazing results. It improves fiber bonding in paper bags, towels and diapers—and is moisture proof. On the medical side, there are indications that chitosen may help in inhibiting leukemia and cancer cell growths.

Although we do not recommend that you start a seashall disposal center in your backyard just yet, seashells may well take over where penicillin left off and become the miracle substance of the century.

Contact Food, Chemical & Research Labs Inc., Dept. IEA, 4900 9th St. N.W., Ballard, Washington.

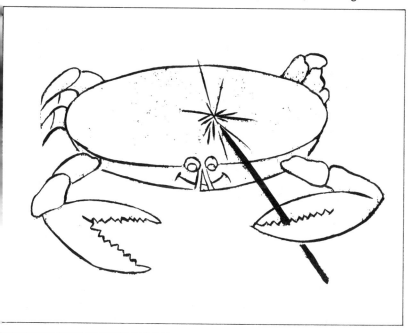

Tote That Couch

Moving furniture around can be a real drag, without a bunch of heave-ho friends—unless you keep it light using *foam furniture*, like a 55-pound full-size couch. And portable furniture stores are cleaning up selling lightweight furniture like that to college kids and other transients.

We found one bright furniture designer, Barry Bursak, who's selling fast-moving portable "pad" paraphernalia from a store called *Granfallons* in Chicago, Illinois. And he is swamped with customers who want to "lighten their load."

Furniture like the couch is no lightweight when it comes to quality. It flips into a double bed at the flick of a finger and comes upholstered in chintz, canvas or cotton at a retail price between $325 and $400. Other developments in this stylish industry include a chrome-and-beechwood chair from Italy that can be packed into a flat box and a 7-foot lamp made of paper that rolls into a small tube.

Local manufacturers will assist you in selecting stock for such a store that is really portable. The best test, of course, is to try and pick it up single-handed.

Pick-up-and-go items are gaining in popularity worldwide not only because of portability, but also economy and functionalism. Makers are stressing the importance of *purpose*, like the multi-use couch.

The tote-able furniture business is just getting off the ground. As more and more Americans pull up stakes (20 million moved last year) they re-evaluate the advantages of owning large pieces of cumbersome furniture. Witness the increase of garage sales and furniture rental outfits.

A portable furniture store should work well in almost any area with a high percentage of transients.

Write: Granfallons, Dept. IEA, 152 W. Huron, Chicago, Illinois.

From Rags To Riches

Here's a great way you can parlay a low investment into big bucks: Outfit a small pickup with car-washing equipment. Scott Alexander and his brother did just that and now gross over $3,200 a month serving regular customers who pay $7.50 weekly to have their cars washed.

Their primary customers are well-to-do owners of luxury automobiles like Porsche and Mercedes with a few Rolls Royces to add class. All the customers save time because the work is done in their driveway or parking lot. The executives are then free to do what they do best: make money.

Other benefits of the wash service are less wear and tear on customer's automobiles and no more worry about damaged finishes or brutal treatment by careless car wash attendants. For these reasons, the service is so popular that it has been expanded to a two-truck operation.

You don't need to be well connected to become successful in this business, and it should be easy to copy in any metropolitan area. It should be especially valuable for those who want to have a nice looking car in areas where weather is a problem.

The best approach to marketing is to obtain the names of car owners from a friendly luxury car dealer. An alternative is to use lists of car owners available from mailing houses that show the make of car and year of registration. Similar lists are often made available by state motor vehicle departments. A simple leaflet under the windshield wipers of cars in office parking lots should bring in plenty of business by appointment only.

Put A Typist In Your Pocket

The next time you want to write an inter-planetary memo, pound it out on your *pocket typewriter!* This amazing technological advancement is already in the prototype stages. And could very well put the secretarial pool in deep water within a few years!

Cy Endfield, an ex-film director, has invented a five-key computerized typewriter that will slip into your pocket along with your calculator. It works on an ingenious code along the same lines as that used by court reporters—that can be learned in less than an hour. The five fingers of the right hand enable you to type as accurately—and as quickly with practice—as with a standard typewriter.

The text appears on a display panel, just as numbers appear on the display of a calculator. The machine does not, however, produce words on paper. It is connected to a high speed automatic typewriter which prints the message on paper, perfectly typed as coded.

The pocket typewriter brings us another step closer to the "office of the future." This concept calls for elimination of excessive transcribing and typing by secretaries, allowing time for more administrative-type duties. Many large corporations nationwide have already established word processing centers which involve the use of sophisticated dictation and typing apparatus. Endfield claims his invention is not a substitute for dictation, but a substitute for the pen. Instead of seeing executives mumbling away into a miniature dictation machine in the future, we will see them furiously pounding away with five flying fingers!

Although the pocket typewriter will cost more than a good five-cent cigar, it will not be much higher than a medium price calculator. The reason is the use of a silicon microprocessor "chip," an advanced form of computer technology. But the most important requirement to owning one will not be the money, but the availability of an automatic typewriter for reproduction to paper.

In a word, the portable typewriter is a "small" but significant sign of the times. Although it is not yet available on the market, it has received an enthusiastic reception from several British governmental agencies, and Endfield is looking for a manufacturer.

Turn Highways Into Fry-Ways!

Imagine replacing the smell of diesel fumes with the sizzling delight of bacon and eggs, crisp sausages, or grilled sandwiches! And imagine washing that repast down with delicious home-made coffee or other hot beverage! Well, you don't have to pull your car into an expensive roadside restaurant to enjoy it all if you have two new products that really intrigued us.

One is a quick-fry pan that plugs into the car's cigarette-lighter socket—and uses no more battery power than a car radio. The pan sells for a suggested retail price of $17.95, and we can really see a need for such a product in these days of high restaurant prices.

It would seem especially useful in a station wagon, where it could perform its culinary chores even when the car is in motion. Owners of vans and campers would be an excellent market, too, since the frying pan could be used both en route and at recreational areas. Passenger-car drivers need only pull off the road and plug in!

The same goes for the $19.95, four-cup coffeemaker, except that it would probably be safer not to use it while the vehicle is in motion. This slight disadvantage is more than compensated for by the fact that the coffeemaker can also operate from an outlet at home or in a hotel room.

If these products whet your monetary appetite, write The Metal Ware Corporation, Dept. IEA, Two Rivers, Wisconsin, 54241 for further information.

Electronic Device To Locate Lost Woodsmen

Even Indians have been known to get lost in the woods, so the swarms of people heading for the boondocks these days should be a perfect market for a new, sophisticated electronic device that can signal, and pinpoint, where help is needed.

Michigan sportsman Donald Bonifield has devised a portable, lightweight two-part "walkie-talkie" unit, called the "Electroway," that emits electronic signals. Small enough to fit into a pocket, the transmitter weighs just about 8 ounces. The 1¼-pound receiver, the size of a cigar box, can receive signals from any number of receivers. Thus one receiver responds to the transmitters of all members of a hunting party.

The receiver operates on a small 12-volt camp-light battery, and the transmitter can operate on an ordinary 9-volt transistor or auto battery. Mated units retail for around $90 a set, but transmitters purchased separately could prove quite profitable as rentals, while providing a unique service.

There's no battery drain unless the transmitter is activated. By simply wiring the receiver connection to an auto or recreational vehicle's horn and headlights, the transmitter can trigger either one, serving as a guide or as an alert to others of an existing problem. The horn would generally be used during the day, the lights at night.

Boating enthusiasts have been quick to spot Electroway as an invaluable aid. While a signal can be sent a mile and a half over land, it can reach 15 miles over water! A signal could be a lifesaver for the lost skipper.

Electroway's applications are endless. One resort owner uses this system as a "homing" device for guests, utilizing a high-power light beam and horn as guides back to his lodge.

Receivers could also be placed strategically as burglar alarms for autos or homes. Triggering the transmitter could set off lights, horns, and even sirens to scare off the intruder.

We've also heard of some people locating Electroway in their autos in supermarket and stadium parking lots. One press of the button, and the car horn blows! Makes it easy—if a bit noisy—to find your car! Write Donald Bonifield, Dept. IEA, P.O. Box 75, Seney, Michigan 49883.

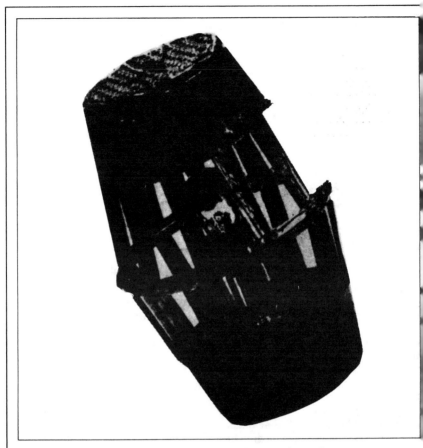

Bug-Zapping Patio Lantern

More outdoor parties have probably been ruined by pesky bugs than by overdone steaks, tepid drinks, and leaky paper plates combined. Until now, your choice of defense was limited to smelly anti-bug lotions, fly swatters, spray cans, and curses.

Now there's a company offering a lantern-shaped electronic bug destroyer that uses an angstrom (black-light) bulb to attract annoying flying insects. When they zero in on the invisible (to you) light—zap!— they're electrocuted. One "Mark 7 Insect Destroyer" is said to clear hundreds of square feet of flies, mosquitoes, gnats, and other pests that go buzz in the night.

Using common house current, the $14.95 (retail) device kills the bugs instantly, incinerating them into an odorless powder. The manufacturer claims the unit is safe for children, pets and birds.

We know of expensive commercial models that get heavy-duty use in areas where insects have developed a resistance to chemicals or where toxic chemicals cannot be used, such as in stables.

If this low-priced unit does what it promises to, there should be a ready market for it among homeowners, campers, outdoor businesses, kennels, and stables. Write Insect Destroyer, 47 West Shore Drive, Dept. IEA, Warwick, RI 02889.

Fruit Slicer Makes Good

An Australian entrepreneur has built a $100,000 a year business using a sharp knife and $114. Sound unreal? Graham McMullen thought so, too, when he started selling sliced and seeded lemons to restaurants and bars. The profits speak for themselves, and McMullen's recognition of the potential market demonstrates how a small businessman can hit the big time.

McMullen realized that no one was selling seeded and sliced lemons. He started in the back room of his house, slicing and selling before going to work at night. Less than five years later, McMullen has moved into a factory and, with his brother and one assistant, produces 18,000 sliced lemons a week.

He's expanded to include oranges as well as olives, cherries and other bar goods. The company receives orders from all over the country and even makes money on the leftovers. A farmer hauls the waste to feed his pigs and cattle; another takes rotten fruit to make compost.

Many American bars and restaurant lounges still have the kitchen staff or more likely, the bartender slice their lemons. Often these garnishes take longer to make than the drink, which slows the productivity of the bartenders. A busy bar or restaurant will go through hundreds of slices in a night. Consequently, there's a good market for this service in the United States.

All you need is a knife and a source of fruit. Canvass bars and restaurants for customers and wait for more business from word-of-mouth referrals. Your prices will vary depending on how much the fruit costs you, but by buying at wholesale prices, you should be able to sell the product at a fairly low rate and make a profit. If you're on a shoestring, do the slicing yourself or hire neighborhood kids to do it (as long as they're careful). If your fingers get tired, Sunkist in Van Nuys, California, sells a commercial sectioner that can give four, six or eight slices.

The costs are low and the profits potentially high, so see if you can cut yourself a slice of the action.

Emergency Fan Belt

Automobile fan belts only seem to snap when you're a million miles from nowhere, in the middle of the desert, or caught in a blinding snow storm. Be it fate or mechanical "revenge," a new emergency fan belt kit on the market promises speedy relief from such misery.

The clip-on belt called "Rescue"™ is designed for use without tools or hassle. It provides temporary relief for all cars and permanently replaces most belts on smaller fractional horsepower applications. This includes shop power tools, lawn mowers and appliances.

The kit includes a 42-inch length of 5/16" diameter polyurethane tubing, a snap-in metal connector, and a razor blade. The belt will operate on most V-grooved pulleys.

It's installed by wrapping it around the pulleys, marking the length required, cutting off the excess and then snapping the two ends together with the metal connector. Package instructions tell how to adjust for tension and stretch compensation.

Rescue reduces the need to have on hand an inventory of different-size replacement belts. When the application calls for a belt longer than the 42 inches, two kits can be fastened together with the metal connectors.

The kit can be sold successfully by direct mail, from gas stations, auto supply shops, hardware stores, and even roadside cafes. The suggested retail price is $4.95. Contact: Emergency Fan Belt, Educational Prods., Dept. IEA, P.O. Box 606, Mineola, N.Y. 11501.

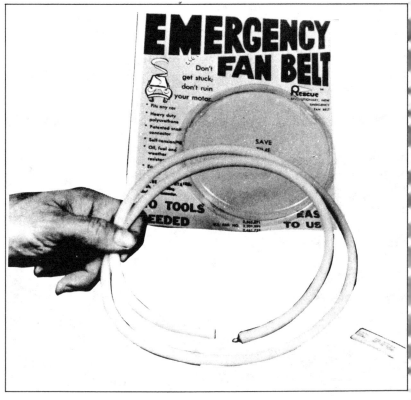

Handle On Safety

Every year thousands of people are injured while bicycling, one of the most hazardous recreational activities around. Now the British have come up with a new product that will surely get a handle on the bike enthusiast market: battery-operated handlebar signal lights!

The Novar Signal Flasher Handgrips replace the regular handgrips, and are operated by simple thumb pressure. Your hand never needs to leave the bars! This handy little item can be seen for several hundred yards at night, so oncoming cars can steer away in time. It is made of impact resistant materials, so it is less likely to break in a fall.

As leisure time increases for American adults, more people will be peddling their way through the evening hours, and the demand for increased safety devices is obvious.

The beams are distributed through Novaco International Technical Accessories, Ltd. in England. The product should find a great market in the states through regular bicycle shops, hobby shops, athletic supply houses and department stores.

For more information on the Novar Signal Flasher, write to N.I.T.A. at Dept. IEA, P.O. Box 27, 17 Park Place; Stevanage, Hertfordshire SGI IBJ, England.

Be A Doll

The cosmetic industry has made millions because men and women are willing to spend millions to have a "doll face." Now you may be able to make your own fortune on people's vanity by immortalizing their faces on a real doll!

We've found a company called Be A Doll, Inc., in New York City, that will have a photo of your face silk screened on a rag doll. This can be turned into a terrific personalized and profitable gift item.

This business idea can be easily duplicated and expanded. If you're handy with a needle and thread as well as silk screening techniques, you can stuff your wallet with ease!

In addition to providing clients with custom-made rag dolls bearing their likeness, business can be expanded to dolls bearing the likeness of real live "dolls."

What woman wouldn't appreciate a doll blessed with Robert Redford's, Steve McQueen's or Humphrey Bogart's kisser? And how many men would reject the gift of a life-sized Brigitte Bardot, Ursula Andress or Farrah Fawcett-Majors doll?

A humorous note can be achieved by producing Chairman Mao, Richard Nixon or Idi Amin dolls. Indeed, an entire store could be stocked with such imaginative gift items.

Write: Be A Doll Inc., Dept. IEA, 99 Prince St., New York City, N.Y.

Add 2 Tsp. Profit . . .

If you've ever dumped half a cup of cream in your coffee by mistake, you know how wasteful regular measuring methods can be. We've found a new product that will put just the right amount in—every time!

This indispensible dispenser called Measure Maid pours just enough of your favorite granulated product. You set a dial and out it comes! The container is made of unbreakable plastic, and it measures from ½ teaspoon up to one tablespoon in ¼ teaspoon increments. It will hold more than two cups (103 teaspoons) of any dry granulated material, and comes with a five-year unconditional guarantee.

The Measure Maid eliminates waste, saving the consumers' money. For example: You could measure the right amount of instant coffee, sugar or even dishwasher detergent every time, avoiding spillage. Until now, the only way to get an exact amount has been to dip in a measuring spoon and level it off, which is time-consuming and results in messy overflow.

Measure Maid has been proven to be helpful to disabled persons who are not able to measure substances easily.

One excellent market for this dispenser is restaurants, which are always looking for methods to get more accurate portion control. The product could be used in the kitchen, as well as on the counter, for pouring sugar, Parmesan cheese and other granulates.

People who have used them in restaurants often want to know where to get one for use at home. The size of the Measure Maid lends itself to mail order, too.

The Measure Maid is the first in a series of similar products that will be coming out on the market soon. It is now being offered in stores at a retail price of $5.95. Contact: Measure Maid Floex Inc., Dept. IEA, P.O. Box 83 Norfolk, Massachusetts 02056.

Ski On Grass!

During the winter snow skiers rocket down slopes throughout the country. But what happens in spring? Expensive ski gear is stowed away; ski schools and ski area operators go into "hibernation" until the next snow fall.

It doesn't have to be this way. Grass skiing is becoming established in Europe where teams compete from all over the Continent. Grass skiing championships were held in Quebec in July 1977.

Now the Rollka brand grass ski has just been introduced to the United States market by Innovation Associates, a Chatsworth, California firm that has been named exclusive U.S. distributor.

Grass skis are essentially miniature caterpillar tractor treads about two feet long that attach to standard ski boots. In use, the grass skis provide the sensations and movements of snow skiing *without the need for snow!* Speeds in excess of 55 mph have been attained by downhill racers in competition.

This opportunity to turn skiing into a year-round activity shouldn't be passed up by snow ski businesses looking for year-round revenue.

For more information, contact Innovation Associates, Inc., Dept. IEA, 9510 Owensmouth Avenue, Suite 6, Chatsworth, California 91311.

TV That Prints!

A revolutionary kind of television has been developed that can deliver printed messages in a viewer's home in minutes! It looks like an ordinary set, but has printout capability and can hand you copy printed in letter size *and full color* on ordinary paper.

The potential of such a system is mind-boggling. Newspapers can be delivered via it. Perhaps just one or two items will be selected for further study by a viewer: stock quotations, recipes, sports or theatre schedules.

Imagine being able to press a button and receive in-depth treatment of a complex national news stories that a TV announcer only covers briefly!

The breakthrough set is called a *Television Multiplex Facsimile* and it's been developed by Matsushita Electric, makers of Panasonic brand electric gear, among other things.

The television uses an ink-jet printing mechanism beneath the tube that weighs less than a golf ball and is the size of a matchbook.

All a viewer has to do is select a channel that is transmitting facsimile copy. This should work about the same as the "simulcast" used by FM radio and TV stations to broadcast concerts and the like now.

When the viewer sees something he wants printed out, a button can be pushed on the set to activate the printing unit while the televised program continues uninterrupted.

Major private companies that have closed-circuit systems can use this technology now to distribute information systemwide. It may be that cable TV companies can move into this realm quickly as well.

Write: Matsushita Electronic Corp. of America, Dept. IEA, Corporate Communications, Dept.-1, Panasonic Way, Secaucus, New Jersey 07094.

Goofy Art Gallery

Cartoon characters have become a way of life in America. Thousands of readers and movie fans follow the escapades of Disney creatures, Snoopy and his friends and the Pink Panther as faithfully as they record their own children's growth patterns.

Imagine, then, the popularity of an art gallery that deals exclusively in cartoon art. Character sculptures, artists' drawings from animated movies, and comic strip inspired paintings could serve as the foundation for this specialty business.

Burt and Edie Rudman of Cedar Rapids, Iowa saw the potential of a cartoon art gallery. Their Gallery La-ingberg is a treasure chest for caricature connoisseurs. They carry a wide selection of "cells"—or transparencies—used as the original drawings for many animated movies, and available for next to nothing from film studios.

A prime source for material would be any major studio that produces animated features. Write to Disney Studios or Hanna-Barbera in Hollywood, Calif., for example, to find out what they have available. There are also many independent producers across the country making Saturday morning children's cartoons who may be willing to sell transparencies—or put them in a gallery on consignment.

And, as a popular cartoon character generally results in an extensive line of products, there are hundreds of art-worthy items available from small manufacturers. The developers of the character will know who is making the spin-off products. You could carry original prototypes or special edition products, depending on what the manufacturers will provide.

There are many name possibilities like Mickey Angelo's or The Gallery at Pooh Corners or Batman's Cave Drawings for this type of business. It is important to check with producers and studios for possible trademark or name usage restrictions in their contracts.

Take a tip from the Seven Dwarfs and "Whistle While You Work."

Write: Gallery Laingberg, Dept. IEA, Cedar Rapids, Iowa.

The Write Scent

Flowery love letters, popular since the days of Marie Antoinette, have never smelled as sweet as they can now! We've found a new writing pen, guaranteed to spark your senses. The pen is filled with ink scented with real French perfume.

The pen set consists of two fine quality ball-point pens that write with Arpege and Chanel No. 5 scented inks. They are attractively designed with elegant 14 karat gold filigree over black and brushed-gold tone, and come packaged in a plush leatherette case.

This little pen set has one gigantic profit margin also: It is successfully retailed between $4.95 and $9.95, yet its wholesale price is around $1.49. That's a minimum of $3.46 gross profit on each set.

With a return like that, who could resist selling them through a mail-order business! These pens make great gift items for your next promotion, and could be marketed to beauty and modeling schools, as well as for fashion shows. They can be sold as graduation gifts for women, and even at flea markets.

For more information on these little jewels, write to Forrest-James Company, Dept. IEA, P.O. Box 11519, Milwaukee, Wisconsin 53211. Success never smelled sweeter!

Photos On Ceramic

We've seen the floodgates open on photographic processes in the past few years. Everywhere you turn there are computer photos, photo T-shirts, and even photos as large as your living room wall!

Now you can capture a fleeting moment in time on ceramic plates that will last beyond your lifetime. Full color snapshots of your family, movie stills, faded old tintypes passed on for generations, and even 14th century religious illuminations can be captured in ceramic, steel or glass using a fantastic new process developed by a freelance photographer from Fullerton, California.

Dish and china manufacturers, portrait studios and others in the booming collectible business are showing great interest in the process, which is claimed to cut costs 25% over traditional decal transfer or hand-painted techniques.

It all started when Sandor Demlinger's family asked him to find a way to produce a portrait of his mother-in-law for her gravestone. He began experimenting and came up with a patent-pending process that involves etching of the image on the ceramic with photochemicals, using a negative of the original to be reproduced. Final step in the process is baking in a fire kiln to melt the design into the material permanently.

One place you can see Demlinger's work is at the MGM Grand Hotel in Reno.

Contact: Sandor Demlinger, Dept. IEA, 1319 No. Riedel, Fullerton, CA.

Renting Hovercraft Is A New Way To Skim Profits

Devices people in tourist locations will rent to amuse themselves come along in endless profusion: boats, snowmobiles, tandem bicycles, saddle horses, even hang gliders. And now there's *hovercraft!*

Flying along 12 inches above any relatively flat surface on a cushion of air, you can take a hovercraft almost anywhere—over water, snow, muddy marshes, sand or grass.

No longer experimental, there should be a good rental/sales market for hovercraft *year round* in almost any tourist attraction.

British Sports Hovercraft, Ltd., with offices at Dept. IEA, 15012 Red Hill Ave., Tustin, California 92680, has designed two models especially for the American market. Both are easy to maintain, unsinkable, and typically rent for $10 per hour to people hungry for something different to do.

maximum speeds of 35 miles per hour, virtually anywhere they want to go, with a six-gallon tank of gas. According to the manufacturer, "a twelve-year-old with five minutes of instruction" can fly the simpler, single version.

From five to 10 units are necessary for a viable rental/sale operation. Two-engined Sea Mouse units wholesale for $2,995; the smaller Stratus model wholesales for $2,000. For recovery of smaller craft, and rental of rides only, the manufacturer suggests purchase of one larger Starduster model, with a two-to three-seat capacity. Marketing plans which detail profitability are also available from the maker.

Promotion and advertising opportunities for a hovercraft rental and sales operation are incredible. Boats in the water will build tremendous interest by themselves, as well as word-of-mouth advertising. But free rides for the press and organized races are other ways to develop year-round business.

Waterbed For Dogs!

Waterbeds continue to ride on a profitable wave as increasing numbers of people discover the pleasure of floating off to sleep. Many pet owners find their dogs and cats enjoy it as much as they do!

Sleeping with dogs and cats can be both uncomfortable and unhealthy. Assigning Spot or Tabby to the floor can aggravate a pet's rheumatism or arthritis. Now there's a way to kick them out of bed without hurt feelings or fear of ill health—the Pet Waterbed!

Veterinarians recommend the bed for the pet who has everything, because it is said to stimulate pet circulation and help tone muscles. It'll also prevent injury to tissue and bones and alleviate joint inflammations. It's even hypo-allergenic!

These waterbeds come in two sizes (18" x 18" and 36" x 36") to accommodate most dogs and cats. Each bed consists of a heavy-duty mattress and hand-crafted, finished birch frame, which can be assembled without tools. The small Pet Waterbed sells for $29.95 and the larger one for $39.95. They come with assembly instructions and a full 90-day guarantee.

Pet Waterbeds are a natural item for sale in pet stores, dog and cat "hotels," or waterbed specialty stores. Even home furnishing stores could use them as a novelty item. The beds are available from Wildwood Products and dealer inquiries are invited. Their address is Dept. IEA, 18107 Highway 18, Apple Valley, California 92307.

Open A Pinball Club

Millions of adults love to play pinball and other electronic games but don't want to go to the typical tacky arcade filled with rowdy teenagers. Even arcades in shopping malls cater to the younger set. One sharp entrepreneur capitalized on this by opening a posh *private pinball club* for members only.

El Casino in Clearwater, Florida, draws adults who pay $25 to $50 for a one-year membership to play their favorite games from pinball to baseball in luxurious surroundings.

Members are given 500 free points on the machine of their choice when they sit down to play; an alternative would be a certain number of free games with the rest at nominal prices. If players "tilt" or "go broke" they must give the machine to the next person with a reservation so no one can "hog" the good machines.

High scorers can use accumulated points to buy tokens for part of the cost of drinks and dinner as an incentive to keep playing. To keep the operation simple, a single specialty is served.

This easy-to-duplicate concept can work well in nearly any major metropolitan area. It turns gaming into an evening of fun, competitive entertainment as well as a chance to socialize. It would work best in a popular "night life" section of town, drawing lots of foot traffic and exposure. Or near a business district, it can attract hungry office workers and executives at lunchtime looking for a *real* break—or an unusual place to take a client.

With imagination, loft warehouse space, a failing bar, or even a basement can become an exclusive, private "key club" for pinball wizards. Food and beverage service would be a profitable plus, but need not be elaborate. Drinks and good-sized sandwiches should be enough. Consider a disco setup for evenings and weekends to add to draw members.

Spider-Grams

Cute may not be the word to describe your neighbor's pet baby tarantula, but believe it or not, spiders are hot this year, and a stock of those little crawly things can make extra cash creep into your coffers!

When a San Diego pet dealer announced he was selling pet tarantulas as Valentine's Day gifts, his three shops were suddenly crawling with customers! He sold his entire stock of 84 tarantulas in three days. That works out to about $900—and more than half of that was profit.

The spiders, known to make friendly pets, range in price from $13.99 for the red-legged variety to $4.99 for the more common brown stock. The animals wholesale from $2.50 to $6 apiece.

The spiders can be marketed in pet stores, novelty and gift stores, fairs, flea markets, or perhaps on a pier, where tourists are apt to buy a souvenir of their trip. They can be sold in conjunction with other small or unusual pets.

The spiders can be sent in the mail first class, in little wooden boxes marked "live specimen," and your customer can have a "spider gram" shipped across town in one day. The box could come with the message attached. The spider-gram could be ordered by phone.

The possibilities are endless, and tarantulas don't mess up the carpet—unless you step on them. You can order tarantulas by the dozen from Gators of Miami, Dept. IEA, 5500 NW 74th Avenue, Miami, Florida.

Put Your
Best Foot Forward

Aches and pains are no match for a fantastic product we recently ran across. The Weihs Gymroller! A 12x12 inch hardwood massaging unit that eliminates sore muscles caused by sports or tension! And produces phenomenal profits. It has been extremely successful at home shows, conventions and gift exhibits nationwide. Dog-tired foot traffic can sit down and try it!

Young and old can use the lightweight Gymroller. There is nothing to set up. Just put it on the floor, plant your feet on it and roll pain away. Bed-ridden patients can rest it on the end of a bed for relief from stationary muscle aches. It can be used at home, in the office, hospitals, or gymnasiums.

The Gymroller works through reflexology, the treatment of health problems by foot massage. Reflexology was developed, centuries back, by the Asians. The Gymroller was designed in Germany in 1964 and introduced to America last year. It promises to be the simplest, most practical and complete massager ever devised. Confucius would have loved it!

There are many nerve endings in the feet tied directly to the vital organs and muscles of the body. Rolling the feet over the specially designed Gymroller exerts pressure on all of these points and stimulates circulation. In other words, a pain in the neck—or anywhere for that matter—can be eliminated with a little fancy footwork!

The simple unit works without any outside power and is constructed of hardwoods. It is light, sturdy and is guaranteed for 10 years. You can also use it to massage hands, legs, shoulders, and back. It is ideal for wheelchair and bed-ridden patients as it will improve blood circulation

The Gymroller is now being manufactured in the U.S. It is a wonderful gift item for friends, family or self! A flyer comes with the Gymroller that indicates all of the reflex points in the feet. It retails for $29.95 and is available for distribution from Helmut H. Lihs, Dept. IEA, 2765 East Broadway, Long Beach, California 90803.

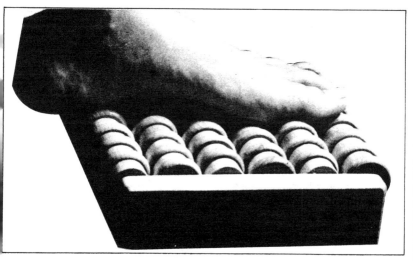

201

Own A Vintage Movie Theatre

Bogart film festivals, Our Gang comedies, Flash Gordon serials, and even horror/sci-fi revivals have brought cinema buffs and nostalgia freaks into movie theaters in droves.

Many people feel that today's movies just don't measure up to the star-studded reels of the Thirties, Forties and Fifties, when you didn't have to worry so much about sending your kids to a matinee.

You can capitalize on the growing interest in old-time celluloid "flickers" by opening a movie theater that shows only vintage films. We've seen several places do this with a one-time "festival" approach, but only a few theaters in the country are "oldie-only."

One is the Rose Bud Movie Palace in Seattle, Washington, an 88-seat house showing the best of Gable, Lombard, Edward G. Robinson, Humphrey Bogart, and the rest of what made up the real Hollywood.

The market is increasing steadily, and there are many metropolitan areas that could support a theater of this type, provided that you locate in the "arty" part of town, perhaps near a college or university, and

price the films quite reasonably. The need to go on a "cheap date" hasn't gone out of style yet!

There are distributing companies in most major cities, and fees for showing these "oldies" are dirt cheap. So you won't have much overhead and margins will be fatter than for a theater showing new releases.

By stocking the lobby with "Thirties" amenities, movie posters for sale, and suitably attired employees, you should have all the atmosphere and patronage you need. Print well-designed, but "funky" programs showing coming attractions, and distribute these on campus and elsewhere in the neighborhood.

Vary the featured films regularly, and promote your own "revivals." One outfit we found charges a membership fee rather than admission, and has discussions after each showing, where films are reviewed. Local critics, faded movie stars who appeared in the film, or cinematographers often appear and spark the discussions.

Write: Rose Bud Movie Palace, Dept. IEA, 202-3rd South Seattle, Washington.

This Will Frost You

There's nothing worse than a tall, cold drink that gets warm by the third sip. Except a drink that's watered down because the ice cubes melt.

Now you can avoid both of these annoying situations with The Frost Mug! This handsome ceramic mug has a built-in coolant that keeps cold drinks the way they are supposed to be—frigid!

The Frost Mug will cool customers and make hot profits in a variety of places, like cookware and kitchen boutiques, department stores, gift and specialty shops. Restaurants can use it to add a new meaning to iced drinks. It will satisfy even the most finicky drinkers because it's attractive, sturdy and practical.

The gel coolant is in the base of the mug and never needs replacement. An hour of pre-cooling in the freezer guarantees a cold drink for up to one and a half hours. Several mugs can be stored in the freezer for a steady supply as needed. And if you still want ice cubes tinkling in the mug, you won't have to worry about them melting and diluting the drink!

The Frost Mug was designed by Robert Weiss, an innovative ceramic designer. Available in rich burgundy, cobalt blue and white, the mug wholesales for $4.50 with freight allowances for quantity purchases. Write to Robert Weiss Ceramics, Dept. IEA, P.O. Box 1069, Healdsburg, Calif., 95448 for more information on this cool item.

Remote Smoke Alarm Fights Faraway Fires

The smoke detector has swept the country like wildfire and has become an important form of security in thousands of homes. It can warn family members of impending dangers and save lives—if it is heard!

But what happens if the fire is in the basement and the family is sound asleep upstairs? Or if the alarm goes off and no one is home?

We have found an alarm system, *Lifesaver II*, that solves the problem. In addition to a standard detection transmitter, Lifesaver II has an extra alarm device in the form of a radio receiver. You can put the free-standing receiver anywhere a standard electrical outlet is available up to 200 feet from the detector, such as in the bedroom, the family room or a neighbor's house.

There are no wires or complicated hookup procedures since the units operate on the ionization principle. If smoke or combustion particles are present, the detector/transmitter sounds a loud, penetrating alarm and simultaneously sends a signal to the receiver, triggering its alarm.

Mount the 9 volt, battery-operated transmitter on the wall or ceiling and plug in the receiver. You can check the entire system with a test button located on the transmitter. If the battery is low, a signal will sound a "chirp" at 30 second intervals for up to 30 days.

A complete set costs about $100. The transmitter is extremely easy to mount, so there are no installation charges to worry about. Several transmitters can be used with one receiver or vice versa if you have need for greater protection.

Lifesaver II is manufactured by Fyrnetics, Inc., a company with solid experience in fire and security products for home and industry. As the market for expanded smoke-detection equipment grows hotter, Lifesaver II will be a forerunner. It is a unique system that is effective *and* attractive. Write to Fyrnetics, Inc., Dept. IEA, 920 Davis Road, Elgin, Illinois 60120 for more information about dealer/distributorships.

A Fish Story

You say you've got sea water in your veins and salt water in your aquarium? And the local tropical fish dealer just hiked up his prices and changed his name to "Jaws?" Don't let it get you down. Get out your diving gear and go slurping!

Slurping in this case has nothing to do with eating. Although the money saved on stocking a fish tank will put steak back in the budget. The "slurp gun" is a revolutionary new underwater device that will bring those tiny critters back aswimming.

The gun is a simple plastic tube equipped with a plunger. When the plunger is retracted, it creates a partial vacuum or current and lures the fish of your choice into the tube.

Once captured, the fish is transferred to a water-and-oxygen-filled plastic bag for transport to the aquarium. The catch is that there are limitations to the size of fish you can slurp, but not many home aquariums are equipped for marlin, anyway.

The slurp guns are manufactured by Aqua-Craft and are made of Butyrate, a strong, non-corroding plastic. They retail for between $18 and $36 depending on length and extras like a rubber handle grip. Professional fish collectors who tested the tool found it easy to master and use in either fresh or salt water.

As more and more collectors of exotic fish are getting into scuba diving, and vice-versa, this nifty item will make a big splash in a variety of locations. Sporting goods stores and diving equipment depots are a natural. Even tropical fish stores can profit by stocking slurp guns. For non-diving fin fans, it is an excellent way to move fish from one tank to another without harm.

They can be displayed—for consumer participation—at sports conventions and home shows with a goldfish-stocked demonstration tank. Boat dealers and scuba diving schools can pull customers in by using the slurp gun as a promotional item. Rental at dockside locations is possible at say $1 an hour, if allowances are made for occasional loss.

The slurp gun can be sold alone or with a net, which helps in the tube-to-bag transfer. Write them at Kenbee's West Diver's Equipment, Dept. IEA, 5705 Glenmont Drive, Houston, Texas 77081.

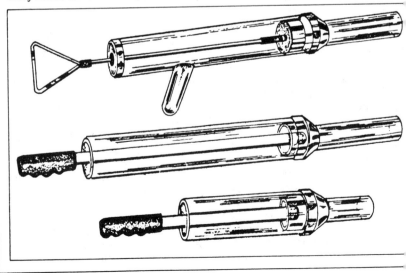

Life Beyond The Tube

Sometimes, the most important member of the family is the television. Adults and kids hook onto the tube and never bother talking to each other. To fight the trend of zombie-like strangers glued to the boob, a San Francisco couple, Pat and Greg Plant, have started a service that helps families find something to do together after they've turned off the TV.

The Plant's service, *Family First*, offers a newsletter with information on trips and special events as well as instructions on arts and crafts and games to play. They sell a calendar with illustrations to color.

As more parents become aware of TV violence and the lack of educational programming, they are turning off the video babysitter. Some families are so accustomed to the television, they have to learn all over again how to work and play with one another. A service that aids them is sure to be popular.

Gathering information on trips and special events is easy. Pick up information from newspapers and local magazines. Contact organizations, tell them about your newsletter, and ask them to mail or call you with data on upcoming events. Libraries are full of books on arts and crafts and games.

The Plants sell their calendar for $4. You might consider an initial charge for the newsletter to help with the cost of having it mimeographed and mailed. Residents of almost any town are going to welcome an opportunity to do things other than watch TV, so you can support the community while the community supports you.

This Idea Isn't Crazy

Kids getting on your nerves? Want to make sure they sit still at the dinner table? Or stay home nights? Well, now you can buckle them into their very own *straitjacket!* It's just the thing for rowdy children, a slightly looney friend, or anyone who wants a great cure for nail biting.

Herb Kardeen, a Canadian escape artist, conceived the idea of marketing jackets imprinted with the message of your choice, which could be anything from "I'm crazy about you" to "Buckle up for safety." The name of your favorite "crazy" is silk-screened across the chest if you prefer.

Kardeen sells the jackets for $200 with complete instructions on how to escape if you're locked in for the evening with little else to do. That's a handsome markup over the wholesale cost, according to our investigators.

We found that the largest manufacturer of made-to-order straitjackets is J.T. Posey, Inc., located at Dept. IEA, 5635 N. Peck Road, Arcadia, California 91006. Their heavy-duty canvas duck model wholesales for $45.90, and they offer a discount of 10 percent on orders of 12 or more. Of course, they don't do imprinting or tell you how to escape.

This idea isn't so crazy once you think about it. There are any number of opportunities to market items like this locally. In T-shirt shops, magic shops, gift shops and even fashion boutiques an imprinted straitjacket would sell to buyers looking for an unusual gift or gag. "Executive" and "kiddie" models would be hilarious gifts. They come in small, medium and large sizes.

If you're touched by this idea, contact the manufacturer for quantity quotes. For further information you can reach Kardeen c/o Malka Glasner, Dept. IEA, 28 Sunnycrest Road, Willowdale, Ontario, Canada M2R-2T4.

Another Life To Live

How often have you heard people say their life is like a soap opera? The next time it happens, don't just sit there listening, make them an offer—they won't be able to refuse!

You can capitalize on the sordid details of friends' or strangers' lives by writing custom-made soap operas for them. And if the details are kind of boring, just invent some!

We found one entrepreneur who is making a bundle creating personalized tear-jerkers for local citizens. He writes a script for $10 and will put it on a cassette for $25. It isn't difficult to see that setting up this business will have you laughing all the way to the bank before you can say Kleenex.

Consider performing the mini-dramas on videotape. Gather a few emotional friends to play the characters. Or scout college theatre departments for students looking for a way to break into show business.

Offer to pay for a copy of their performance instead of laying out hard, cold cash. Copies of a video tape will cost about $12 for 30 minutes.

Start on friends. Just have them supply a few bits of information about the people they want included in their soap opera. A little creativity is all that's needed to write a juicy plot. Everyone gets to be a star! With a customized script!

The growth of this business will be highly dependent on word-of-mouth referrals. And that won't be a problem after a few soaps are in circulation. But it wouldn't hurt to put an ad in the Personal Classifieds of the local paper to reach a full audience.

This is not a wishy-washy business. It has the potential of bubbling into big bucks. So the next time you see someone crying in their beer—get out a pencil and paper, and write your own success story.

Sell Tiny Tables

Miniature furniture is bigger than ever! Doll houses are no longer kid stuff—adult collectors have swooped down on hobby shops, flea markets, antique stores, and thrift shops, in search of these tiny domiciles, buying them up as if they were the latest real estate gambit.

Decorating these tiny homes calls for even tinier furniture, and there just isn't enough of it around these days to satisfy the growing demand. Manufacturers and dealers can't keep up with orders!

Perhaps reacting against a world obsessed with grand dimensions, dealers and collectors are crying out for suppliers. The field is growing so rapidly there's now even a monthly newsletter: *The Miniature Entrepreneurs Newsletter*, 111 Brighton Terrace, Brooklyn, NY 11235. The subscription rate is $6 a year.

If you're imaginative and good with your hands, consider building your own miniature furniture. Copy the designs of contemporary furniture makers, or research period pieces. Basic books on furniture-making are readily available; simply reduce the dimensions.

Samples for easy duplication can be secured from Sam A. Wooden Factory Co., Ltd., Dept. IEA, Central P.O. Box 7856, Seoul, Korea.

This company manufactures a complete line of miniature furniture, including beds with real mattresses, upholstered chairs, china cupboards with pull-out drawers, tables, ottomans, stools, bureaus, and many other fine woods and fabrics.

Window Greenhouse Improves The View

Even a villa overlooking gorgeous country landscape can have at least one window in the house that looks out on a less-than-pleasing view. And there are millions of people who have to look at brick walls or parking lots.

Until now, about the only thing to do was draw the blinds or paint the window black! But we've found a new product that will turn any problem window into a lush greenhouse for plants.

It's a clear acrylic bubble sealed in a white aluminum frame and mounted on a 4½-inch pine frame.

No crossbars block the outside view, and plants can be placed on adjustable redwood shelves. The bubbles come in seven sizes, ranging from 38 inches by 58 inches, to 74 inches by 44 inches. And they are ready to install in minutes.

Suggested retail prices from $325 to $375 include all parts and instructions for vertical or horizontal mounting. Optional accessories include grow lights, heater/fan combination, and extra brackets.

Greenhouse windows available in the past had to be installed by a carpenter, while a home handyman can put up one of these, at less labor cost. Another advantage is the one-piece acrylic construction, which does a better job of insulating against drafts than a multi-pane glass version.

Sol-R, makers of the "Living Window" is looking for dealers and distributors to handle this new greenhouse window. It should find a ready market in home improvement centers, garden departments, and even plant stores. Window Greenhouse Bubble Box, Dept. IEA, P.O. Box 1222, 20 Beharrellst, West Concord, Mass. 01942.

You've Come A Long Way, Baby

Finding a good baby sitter is a problem for millions of proud parents who don't want to trust their pride and joy to just anyone—or are reluctant to have an unknown baby sitter in their homes. With on-the-go lifestyles, both parents working, or single-parent situations, the hassles multiply.

Recognizing this, a savvy nineteen-year-old has established a "Sitter Power" service patterned after temporary help agencies. Ilene Beth Fletcher's Community Service Agency, Inc. now boasts 25,000 clients and a pool of over 350 baby sitters on

24-hour call. About 100 of them are *specially trained to work with handicapped children.*

Each sitter is experienced and thoroughly screened before hiring. Of course, they can work full or part-time, so it's a virtually ideal job for lovers of children. The parents go for the idea, too, judging by the number of clients who keep returning.

This idea could work on a smaller scale in almost any metropolitan area and capitalize on a real need in the marketplace. The service for parents of handicapped children should be a winner by itself. Convenient, in-the-home sitting is an advantage to play up when marketing the service.

This Something-For-Nothing Business Measures Up Well

When you lease building or office space by the square foot—how do you know you get what you're paying for? Do you *really* go down on your hands and knees and actually measure the space to make sure you're not being cheated—unintentionally or otherwise?

Well, you can bet no one else bothers—or knows how—to do it, either. You just assume that the 7,500 square feet mentioned in the lease is correct—and pay accordingly.

Space Audit is so certain that you're paying for more space than you have, that they will measure your office free. Then if the square footage is less than that described in the lease, you seek a rebate from the landlord and split it with Space Audit. If the floor space is correctly described, the northern California firm makes no charge.

It's a "can't lose" proposition for the businessman, who is happy to split his savings with Space Audit and pays nothing if the firm can't save him money. And the measuring company can't lose either, since most buildings are improperly measured.

Starting such a business in your town should be extremely simple and require practically no investment. You need nothing more than standard measuring tapes, meticulous procedures, and a little training in something like basic mathematics, engineering, mechanical drawing or architecture.

You could also offer your services to landlords, helping them avoid 'future problems and assuring them that they are not giving away *too much* space. The important thing is that you be completely objective, go for precise measurements, and gain a reputation as a disinterested professional.

Space Audit, Dept. IEA, 1400 Coleman Ave., Santa Clara, CA 95050.

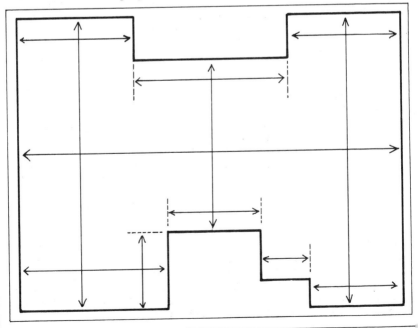

"Revenooers" Won't Care About This Home Brew

America has a huge thirst for liquids other than water. Throughout our history, folks have been trying to slake that thirst with home-brewed elixirs. Some of these potables are legal—like a specified amount of wine and beer (not for sale). Some—like hard liquor—are guaranteed to bring the "Revenooers" down on you with hatchets and handcuffs.

We heard of a new product, however, that has tremendous potential—and won't even get Elliot Ness upset; home-brewed fully carbonated soft drinks! Housewives who are tired of lugging back soft-drink bottles—or cluttering up the house with non-return cans—should be an immediate market for the simple, non-electric "Home Soft Drink Factory." Especially when they consider the constantly rising price of commercially bottled soft drinks!

Kids will no doubt love to make their own sodas, which they can do by merely adding a bottle of cold tap water and pushing a button to activate the carbonator. The unit, which takes up very little room on the kitchen counter, can produce nine popular soft-drink flavors—two of them are even low-calorie!

Selling for about $40 in the appliance section of department stores, "The Home Soft Drink Factory" utilizes bottles of flavor concentrates, which sell for about $2.50 a quart. If do-it-yourself soda pop is your cup of tea, write Soda Stream U.S.A., Dept. IEA, 145 B. Commerce Rd., Carlstadt, New Jersey 07072.

Language Barrier Broken!

We've uncovered an amazing pocket computer that allows travelers to communicate in languages they don't even know! This new product is the *Language Translator* from Craig Corporation. It stores up to 7,000 words and translates from one language to another at the touch of a button.

Simply enter the English word or phrase you want translated on the keyboard, and the foreign equivalent appears on the display screen. Four separate language memory capsules can be used at once, allowing anyone to cross-translate between French, Japanese, German, Swedish, Polish, Russian, Italian, Spanish and English.

On the back of the unit are 50 common phrases such as "How much does this cost?" or "May I please have the . . . ?" A user presses the number of the desired phrase and enters the missing word to complete the sentence or question. Long sentences creep across the screen like worms.

You can converse by having the other person enter the answer on the unit in *his* language for translation to yours. You can negotiate prices, order from menus, read newspapers, and understand street signs. Students can use it to achieve fluency faster, but it isn't a substitute for practice.

This item, which is about to be introduced in the marketplace, has incredible potential. Travelers are a natural, but there are many other markets, ranging from international businesses to police officers in bilingual neighborhoods.

The Language Translator is going to retail for $199.95 per unit (including an English capsule); additional language memory units will sell for $24.95. Contact Craig Corporation, Dept. IEA, 921 W. Artesia Blvd., Compton, California, for further information on a product that should sell like wildfire.

New Way To Learn

Remember when going to school meant listening to a teacher do a five-hour monologue? Remember getting rapped on the knuckles or stuck in a closet if you didn't pay attention?

Well, students using the Lozanov Method are told *not* to pay attention to the teacher, and loll around on the floor listening to classical music instead! What's more, they are learning tough foreign languages *five times faster* than conventional classroom methods.

The Lozanov Method, or "suggestopedia" as it is known, is a proven method of learning now being used widely in Canada, Austria, and most other European countries. It is based on the fact that both hemispheres of the brain—the logical left and non-logical right—are better when used together to learn.

In traditional methods, the two sides of the brain fight with each other. One wants to concentrate while the other wants to look out the window and daydream, absorbing signals that have nothing to do with the task at hand.

What the Lozanov Method does is coordinate the effort of the whole brain, by creating a relaxed atmosphere, with no pressure, in which the student becomes convinced that learning is easy and natural. Test results prove it works.

Students are given new names and backgrounds, so that what they do in class as a different person won't be as embarrassing. Instructors read lessons three times, in three different positive tones of voice, and then repeat the process while classical music plays, to open the *whole* mind. In the next classes, students role-play spontaneously in their new identities using what they've learned before.

After a 25-day cycle of listening and role-playing, most students have a working vocabulary of 2,000 words they can speak, read or write fluently. Side benefits of the positive atmosphere include a better self-image and social skills for many students.

The Canadian government is using suggestopedia in a program for civil servants, and in the United States, about 10 universities have researched it. There are two outfits teaching it here commercially right now. One is Mankind Research Unlimited, in Silver Springs, Maryland. The other is a private school in San Francisco called Language in New Dimensions.

MRU has purchased U.S. commercial rights from Bulgaria; apparently the Bulgarian approach is closest to the true Lozanov Method; others teach variations based on the same principals.

The best thing about it is that, unlike "cramming" in which quickly learned material is rapidly forgotten, standard testing of students on well-accepted tests, show that scores in the 90's at the end of the program are common, and *actually improve* after the course is finished. Educators are non-plussed about this "negative forgetting" mystery.

For additional information on this exciting new opportunity, contact the Lozanov Learning Institute, Dept. IEA, 5408 Silver Hill Rd., Washington, D.C. 20028.

Beauty On Wheels

Farrah Fawcett-Majors can afford to have her own hairdresser on the set, but most people have to travel to find a stylist they can trust. Why not take this service to them, with a mobile beauty salon!

A new hairstyle is a morale booster for the thousands of women (and men) living in retirement communities, nursing homes, or confined in hospitals. Growing numbers of working women have difficulty finding time to get away from the office—and who wants to waste precious weekend time in a beauty shop?

These are just a few of the markets where a smart businessman could "clean up" by hiring beauty operators to work regular routes in specially-equipped vans or motor homes. It would be advisable to concentrate on high density retirement/hospital areas, office complexes or shopping centers to increase volume and cut travel time between stops.

Outfit a mobile unit with chairs and hair dryers, as well as extra-capacity water storage tanks needed for frequent hair washing. The van would need to be self-contained, as water and electric hookups may not be available everywhere.

A good operator can do three or four of the new "blow-dry" cuts in an hour, and charge $15 to $20 a head. Permanents and hair coloring, more popular with an older clientele, take longer, but should cost more because of the extra time necessary.

Best bet to prevent an operator from "free-lancing" without sharing receipts with you is to have customers call ahead to arrange appointment times within a prearranged visit schedule. Then have the operator keep a log that you can cross-check against the schedule which you provide.

Work with the retirement communities, convalescent homes and the like, to have them promote your service as an added "benefit" for residents. The only advertising necessary to reach this market is word-of-mouth and bulletin board notices. Your visit can even become a welcome social event.

Promoting your service among office workers, or employees of companies like banks or insurers that employ large numbers of women, can be done in much the same way. Make sure your visits are timed for early morning, lunch hours, or just after quitting time.

Pack Up All Your Troubles

The most infuriating situation to a traveler—next to missing the plane—is being told the luggage did not arrive on the same flight. And because of ground transportation problems, the airline cannot guarantee quick delivery when and if the luggage does arrive.

Although it inevitably reaches its airport destination, thousands of pieces of luggage sit in "lost and found" depots, waiting for delivery. Taxicabs are generally too expensive and are unreliable, as delivery service is not a top priority for them.

We found an enterprising young man in the Midwest who realized the extent of the problem and has grabbed the bag, so to speak, and run with it. He has established a 24-hour luggage delivery service, charging the airline for each stray bag delivered, based on destination.

Working with one van, one additional employee, a pocket pager for contact with the airport and a contract with four carriers, Kevin Warrenton is returning up to 4,000 pieces of luggage a month to grateful passengers.

Luggage delivery is a service that can be established in any city with a major airport—and that's just about every city. Your major investment is going to be for a secondhand van and cargo insurance. If you have no other job commitments, there is no need for additional assistance, so you can keep overhead to a minimum. A service of this type requires a delivery license obtained at the local Motor Vehicle or Transportation offices.

Prepare a proposal for each airline you want to deal with. A tip from Warrenton—airlines are reluctant to sign contracts based on a flat monthly fee. Therefore, establish delivery zones in the city and charge per bag to specific areas. Kand G. Delivery, Dept. IEA, Des Moines, Iowa, D.O.T. 69268.

In The Old Kit Bag

Almost anything you want to make or build is available in a kit these days. Houses or hunting knives, clocks and clothes can be purchased as kits and constructed at savings of 20 to 50 percent. And the popularity of kit-building is growing because people find they end up with a better quality piece of merchandise than one that is mass-produced. You remember the old adage: "If you want it done right, do it yourself."

The time is right to jump on the sawhorse and construct a booming business with a kit shop. By following the pattern of one entrepreneur we found, it's as easy as falling off a log.

Kits range from decorative to practical. As most department stores and large home decorating centers stock decorative or arts and crafts kits, it is advisable to go with the useful aspect. These can be home related, like comforters and grandfather clocks, or strictly for entertainment with guitar, flute and harp kits.

Sports and outdoor fans will be attracted to money-saving items like sleeping bag and insulated clothing kits, snowshoe and canoe kits. Although there are complete house and boat kits avialable, they are, to say the least, very cumbersome for display purposes. The toy or hobby-building market is primarily a specialty market, but does not preclude your stocking a random selection.

The Hobby Industry Association of America, Dept. IEA, 319 E. 54th St., Elmwood Park, New Jersey 07407, is an invaluable source of information.

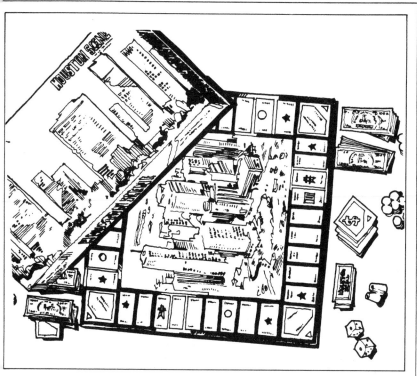

Play Monopoly For Real

Monopoly is the most popular game in the world. It brings out the entrepreneur in everyone and since its introduction in the 20's, has been the top selling board game in history. It makes the Pet Rock look like it's standing still and runs circles around the Hula Hoop, in overall sales.

Now an enterprising outfit in Houston is marketing an offshoot called "Houston Scene." Instead of Atlantic City's Boardwalk and Park Place, the new game involves Houston stores, restaurants and landmarks. You can still accumulate great wealth, but the game is basically sold on a "get to know your city" basis. It sells for $11 and can be played by two players aged nine or older.

The concept offers tremendous potential for any city or town—or county—or state. It not only immortalizes the selected location, but serves as an excellent advertising medium for localized businesses. Once you have decided on game strategy, the most important factor in successful gamesmanship, you can get a graphic firm to design the board layout and game accessories.

The most profitable step in getting your game together is selling board space to local businesses. What hotel or restaurant wouldn't be delighted to see their name "advertised" on a hot new board game!

A toy manufacturer specializing in games and jigsaw puzzles may be interested in production, but may also want to buy the rights. You can have a good printer do the work and market the game yourself, by getting radio or television exposure on local shows and through mail order.

Jaskels, Dept. IEA, 4725 W. Hamon, Houston, Texas 72093.

Rise And Shine

The only thing worse than insomnia is not being able to wake up in the morning. For many oversleepers the alarm clock isn't dependable.

We found an entrepreneur, Richard Senac of New Orleans, who was wide awake when he devised his unique solution—a telephone wakeup service called Roosters Inc. Instead of a pleasant voice announcing the day, sleepyheads are greeted with a 21-gun salute, a bugler sounding reveille, or other equally resounding noises.

This clever idea is very easy to set up as a part-time business. All you need is a telephone, a sound effects record, and some sleepy customers. No experience is required, although it is helpful if you are an early riser. As the business grows it will be necessary to add additional phones, records, and bright-eyed, bushy-tailed employees who enjoy getting up at daybreak.

Finding customers will be a snap. Have flyers printed and distribute them to offices, factories and campuses in your town. And consider having someone in nightclothes do the job for a real eye-catcher! Design a simple registration form that includes spaces for name, billing address, phone number, and wake-up time. In addition, offer eight to ten noises selected from the record with the option of the same noise everyday or a random selection.

Before setting prices, check with answering services in the area that offer a wake-up service. Many charge on a per call basis, but it is much better in this case to set a flat monthly fee of $8 to $10 for five-days-a-week service. Just imagine, with 20 quick phone calls (average length is 30 seconds) a day before you go to your regular job, you'll never have to lay awake at night worrying about money!

Human Pinball Game

If you combined the thrill of skateboarding with the skill involved in playing pinball, you would have the hottest money-making game in the United States!

International Sports and Recreation Corp. did just that and came up with *Skate Ball*—a human pinball game that is guaranteed to rack up profits for fast-moving entrepreneurs. Skate Ball is, according to its developers, the first fair method of record keeping to come along in competitive skateboarding. And it's fun!

A Skate Ball course can be set up either indoors or outdoors, depending on annual climate variations and ranges. Skateboarding is currently a $20 million a year business in the U.S., and we can see that Skate Ball courses will add a hefty jackpot to the industry's overall attraction and success. The game can be an added event at existing skateboard parks or established as a separate business. Sixteen courses have been set up in several major cities like Los Angeles, Las Vegas and Chicago. The total market, though, is still uncharted, and wide open.

For 25 cents players on skateboards—or roller skates—zoom over sensors mounted in a fiberglass surface and score points based on ability. Bells ring, buzzers sound and lights flash as the human pinballs hit 100 to 1000 point targets. Four courses are available—beginner, intermediate, advanced and the grand mogul slalom course.

Contact International Sports and Recreation Corp., Dept. IEA, 1001 Northwest 62nd Street, Fort Lauderdale, Florida, (305) 491-1811, if you feel Skate Ball could light up your future in business.

Fanning Up Profits

In the past few years, hand-held fans have changed from a functional cooling device to an art form gaining space in homes and museums across the country. We found an enterprising young woman, Cary Matthews, who has a very successful business designing and constructing fabric fans. Her specialty is the uchiwa, a traditional Japanese non-folding fan that is mounted on a bamboo handle with embroidery thread.

This type of business can be set up in a minimal amount of space with a very low investment. A work table and storage shelves will turn a den or spare bedroom into a manufacturing area resulting in good profits. One of the uchiwa fans can be made in an hour at a material cost of approximately $4. The completed product will sell for between $15 and $30 depending on size and quality.

Today's eclectic decorating themes offer a broad market for fans. They are used by interior decorators and designers as accessories to be hung on walls, suspended from ceilings or bound together as lamp shades. They make a beautiful gift item for anyone with an interest in art. And of course, they are extremely useful on hot, muggy summer days.

The outer shape can be formed with plastic strips or paper-thin lengths of pliable bamboo. The inside panel is fabric or heavy rice paper either pre-printed or painted with bright designs. Glue and embroidery thread bond the inner and outer shapes. The library is an excellent source of information on design and construction of fans. There are many books available geared to oriental arts and crafts.

Taking several samples to gift shops, boutiques and department stores will ensure your getting display space. The same approach is advised for decorators although an introductory phone call or letter is recommended. There is also good potential for mail order because you can work on an "as-ordered" basis.

Sparkling Teeth Everywhere!

Now you can brush your teeth anywhere, anytime! Lapident, a revolutionary new toothbrush, carries its own supply of toothpaste, in a nifty refillable handle-dispenser.

The availability of Lapident means that workers and children can carry them in their lunch boxes for brushing after every meal. They're handy for college students to carry for quick brushes between classes. It's perfect for traveling as well.

To load the toothbrush, you unscrew the back clip, remove the brush and fill the hollow shaft with your favorite toothpaste. When filled, all you have to do is turn the handle to the right until the desired amount of toothpaste appears on the brush.

After using Lapident, the brush is covered with a clear plastic cap. This prevents the toothpaste from drying up, and makes Lapident ideal to keep in coat pocket or purse!

The 5¾-inch toothbrush comes in four colors: red, blue, yellow and green. The shaft and cap are made of plastic, and the bristles are nylon.

It's a great item for sale by direct mail or to drugstores, supermarkets, novelty stores and wherever toiletries are sold. Prices from the factory distributor are $8.55 per dozen (delivered), with a minimum order of 20 cases (12 dozen per case).

Inquiries for exclusive wholesale distributorships are welcome.

BRM Distributors, Inc., Dept. IEA, P.O. Box 2351, Hialeah, FL. 33012.

Complete Start-Up Manuals Available By Chase Revel & IEA Staff

EACH MANUAL CONTAINS EVERYTHING YOU NEED KNOW TO START AND SUCCESSFULLY RUN A SPECIFIC BUSINESS:

The pitfalls—how to avoid them.
Profit—how much to expect.
Exact Costs—of everything to set up, open, and operate.
Equipment—what to buy and where to find it.
Ways to save money on equipment, fixtures, etc.
Rent—how much to pay.
Location—how to choose the best.
Leases—how to negotiate important points.
Licenses & Permits—what to expect and how to get them.

Merchandise—what to buy, how to buy, where to buy.
If Retail—how to lay out your store and display your wares.
Quick, cheap and impressive decorating ideas.
Signs—how much, how big, where, and what to say.
Employees—whom to hire, where, and what to pay.
Advertising—how, where, when, and how much.
Promotion—best gimmicks completely detailed.
Insurance—what you need and how much.
Knowledge—where to find it, buy, or rent it.
Financing—how to finance your opening costs.
Financing—how to finance your sales to customers.
Customers—how to bring them in and keep them.
Pricing—what price to sell your products or services.

AUTOMOTIVE

9.	Tune-Up Shop	$35.00
18.	Consignment Used Car Lot	$29.50
35.	Do-It-Yourself Auto Repair Shop	$29.50
44.	Muffler Shop	$35.00
48.	Auto-Parking Service	$29.50
50.	Auto-Painting Shop	$35.00
54.	Ten-Minute Oil Change Shop	$35.00
68.	Self-Service Gas Station	$35.00
76.	Car Wash	$35.00
77.	Vinyl-Repairing Service	$29.50
108.	Used Car Rental Agency	$35.00
146.	Automobile Retailing	$29.50
157.	Cross Country Trucking	$35.00

FOOD

6.	Pizzeria	$29.50
16.	Hamburger Stand	$29.50
19.	Cheese & Gourmet Food Shop	$35.00
25.	Popcorn Vending	$29.50
36.	Old-Fashioned Ice Cream Bar Stand	$29.50
55.	Fried Chicken Takeout Restaurant	$29.50
56.	Mobile Restaurant	$29.50
59.	Coffee Shop	$35.00
73.	Hot Dog Stand	$29.50
79.	Yogurt Bar	$35.00
83.	Cookie Shop	$35.00
94.	Homemade Cake Shop	$29.50
119.	Salad Bar Restaurant	$35.00
124.	No-Alcohol Bar	$35.00
125.	Health Food Store	$35.00
126.	Donut Shop	$35.00
127.	Shrimp Peddling	$29.50
128.	Soup Kitchen	$35.00
164.	Churro Snack Shop	$35.00
156.	Sandwich Shop	$35.00
158.	Specialty Bread Shop	$35.00

173.	Convenience Food Store	$35.00

MANUFACTURING

29.	Ghost Dog Making	$29.50
61.	Stained Glass Window Manufacturing	$29.50
64.	Bust-Developing Product	$10.00
66.	Custom Rug Making	$29.50
75.	Hot Tub Manufacturing	$35.00
91.	Burglar Alarm Manufacturing	$29.50
93.	Burlwood Table Manufacturing and Retail Store	$29.50
120.	Sculptured Candle Making	$29.50

PUBLISHING

23.	Rental List Publishing	$29.50
26.	"Who's Who" Publishing	$35.00
67.	Newsletter Publishing	$35.00
110.	Free Classified Newspaper Publishing	$29.50

RECREATION / SPORTS

4.	Tennis & Racquetball Club	$35.00
5.	Athletic Shoe Store	$35.00
82.	Skateboard Park	$35.00
88.	Roller Skate Rental Shop	$29.50
90.	Roller Skating Rink	$29.50
100.	Pinball Arcade	$35.00
109.	Windsurfing School	$29.50
172.	Physical Fitness Center	$35.00

RETAIL

2.	Plant Shop	$35.00
7.	Pet Shop	$35.00
11.	Furniture Store	$35.00
14.	Adult Bookstore	$14.50
22.	Bicycle Shop	$35.00
24.	Liquor Store	$35.00
32.	Antique Store	$35.00
43.	T-Shirt Shop	$29.50

60.	Earring Shop	$29.50
65.	Sunglass Shop	$29.50
72.	Mattress Shop	$35.00
84.	Computer Store	$35.00
106.	Gift Shop	$35.00
107.	Women's Apparel Shop	$35.00
117.	Used Bookstore	$35.00
118.	Handcrafts Co-Op	$35.00
129.	Pipe Shop	$35.00
131.	Backpacking Shop	$29.50
132.	Hobby Shop	$35.00
133.	Discount Fabric Shop	$35.00
134.	Paint & Wallcovering Store	$35.00
139.	Christmas Tree Lot	$18.50
140.	Christmas Ornament Store	$18.50
141.	Tropical Fish Store	$35.00
142.	Gourmet Cookware Shop	$35.00
143.	Flower Shop	$35.00
144.	Do-It-Yourself Framing Shop	$35.00
152.	Intimate Apparel Shop	$29.50
153.	Flat-Fee Real Estate Agency	$35.00
154.	Travel Agency	$35.00
161.	Children's Apparel Shop	$35.00
162.	Coin Laundry	$35.00
163.	Shell Shop	$35.00
167.	Video Store	$35.00
169.	Vitamin Store	$35.00
170.	Family Hair Salon	$35.00
171.	Phone Store	$35.00

SERVICES

12.	Window-Washing Service	$29.50
13.	Instant Print Shop	$35.00
17.	Quit-Smoking Clinic	$35.00
28.	Tool & Equipment Rental Service	$35.00
31.	Parking Lot Striping and Maintenance Service	$29.50
34.	Janitorial Service	$29.50
37.	Dry-Cleaning Shop	$35.00
38.	Copy Shop	$29.50
47.	Trade School	$35.00
51.	Employment Agency	$35.00
52.	Furniture-Stripping Service	$29.50
53.	Carpet-Cleaning Service	$29.50
58.	Day-Care Center	$35.00
80.	Weight Control Clinic	$35.00
95.	Digital Watch Repairing Service	$35.00

105.	Kitchen-Remodeling Service	$35.00
130.	Roommate-Finding Service	$29.50
136.	Secretarial Service	$35.00
137.	Furniture Rental Store	$35.00
145.	Insulation Contracting	$35.00
148.	Telephone Answering Service	$35.00
150.	Exterior Surface Cleaning	$29.50
151.	Consulting Service	$35.00
155.	Chimney Sweep Service	$35.00
159.	Security Patrol Service	$35.00
160.	Maid Service	$29.50

TOURIST

1.	Dive-For-A-Pearl Shop	$29.50
3.	Balloon Vending	$29.50
8.	Handwriting Analysis By Computer	$29.50
10.	Flower Vending	$29.50
27.	Antique Photo Shop	$29.50
39.	Stuffed Toy Animal Vending	$29.50

UNUSUAL

15.	Mail-Order Business	$35.00
20.	Swap Meet Promoting	$29.50
21.	Art Show Promoting	$29.50
33.	Pet Hotel & Grooming Service	$35.00
40.	Adults-Only Motel	$18.50
42.	Mini-Warehouse	$35.00
46.	Psychic-Training Seminars	$35.00
49.	Rent-A-Plant	$29.50
57.	Bonsai Collecting	$29.50
63.	Lie Detection By Voice Analysis	$10.00
70.	Homemade Candy Stand	$29.50
71.	Seminar Promoting	$35.00
89.	Free University	$35.00
92.	Import & Export	$29.50
98.	Liquidated Goods Broker	$29.50
122.	Plastics-Recycling Center	$29.50
135.	Do-It-Yourself Cosmetic Shop	$35.00
138.	Pet Cemetery	$29.50
147.	Mail Receiving Service	$29.50
149.	Sailboat Leasing	$35.00
166.	Jojoba Plantation	$35.00
168.	Financial Broker	$35.00

OTHER BOOKS AVAILABLE BY CHASE REVEL AND THE IEA STAFF

How to Raise Money to Start Your Business

by Arnold Van Den Berg

Arnold Van Den Berg, a financial consultant with more than a decade of experience in the field, maintains that financing is only "difficult because people don't do the right thing." Van Den Berg, who started his own consulting firm on borrowed capital, today is one of the most successful consultants in the country and handles portfolios in the millions of dollars. He will present this session in "plain, easy-to-understand English."

Many unique ways of raising money are covered:

How to prepare a loan request that will improve your chances by 200%.

What a banker looks for and what scares him away.

The successful way to obtain SBA loans which are easy and fast if you know the angles.

Finding out which lenders may be amiable to you and which ones won't.

Inside tricks to attract investment capital.

Other easy sources which are frequently overlooked.

Methods for obtaining expansion capital.

Presented in simple, easy-to-understand language.

Order #301 $16.95

Hottest New Businesses and Ground-Floor Trends

by Chase Revel

Chase Revel, MBA and the foremost authority on small business development in this country, noted by the newspapers as " . . . a forecaster of new trends who seldom misses," conducted this seminar. Revel has owned 18 successful businesses in the past 20 years, is director of IEA, president of one of the largest management consulting firms, editor and publisher of *Entrepreneur* Magazine and chairman of the board of a large electronics company. Here's some of the topics he will cover:

What will be the hottest new businesses in 1979?

Which ones will show the most profit?

Which businesses will decline in acceptance?

What business categories offer the most growth potential?

What trends are developing now that will create new profit opportunities?

An amazing criteria for spotting ground floor gold mines before everyone else jumps in!

How technology will create some amazing new consumer businesses.

New products now in development that offer fantastic profit opportunities!

The reasons why certain businesses will double volume in the next few years!

How to spot fads at birth that mean gigantic short-term profits!

The fads developing now!

The ways people are capitalizing on changes in our society!

A sure way to create a business that will be immediately accepted!

How to determine whether your business idea will work and whether it is worthwhile.

The businesses to stay away from!

The McDonald's of 1980.

Order #302 $16.95

Advertising and Promoting Your Business or Product

by Ronald Tepper

IEA public relations director and the man who helped introduce the Beatles to America, he is one of the top PR specialists in the nation, with over 17 years' experience in practically every type of product or service, including political campaigns. Tepper began his career as a newspaper reporter, so he knows the business from both sides of the fence. Here's a few of the items he covers:

What is promotion—how you use it to double your sales at virtually no cost.

The proven gimmicks and angles.

What is publicity and how you use it to market a new product or service.

How you can publicize and promote your business and/or products.

How to get TV coverage for your product, service business or retail store.

Basic steps in PR, promotion and merchandising.

The best advertising vehicles and how to evaluate them.

Putting ads together—how you do it and the free assistance you can get.

Market research—how you conduct your own research and how it is utilized to increase sales.

News releases, features and interviews—sure-fire business builders.

How to make newspaper and magazine writers come to you.

The key promotional techniques that lead to increased sales.

Promotional ideas for service, retail and manufacturers to utilize.

How $50 can get you $1 million worth of publicity—and sales.

Order #303 $16.95

How to Intelligently Buy a Business

by George Murray

George Murray, Director of IEA's vast research department, is past director of corporate planning for Mattel, Inc., having served that international conglomerate during their biggest growth years. George personally investigated and thoroughly evaluated well over 1,000 prospective business-acquisition candidates (both large and small) for Mattel. If anyone knows what to look for when analyzing a new or existing business opportunity, it's George Murray.

The advantages of buying a going business; the disadvantages.

The dangers and ways you may lose everything.

Common mistakes buyers usually make.

The usual reasons business are sold.

Methods of uncovering the REAL reason a business is being sold.

Questions you must ask yourself before buying.

Checklist of information needed to evaluate a business.

Information you must expect from seller.

Methods to determine the VALUE of the business.

Ways to arrive at the correct price to pay.

How to find hidden liabilities.

Tricks sellers use to create false value.

Techniques to determine if sales figures are valid.

How to buy a business with no cash.

Financing techniques—using leverage to the optimum.

Tax considerations that can make or break a sale.

Using brokers, lawyers and accountants effectively.

Pros and cons of buying franchises and dealerships.

Negotiation tactics.

Order #306 $16.95

Legal Ins and Outs
of Small Businesses

by William Synder

William Snyder, Attorney at Law, Professor at Santa Monica College, Member of California and American Bar Association, Chairman of legal committee of California Apartment Association and member of the ABA division of Business and Banking. Mr. Snyder's law firm, Meller & Snyder, handles hundreds of small business clients and is intimate with their everyday legal problems.

Whether you should incorporate.

Legal problems with sole proprietorship or partnerships.

How to collect bad checks.

Methods of motivating slow payers.

Legal processes for collecting bad debts.

The dangers of being a corporate officer and the personal liabilities.

Your liability for salesmen and employee actions.

Protecting ideas and business secrets.

The dangers of advertising guarantees.

The liabilities of manufacturing a product.

Practically any legal business question answered.

Order #305 $16.95

How to Set up a National or Local
Product Distribution System and
Sources of New Products

by Don Dible

Dible is author of the best-selling *Up Your Own Organization* and a former engineer who gave up a safe, secure aerospace job to form his own successful manufacturing and distributing company.

Here are the proven, step-by-step methods of manufacturing and distributing, including how to:

Dream up hot, new, unique products through a sure-fire, 10-point checklist.

Establish an instant dealer network.

Sign up commissioned sales reps.

Find subcontractors.

Start manufacturing on a "shoestring."

Price your product.

Start part time.

When and when not to patent your product.

Actual case histories plus questions and answers.

Order #304 $16.95

How to Prepare a Successful
and Thorough Business Plan

by George Murray

One of the nation's leading business consultants, he has spent more than two decades in the field of planning and starting new businesses.

A checklist of important items to be included:

Operational process and goals.

Evaluating competition.

Realistic market research methods.

Sources of back-up data and analysis.

Use of professional legal and accounting aspects.

Start-up expenses and cash use.

Projections of cash flow and profit/loss.

Packaging your plan for optimum response from loan officers and investors.

Order #317 $16.95

Best Promotional Gimmicks

by IEA Research Staff

Here are scores of detailed descriptions of promotions, with photos, that actually worked phenomenally. You can easily adapt, and even copy, them for any type of business. Written in "feature-story" style, these interesting accounts will point the way for *you* to get free publicity in the news media. Ideas range from building sales by giving away a free newspaper with every gasoline fill-up to a "Midnight Pajama Sale" at a college book store!

Order #111 $7.50

Basic Steps for Starting a Business

by Chase Revel

Here are the proven basic steps that will save you thousands of dollars and dozens of headaches. You'll learn hundreds of maneuvers to help you through the "start-up" maze, what to do and what not to do—the how's and when's you must know for success.

Includes:

The legal choices, licensing, federal, state and local permits and how to get them.

How to avoid headaches and problems at the business license bureau.

Pros and cons of incorporation or partnerships and name choice.

Checklists for leases and location negotiations.

How to spot future problems with a location and ways to prevent it.

The sure-fire way to obtain credit quickly regardless of your personal credit.

How to hire and employment tax considerations.

Why you shouldn't buy insurance from your regular insurance man.

The reasons you shouldn't open your account at the nearest bank!

A trick that will immediately impress the banker!

Hidden banking problems.

How to deal with suppliers and obtain credit immediately, and much more.

Order #308 $16.95

The Low-Cost and Proven Way
to Enter Mail Order, with
Case Histories and
Sure-Fire Techniques

by Jay Abraham

One of the most phenomenally successful mail-order experts in the country, he is best known for taking a company that was grossing $20,000 a year and developing it into a $13-million-a-year business through mail order!

Many consider mail order the best business of all because the money comes *to you!* Here is revealed the whole spectrum of this money-making business: how to get into it; do it; make it to the top; pinpoint hot new products; and when, where, and how to advertise.

Order #312 $29.50

Shortcuts and the Sure Way to Obtain
SBA Financing

by IEA Staff and a former SBA officer

SBA money *is* available, and it *is* easy to get if you follow this step-by-step guide. Last year, the SBA guaranteed $2.1 billion in loans for businessmen. The trouble is that most small businessmen have the erroneous opinion that: minorities get all the SBA money, the paperwork is impossible, and the waiting period is up to nine months. These beliefs are simply not true. This book tells you how to get money quickly and uses sample forms, checklists, and inside tips to help you get your share of the pie!

Order #85 (New Business) $24.50
Order #86 (Existing Business) $24.50

How to Easily Sell Your Business
for the Best Price

by Richard Haisman

Haisman is an IEA correspondent who has been a business broker for almost two decades.

The ins and outs, tricks and gimmicks for a quick sale at your price.

Veteran of 100s of business sales discloses his winning techniques.

Shows how to highlight good points. Specifies exactly what items make a business "saleable."

Order #99 $18.50

How To Pick A Recession Proof Business

by George Murray

Certain businesses actually grow during a recession and some are not affected. This seminar will point out which ones and the reasons. Numerous businesses are covered.

Also, ways you can predict the drop in other businesses.

Methods by which you can beat competition during recession.

Ways you actually make landfall profits.

Areas of your business operation that should not be cut back during slow periods.

The signs that will warn you of a coming recession.

Places you can borrow money easily during recession.

Important advertising and marketing techniques during recession.

Businesses to stay away from because of their recessionary problems and much more.

Order #225 $16.95

How To Prevent Bad Checks, Pilferage, Embezzlement

by Mark Peters

Many small businessmen lose thousands of dollars each year because they don't know how to thwart bad check passers, stop shoplifters, prevent pilferage and internal theft. Many are also embezzled without ever realizing it.

Ways to outwit the bad check passer.

Techniques for spotting the check passer that can be taught to employees.

Signals that give away the potential shoplifter.

Methods to prevent employee theft.

Control systems that reduce pilferage.

Ways to reduce the chance of burglary.

Techniques that will scare away potential armed robbers.

The various, unusual ways you can be embezzled.

Order # 226 $16.95

How To Franchise Your Business

by Chase Revel

Have you ever wondered if you could franchise your own business? If you have a successful business, it's a logical question.

Can you franchise it with any expectation of success?

Does your business lend itself to franchising?

Covers every question on the subject such as:

The key requirements for successful franchising.

Feasibility studies.

Disclosure statements.

Financing.

Operating manuals.

Marketing materials.

Franchise sales techniques.

Order # 213 $24.50

Advertising Techniques for Small Business

by John Hiatt

Powerhouse advertising that results in SALES! Whether it be for a product, service or company image. The most effective forms of promotion at your disposal, paid for space, air time, specialty items, direct mail, newspapers and billboards.

How to design & write an ad that sells!

How to pick media effectively.

How to negotiate with suppliers.

How to plan a total advertising campaign.

How to identify your audience.

How to determine if an ad is good before it's run.

Trade outs to help keep costs down.

Insiders professional secrets on the formula for a super-sell ad!

Order # 224 $16.95

Businesses You Can Start For Under $1,000

by Mitchell Milgaten

The name and address of every person who has been burglarized is worth $50 to $500 to you.

Tree stump slabs available free from the forest bring $300 to $500.

A daily compilation of apartments for rent nets over $50,000 a year.

A weekly two-page letter on your hobby can net $10,000 to $100,000 annually.

Dig up miniature trees in the forest and get $50 to $100 for each one.

Dip ice cream in chocolate. Creator of the idea sold $40,000 in his first 10 days.

Put on a weekly art show and make $500 a week.

Take photos of golfers (without their knowledge) and make $300 a day.

You can have a fully equipped hamburger stand for only the rent and $100 of food supplies.

A lady bakes rich homemade cakes in her home and made $84,000 the first year.

A Montreal man hands roses to ladies in restaurants. Former truck driver nets over $50,000.

Provide TV and room service for dogs. Pet hotels in big demand.

Plus many more.

Order # 211 $16.95

Tax-Saving Angles and Techniques for Small Business People

By Egon Van Den berg

Many businessmen waste hundreds of thousands of important profit dollars each year because of inept bookkeepers who don't understand tax-saving methods. Multi millionaire Chase Revel states: "I paid as high as 74% of my income before I learned small business tax saving methods. Some of us think we know it—but we don't." This seminar outlines dozens of techniques in plain English to help you save money and taxes.

The many ways you can capitalize on your position as business owner.

Various tax advantages and disadvantages of proprietorships, partnerships, limited partnerships and corporations.

Understanding the tax-saving chapter selection.

Choosing when to lease or buy equipment, etc.

Delaying taxes with advertising.

Obtaining and using investment tax credits.

Using executive perks to your advantage.

Tax cost of employees.

Reducing costs with independent contractors.

Using inventory evaluation systems to delay or reduce taxes.

Timing purchases for best tax advantage.

Order # 323 $16.95

How To Protect Your Ideas or Product

by George Murray

How many people have had a great idea, product or service stolen from right under their nose? Or how many have had a great product and did not know how to protect it?

No area is more mystifying than patents, copyrights and trademarks, but this session will clear up all your doubts because George Murray will explain each in layman's terms.

How you can research a patent for as little as 50 cents instead of the hundreds (and sometimes thousands) of dollars it normally takes.

How to read a patent.

How to protect your own product without an attorney.

The new copyright law and how it will affect you.

Plus dozens of other ins and outs of patents, copyrights and trademarks that will not only save you thousands of dollars but will also help you to protect your product, invention, etc., so that it can't be stolen.

This session is a must for anyone who has—or is—developing a new product, service or invention.

Order #229 $16.95

220

Negotiating Techniques

Few people have the talent necessary to negotiate the best for themselves and most of those who do have the talent fail to recognize it and use it effectively. Negotiating is an art and it can be taught. Unfortunately, many people who are in the midst of negotiating some deal, job or even a raise give themselves away and end up with a worse deal than their opponent would have made without any negotiation.
How to determine if the quoted price is firm or negotiable.
How to spot weaknesses.
How nonverbal gestures will tell you what your opponent is planning.
How to turn a bad offer into a favorable situation.
Methods of intimidation which will undermine your opponents confidence.
How to pick questions and comments that will uncover the opponent's true motives.
Psychological strategies for successful results and much more.
The degree of success you have in business is often determined by your negotiating skills. Here's the chance of a lifetime to improve both.

Order # 228 $16.95

How To Sell Your Ideas

by Chase Revel
Here's how to profit from ideas and new products concepts. A complete guide to the processes and methods of capitalizing on your own ingenuity. Included are such topics as protecting an idea, pre-sales preparation, determining your best prospects, packaging your idea to make it look more valuable, deciding what your cut should be, approaching the prospect, closing the deal, and monitoring the progress of the concept.

Order #316 $16.95

Special Report: Sculpture by Computer

by IEA Research Staff
The inside story of a hot new business combining computer technology and a special photographic technique that lets you produce a near-perfect head-and-shoulders sculpture out of almost any material, for a retail price of as little as $150! And in only one hour! With absolutely no sculpting experience you can enlarge, reduce, and copy items as small as a thimble and as large as an automobile. There's a big market for doing people, pets, race and show horses, etc. Here's a complete run-down on what it is, how it's done, and the market for this hot new business prospect.

Order #96 $10.00

The Truth About Small Business Profits

by Chase Revel
Tells who is really making a bundle—how much and who isn't. Unquestionably the most useful book ever prepared on small business! Chase Revel blows the lid off of over 100 different small businesses—all torn apart, totally analyzed and revealed in shockingly accurate detail. NOT THE "EDUCATED" GUESSES of a classroom instructor—but real life dollars and cents figures taken from actual case studies on over 100 different existing businesses. This is the one way you can find out exactly how much any small business can be expected to make and how to make it.

Order #520 $9.95

Pros and Cons of Buying Franchises and Distributorships

by Chase Revel
How to discover the difference between good and bad franchises and distributorships. Why a franchise (or distributorship) might not be good for you but fine for someone else. Critical areas you must define about the future dealing with the franchise company. The first signal that tells you not to buy a franchise or dealership company. Which franchise may well become the McDonald's of the 1980s.

Order #315 $16.95

Women Getting into Business

by Betty Wuliger
Here is a practical, down-to-earth guide aimed especially at women. Tells you how to start your own business and how to put every dollar to work for you. Here is everything you need to know, every step of the way, including such crucial subjects as your personal qualifications, financing, location, credit, the business plan, personnel, competition, partnerships and corporations, insurance, and a dozen key areas you may never even have considered.

Order #309 $16.95

Businesses You Can Run & Still Keep Your Job

by George Murray
Most big companies have branches all over the world. They've developed techniques to motivate the branch managers and control the operations from afar. You can use the same techniques.
Types of businesses best for absentee ownership.
Businesses not suited.
The key ingredients for a smooth & profitable operation.
Methods to obtain dedicated managers.
Pros and cons of choosing a mature manager or an enthusiastic young buck.
Ways you can determine the honesty of your manager.
Where to find experienced managers.
The most successful compensation/incentive programs.
Inventory control systems that prevent losses.
Easy cash control methods.
Pitfalls you can avoid.

Order # 218 $16.95

Hidden Franchise Laws

by Vernon Haas
Haas is an attorney and chairman of the American Bar Association Subcommittee on Franchise Law.
What constitutes a franchise? What are the responsibilities of the franchisor and the franchisee? How are both parties protected from third-party litigation? You must know the answer to these and myriad similar questions—all covered in layman's language in this report—if you want success instead of failure. Franchise advertising seldom explains the hidden related laws, and the prospective franchisee is at the mercy of half-truth and bad advice. This book points out and takes you around the pitfalls.

Order #87 $7.50

Special Report: Booming New Business—Videocassettes/Videodiscs

by IEA Research Staff

Here is a giant new market, but where is it going? As consumer acceptance for home/business videocassette recorders matches the equipment's ever-decreasing price tag, there is bound to be a continually expanding market for pre-recorded videocassettes. This overview report tells you what it's all about, how it's used, and how you can profit from this exciting new opportunity.

Order #97 $10.00

USE ORDER CARD ON FOLLOWING PAGE.

ORDER FORM

See Pages 218-222 for List of Titles and Prices.

*FREE with 2 or more items ordered:
Special Report #200 NEGOTIATING TRICKS
*As there is a limited quantity available, this offer is
on a first-come, first-serve basis.

10% Discount on 5 to 9 items.
20% Discount on 10 or more items.
Complete Start-up Manual Library,
50% off: $1,995.00

Institutions, Colleges and Libraries receive 20% Discount on ALL items except Complete Manual Library.

ORDER FORM. MAIL TO:
IEA RESEARCH, Dept. 819, 631 Wilshire Blvd., Santa Monica, CA 90401

PLEASE SEND THE FOLLOWING ITEMS:

NO. _____ TITLE _____ PRICE _____

NO. _____ TITLE _____ PRICE _____

NO. _____ TITLE _____ PRICE _____

NO. _____ TITLE _____ PRICE _____

NO. _____ TITLE _____ PRICE _____

(Use additional card or sheet
of paper for more titles)

Total _____

LESS QUANTITY DISC. _____

SUBTOTAL _____

Calif. Residents Add 6% Sales Tax _____

**PAYMENT
ENCLOSED $ _____**

Add $4.00 per Manual for First Class
Mail on Special Rush Orders.

Or Charge to my

First Class Postage & Handling _____

☐ BankAmericard/VISA ☐ Master Charge

TOTAL _____

Charge Card # _____ Exp. Date _____ Master Charge Interbank No. _____

x _____

Sign if charging

SHIP TO:

NAME _____

ADDRESS _____

CITY _____ STATE _____ ZIP _____

| RC | AM | SHP | FCP | CL | ENNM | AD | CK |